W9-CBX-852

CRITICAL ACCLAIM
FOR *TRAVELERS' TALES*

"The *Travelers' Tales* series is altogether remarkable."
—Jan Morris, author of *Journeys*, *Locations*, and *Hong Kong*

"For the thoughtful traveler, these books are an invaluable resource. There's nothing like them on the market."
—Pico Iyer, author of *Video Night in Kathmandu*

"This is the stuff memories can be duplicated from."
—Karen Krebsbach, *Foreign Service Journal*

"I can't think of a better way to get comfortable with a destination than by delving into *Travelers' Tales*...before reading a guidebook, before seeing a travel agent. The series helps visitors refine their interests and readies them to communicate with the peoples they come in contact with...."
—Paul Glassman, Society of American Travel Writers

"...*Travelers' Tales* is a valuable addition to any pre-departure reading list."
—Tony Wheeler, publisher, Lonely Planet Publications

"*Travelers' Tales* delivers something most guidebooks only promise: a real sense of what a country is all about...."
—Steve Silk, *Hartford Courant*

"These anthologies seem destined to be a success...*Travelers' Tales* promises to be a useful and enlightening addition to the travel bookshelves. By collecting and organizing such a wide range of literature, O'Reilly and Habegger are providing a real service for those who enjoy reading first-person accounts of a destination before seeing it for themselves."
—Bill Newlin, publisher, Moon Publications

"The *Travelers' Tales* series should become required reading for anyone visiting a foreign country who wants to truly step off the tourist track and experience another culture, another place, first hand."
—Nancy Paradis, *St. Petersburg Times*

"Like having been there, done it, seen it. If there's one thing traditional guidebooks lack, it's the really juicy travel information, the personal stories about back alleys and brief encounters. The *Travelers' Tales* series fills this gap with an approach that's all anecdotes, no directions."
—Jim Gullo, *Diversion*

DANGER!

true stories
of trouble
and survival

DANGER!

true stories
of trouble
and survival

Collected and Edited by
JAMES O'REILLY, LARRY HABEGGER,
AND SEAN O'REILLY

TRAVELERS' TALES
SAN FRANCISCO

Danger!: True Stories of Trouble and Survival
Collected and Edited by James O'Reilly, Larry Habegger, and Sean O'Reilly

Cover and interior design by Kathryn Heflin and Patty Holden
*Cover photographs: Copyright James Nachtwey/Magnum Photos, Inc. Uganda, boy waits
as army searches his home.*
Copyright Kennen Harvey/Tony Stone Images. Climber falling from overhang above.
Copyright Corbis/Jeff Vanuga. Burning tree.
Copyright Joel Sartore/National Geographic Society. Western town, Salmon, Idaho.
Page Layout by Cynthia Lamb, using the fonts Bembo and Newton

Distributed by O'Reilly and Associates, Inc. 101 Morris Street,
Sebastopol, California 95472

Library of Congress Cataloging-in-Publication Data

Danger! : true stories of trouble and survival / collected and edited by James
    O'Reilly, Larry Habegger, and Sean O'Reilly.—1st ed.
        p.   cm.
    ISBN 1-885211-32-5
    1. Natural disasters–Anecdotes.   2. Disasters—Anecdotes.
3. Voyages and travels—Anecdotes.   I. O'Reilly, James.
II. Habegger, Larry.   III. O'Reilly, Sean.
GB5018.D25   1999
904—dc21   99-18518
                                                    CIP

First Edition
Printed in the United States of America
10 9 8 7 6 5 4 3 2 1

A man wrestles eternally upon a span, above a chasm. Locked in his arms is a dark angel, the Phantom Lord—not death itself but fear of death. The man falls, finally, but the Phantom Lord falls with him. In the man's surrender lies the Phantom Lord's defeat.

—ANDREW TODHUNTER,

Fall of the Phantom Lord: Climbing and the Face of Fear

Table of Contents

Part Two
GOING TO THE EDGE

Part Three
HEART OF DARKNESS

Part Four
CROSSING TO SAFETY

Danger! An Introduction

TIM CAHILL

Danger is entirely about mortality. It is an elucidation and illumination of the final mystery of human experience, a matter, if you will, of life and death.

Concepts of cowardice and courage exist in continuous collision, of course, and often times dwell within the same person, at the same time. This is what we might call the surface tension of danger. Other verities, vaguely translucent, drift beneath the surface of our terror. What, for instance, is the nature of fear? In what ways do we value a human life, and more particularly, our own? When is it preferable to die rather than endure anymore? Is there honor in dying with companions when it is possible to save one's self?

Danger presents choices that challenge the boundaries of our moral systems. Decisions, often made in seconds, may eventually define an entire lifetime. Whether we know it or not, danger compels us to commit philosophy, and in a big damn hurry, to boot.

In this book, the reader will encounter some who voluntarily place themselves in the proximity of danger: search and rescue workers, gang members, climbers, divers, war correspondents. A mountaineer and ski guide barely survives an avalanche, a diver is trapped in an underwater cave, a climber experiences a crisis of courage.

Others who encountered danger were actually looking for adventure, which is quite a different thing. In one story, innocent tourists, trekking the mountains of Kashmir, are taken hostage by militants. One author, researching English soccer riots, finds himself at the center of a riot about to "go off." A woman is mauled by a hyena, a helicopter crew ditches in a sea roiled by the storm of the century.

We learn here of odd and unfamiliar perils encountered in the jungles of the Amazon, and in the civil wars racking Africa. A woman is bloodied by a cougar in Alaska, a man is racked by malaria in the Congo, and a young woman fends off a young thug on a bus in Los Angeles.

Often the stories are poetic and sometimes thoughtful: a matter of survival recollected in tranquility. Other pieces are written in the present tense, and while the events are precisely recollected, little effort is made to divine their meaning.

No matter. A reader is not going to walk away from this collection unscathed. What moves us here, as I have suggested, is the concept of mortality. This book might be seen as a collection of clues to the final mystery. No living human being has ever solved the ultimate puzzle, of course, but then again, we never stop trying, and that is because we are human.

These stories linger in the mind, simmering away until they burst up into full boil: what would I have done in that situation? How is it that a trained soldier and an urban commuter describe danger in very similar terms? Is the survivor's guilt justified?

One last point: each and every story in this collection is compulsively readable, as matters of life and death always are.

Tim Cahill is editor-at-large of Outside *magazine and is the author of six books including* Jaguars Ripped My Flesh *and* Pass the Butterworms. *He also co-wrote the IMAX film* Everest. *He lives in Montana with Linnea Larson, a couple of cats, and a dog.*

PART ONE

Dangerous Territory

PETER MAASS

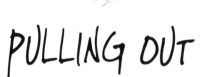

PULLING OUT

Journalists may find an island of safety in a war,
but for others there is no escape.

It was 5:45 in the morning, and the alarm clock next to my bed sounded as loud as a mortar explosion. I heard the sound again, a rumbling noise like thunder, and I knew it was not my alarm clock, a palm-sized device that beeped quietly when it tried to wake me up. It was often like that: something would shake me out of my sleep, a sharp sound or a bad dream, and I would keep my eyes closed and give my mind a few seconds to clear up and figure out where I was, whether I was in a bed or on the ground or under a desk, in a hotel or military barracks or somebody's living room, clothed or un-clothed, safe or vulnerable.

I remembered where I was. Vitez, central Bosnia. I had ar-rived the previous evening with three colleagues, parking my jeep next to a sign that said "Kasem's Gas Station." I knew Kasem's because I had slept there on previous trips. Now came the hard part: what was happening around me? A thunder-storm? I hoped so, I deeply hoped so, but I didn't hear any wind or rain. I had to accept the possibility that I had been woken up by artillery fire. A training session? No, the Bosnians didn't have enough ammunition to spare. Okay, it was the real thing, but the battle might be taking place on the other side of Lasva Valley, and I was hearing the echo. I opened my eyes after another thunderlike rumble, closer this time.

No, it can't be. I was like a person who refuses to believe his checking account is in the red, and does the calculations over and over again until he can't avoid the bottom line. I was caught on top of a thousand gallons of gasoline in a mortar attack.

It was dark when we had pulled into Kasem's eight hours earlier, and none of us noticed the fresh combat trenches surrounding it. We didn't pay much attention to the fact that the pump jockeys had AK-47s slung over their shoulders. Everybody's got a gun in Bosnia. I asked one of the soldier-attendants whether there had been trouble recently, and he casually replied, "Yeah, we got robbed three nights ago." In a war, robberies are the least of your worries. I felt fortunate that Kasem's had a few vacant rooms on the second floor, and paid $25 to check into the front line.

I should not have been surprised about what happened next. Nothing lasts for very long in Bosnia; safety passes into danger, danger passes into safety. We all knew this, but it was easy to become forgetful when you were safe and feeling good. When I checked into Kasem's and was the first to take a shower, I thought things were going well. I shared a room with Sasha Radas, my interpreter, and the adjacent room was taken by Cathy Jenkins and Adam LeBor, British journalists. We pooled our food and enjoyed a good meal that night, by local standards. Slabs of salami, some fresh fruit, cookies and a bit of brandy to top it off. In a country where most people went to sleep hungry and cold, we were warm, clean and had plenty of spare gasoline for our jeep. Vitez was quiet, as was the long stretch of territory to Tuzla that we were planning to drive through on the next day. I slept well, until 5:45 a.m.

There are some journalists who enjoy being under attack, the war junkies, but I am not among them. My hero is not George Patton or Peter Arnett or Robert Duvall in *Apocalypse Now*, loving the smell of napalm in the morning. My hero is Captain Yossarian from *Catch-22*. Like Yossarian, who knew the odds of being shot out of the sky during World War II and didn't like them, I consider myself a realist, not a coward. When I accepted the assignment to cover Europe's worst war in several generations I knew only that wars are a fundamental human experience and that I should try to learn why. I also knew that covering a war can do good things for a young journalist's career. It took a while to learn of the drawbacks, such as waking up to a mortar attack.

When I could no longer pretend that the shells landing around Kasem's were thunder, I slipped out of bed, threw on my clothes, lowered my flak jacket over my head and pulled down the groin flap as low as it would go. The sound of mortars was joined by its evil twin, the sound of machine-gun fire. My colleagues performed the same hurry-up dressing routine and crouched with me in the hallway, where we had little time to ponder our next move before the first bullets zipped through the windows, shattering the glass and sending us face-first to the ground. Our reaction was immediate, beyond instinctual. We crawled like alligators to the next safest place, the stairwell, abandoning our bags in the hallway. We had the same thought on our minds, *One direct hit and we're vapor.* It could happen any second. I wanted to click my heels twice and be in Kansas.

Tragedy and absurdity were moons circling the Bosnian war. I realized this as we crouched in the stairwell trying to sort out the least bad option. We could stay where we were.

We could try to find the basement, if one existed, and wait out things there. Or we could make a run for it, jumping out the second-floor window or dashing out the door on the ground floor. Instinct tells you to run, to tear the hell out of the corner you're in and run, quite literally, for your life, run faster than you have ever run, faster than you imagined you could run. But, in fact, the run-for-your-life option was less preferable than staying put atop the gasoline. If we made it outside, which direction should we head? Which direction were the shots and mortars coming from? I hadn't a clue. There was also a terrified bear in a cage out back, and what if he had gotten loose? The bear was named Mackenzie, after the U.N. general.

Then the phone rang. You assume that everything around you stands still when your life hangs in the balance. Just as your body shuts down its nonessential functions—you don't feel hungry anymore, you don't need that cup of coffee to wake you up, and you can skip the visit to the toilet you were planning—you assume that phones will not ring, that dogs will not bark and that flowers will stop growing. Time is standing still for you; it should do the same for everybody else. But there we were, listening to mortars and machine guns firing at us, and the phone rang downstairs. The guns stopped firing for a moment. Perhaps our attackers heard the ring and thought it was a signal. Or maybe it was our attackers on the phone, calling to demand our surrender. Better yet, perhaps it was somebody from the British Army, which had a base just two miles away, who had heard that foreign correspondents were in trouble at Kasem's. If only.

The guys with the AK-47s were not answering the phone. They had disappeared, taking up positions in the trenches around the station, from where they returned fire. Sasha, the interpreter, agreed to crawl downstairs and answer the phone. It was a brave act, because the phone was in a glass-enclosed office visible from three sides. He slithered into the office, hid under the desk, slipped his hand onto the desktop to grab the phone, pulled the receiver under the desk and put it to his ear. It was a woman calling who said she was the girlfriend of one of the pump jockeys. She lived nearby and heard the battle. Was her lover still alive? Sasha couldn't say. He asked her whether she knew anything about our attackers and could do anything about it. She whiffed on both queries.

Sasha crawled back to the stairwell. Time limped along at the pace of an old woman crossing a busy street. *Hurry up*, you think, *Hurry fucking up*. All that I remember of those minutes in the stairwell, looking at the faces of my colleagues trying, as I was, to look as though they weren't terrified, is that I took the jeep keys out of my pocket, dangled them in the air and announced that I was putting them in my right front pocket. The reasoning was simple—if I got hit and we needed to make a run for it, the others should know where the keys were. It was gruesome logic but hardly unusual. Before going to Bosnia, many journalists took out special war insurance policies. If you lose a finger, the insurer pays you say, $10,000; for a thumb, you get $15,000; a lost hand nets $30,000; a leg is worth $40,000 if the amputation is below the knee, and $60,000 above the knee. A British colleague's policy awarded him $150,000 if he suffered "irredeemable dementia" after covering Bosnia.

There were shouts outside, and the gunfire ceased again. A linebacker-sized soldier with a black ski mask over his face and an assault rifle in his hands burst into the station. This was re-assuring, because, after all, he was not shooting. "*Novinari! Novinari!*" we shouted, telling him we were journalists. The war was still at a stage when announcing yourself as a reporter was a protective measure rather than an invitation to fire. We held up our United Nations press cards. We didn't know whether we had been captured or liberated, or by whom, or what this jittery soldier planned to do with us. He had no markings on his camouflage uniform. Was he a Croat? Muslim? Serb? British? We dared to ask.

"You don't want to know," he snapped. "Who else is here?"

We told him no one, but he ran past us to the first floor and began kicking in the doors, SWAT-style, bursting into each room with the speed and precision of a gentleman who had done this many times before. Sasha whispered, "Maybe he is trying to show off." It was not a joke; at times like that, your mood is manic. One moment you are sure you are going to die, the next moment you think everything is okay, the masked storm trooper is just showing off, and you can relax now. But our trooper was not showing off. After destroying as many doors as he could find, he ran back downstairs and barreled through a couple of glass doors he found there. He located the basement we had thought of sheltering in.

Another masked soldier carrying the obligatory AK-47 ran inside and crouched next to a wall a few feet away. He was smaller, about six foot two, and his eyes were wild and bloodshot. "Who are you?" asked Sasha. The guy smiled through his hood and whispered one word: "*Ustashe.*" This was the name of Croatia's World War II pro-Nazi movement, and five decades later Croat extremists in Bosnia proudly referred to themselves as Ustashe, a one-word boast that meant, "We're the meanest sons-of-bitches around." More of them piled into the gas station.

The entire valley had turned into a battle zone between Croat forces and the Bosnian Army, allies until dawn broke, when Croats assumed the role of Judas, hoping to lop off a chunk of Bosnia for themselves. The gas station had been controlled by the Bosnian Army when we checked in but the management was changing hands, Bosnian-style. We told the

Croats we just wanted to get out of the place and shelter at the British base down the road. No problem, they said, but you can't leave now because it's unsafe. We suggested they contact the base so that the British armored personnel carrier could fetch us. They said they would see what they could do.

My sympathies had shifted. Until the Croats seized Kasem's, they were attacking it and, by extension, attacking us. Now that they were in control of it, the Bosnian Army was counterattacking and, by extension, attacking us. I had the simplest of wishes, to get out of the madness.

A few minutes later, a soldier told us to get outside. I moved downstairs as quickly as possible with my backpack, computer bag, helmet, and flak jacket. The pump jockeys were in the office again, but now their hands were raised in the air, and they were staring at the wrong end of an assault rifle. Their faces bore the look of death. Ustashe do not take prisoners.

I stepped outside. There was no British APC in sight. Sasha dashed out and said the soldiers wanted us to *run* to the British base. They didn't know we had a jeep in the parking lot, but even so, I didn't like the idea of driving through a battle in a soft vehicle. We could return to the building and wait for better times. I noticed a few houses burning a couple hundred yards away, saw a company of nervous soldiers crouching for cover behind the station and realized that better times would not be coming to this spot. I ran to the jeep, past an unexploded grenade that lay on the ground like a gum wrapper, opened the trunk and threw out one of the jerrycans of gasoline. The fewer explosive materials we carried the better. My colleagues jumped into the jeep, and they had the same thought on their minds: he better not flood the engine again. Thankfully I didn't, and, as we screeched out, one of the Ustashe soldiers gave us a straight-armed Nazi salute. It was his way of saying good-bye.

My Russian jeep had a top speed of 65 miles an hour, or about a quarter of the speed I would have liked. I weaved from one side of the empty road to the other, making it more difficult for snipers to get off an accurate shot. It's a trick I learned in Sarajevo. It might be useful when I return to my hometown of Los Angeles, where commuters occasionally face gunfire on the freeways. There was total silence in the jeep, everyone scrunching down into their helmets and flak jackets like turtles trying to sleep. At moments like that I would try to believe that my fear exceeded the danger, that I was merely being paranoid, but the sound of gunfire contradicted such hopes. Sasha interrupted my thoughts. "Oh no," he said, pulling something from his pocket. "We forgot to return our room keys."

We barreled into the British base. We had survived, we had gotten a second chance to live as normal people. *Okay*, God was saying, *I'll let you out of this one, but I hope you learned your lesson.* This was only one of my second chances I got while covering the war. Each time I got one, I continued the same unsafe behavior that put me into the position of needing to pray for deliverance from a lethal corner I had boxed myself into. Sooner or later, the odds would catch up with me, as they had caught up with friends of mine. It was just a matter of time.

We dashed into the command post. The duty officer was an incarnation of David Niven, standing straighter than a telephone pole and speaking without moving his jaw. "Right, there's quite a bit of fighting going on out there this morning, so you were bloody lucky to get out of it so well," he said crisply. "I would suggest that you march down to the canteen and have some breakfast and tea. I should think you could use a good meal after a fright like that." When Brits get nervous they drink tea. So long as they are drinking tea, everything is okay. Never mind the mortars, would you like one lump of sugar or two?

The base was a neutral haven. Shells screeched overhead, a few every minute, each one making a horrible sound as it sliced through the air, a gut-splitting noise that made you want to retreat as far away from the front line as possible. The biggest shells were fired by the Croats from a 155-millimeter howitzer known as Nora, which used to be pointed at the Serbs, but now was firing from its hilltop perch at the Bosnians, making the British soldiers mutter things like, "Nora's up to no good today." It was hard to understand why a weapon of death was given a name that belonged to plump aunts. There were lots of things that were hard to understand. Why, as I mentioned before, when the only people outside were soldiers trying to kill other soldiers, did a fat pensioner pedal past the base on an orange bicycle? I still chuckle over the explanation given by the officer who observed the scene with me: "Bosnian mind fuck."

The breakfast was great, an affirmation of the parallel universe that I had just escaped to. As I dug into my corn flakes, the captured pump jockeys a few miles down the road were probably being marched out of the gas station and ordered to stand in front of a ditch. As I got up from the table to fetch more jam for my toast, their Croat captors might have been taking aim. And as I sat back down and had another sip of English breakfast tea with two lumps of sugar in it, the young Bosnians who had been my hosts the night before were probably being shot dead. The war spun off lots of parallel universes. There was, for example, the parallel universe of diplomacy, in which diplomats would sit down in plush chairs in Geneva or Brussels or New York and concoct peace plans that worsened the fighting.

Bosnian mind fuck.

The executions that I assumed were taking place down the road were less troubling than the suddenly bleak outlook for several million Bosnians who supported their government and its notion of a pluralistic country in which everyone would live together peacefully. After a year of warfare, the government had lost two-thirds of its territory to nationalist Serbs, and the attack that woke me at Kasem's gas station was a sign that the remaining third was in trouble. Croats in Bosnia, backed by Croatia proper, wanted Kasem's gas station, wanted Vitez and wanted most of the territory not yet seized by Serbs. They figured that if the Western world was letting Serbs carve off a slice of Bosnia, why shouldn't Croats have a slice, too?

As I sat in the British canteen, a soldier next to me swallowed the last of his breakfast sausages and let out a huge battlefield burp. He got up from his chair, grabbed his SA-80 rifle with one hand and his food tray with another and shook his head in pity. "If the West is going to give weapons to these poor bastards, it better be done real soon," he said. "They're going to get killed, the whole lot of them." An obedient soldier, he then headed outdoors to help keep the West's death watch.

Peter Maass was a foreign correspondent based in Asia and Europe. His atricles have appeared in the Washington Post, The New York Times, The Wall Street Journal, *and* The New Republic. *He is currently a staff writer for the* Washington Post *and lives in Maryland. This story was excerpted from his book* Love Thy Neighbor: A Story of War.

DITCHING AT SEA

*Looking for a sinking boat in a great storm,
a rescue helicopter and its crew find
themselves in desperate straits.*

THE RAIN BAND IS A SWATCH OF CLOUDS 50 MILES WIDE, 80 miles long, and 10,000 feet thick. It is getting dragged into the low across the northwest quadrant of the storm; winds are 75 knots and the visibility is zero. Satellite imagery shows the rain band swinging across Ruvola's flight path like a door slamming shut. At 7:55 p.m., Ruvola radios the tanker pilot to confirm a fourth refueling, and the pilot rogers it. The refueling is scheduled for five minutes later, at precisely eight o'clock. At 7:56, turbulence picks up a little, and at 7:58 it reaches moderate levels. *Let's get this thing done,* Ruvola radios the tanker pilot. At 7:59 he pulls the probe release, extends it forward, and moves into position for contact. And then it hits.

Headwinds along the leading edge of the rain band are so strong that it feels as if the helicopter has been blown to a stop. Ruvola has no idea what he's run into; all he knows is that he can barely control the aircraft. Flying has become as much a question of physical strength as of fitness; he grips the collective with one hand, the joystick with the other, and leans forward to peer through the rain rattling off the windscreen. Flight manuals bounce around the cockpit and his copilot starts throwing up in the seat next to him. Ruvola lines up on the tanker and tries to hit the drogue, but the aircraft are moving around so wildly that it's like throwing darts down a gun barrel; hitting the target is pure dumb luck. In technical terms, Ruvola's aircraft is doing things "without inputs from the controls"; in human terms, it's getting batted around the sky. Ruvola tries as low as 300 feet—"along the ragged edges of the clouds," as he says—and as high as 4,500 feet, but he can't find clean air. The visibility is so bad that even with night-vision goggles on, he can barely make out the wing lights of the tanker plane in front of him. And they are right—*right*—on top of it; several times they overshoot the drogue and Spillane thinks they are going to take the plane's rudder off.

Ruvola has made twenty or thirty attempts on the drogue—a monstrous feat of concentration—when the tanker pilot radios that he has to shut down his number one engine. The oil pressure gauge is fluctuating wildly and they are risking a burn-out. The pilot starts in on the shut-down procedure, and suddenly the left-hand fuel hose retracts; shutting off the engine has disrupted the air flow around the wing, and the reel-in mechanism has mistaken that for too much slack. It performs what is known as an "uncommanded retraction." The pilot finishes shutting down the engine, brings Ruvola back in, and then reextends the hose. Ruvola lines up on it and immediately sees that something is wrong. The drogue is shaped like a small parachute, and ordinarily it fills with air and holds the hose steady; now it is just convulsing behind the tanker plane. It has been destroyed by 45 minutes of desperate refueling attempts.

Ruvola tells the tanker pilot that the left-handed drogue is shot and that they have to switch over to the other side. In these conditions refueling from the right-hand drogue is a nightmarish, white-knuckle business because the helicopter probe also extends from the right-hand side of the of the cockpit, so the pilot has to come even tighter into the fuselage of the tanker to make contact. Ruvola makes a run at the right-hand drogue, misses, comes in again, and misses again. The usual technique is to watch the tanker's wing flaps and anticipate where the drogue's going to go, but the visibility is so low that Ruvola can't see that far; he can barely see past the nose of his own helicopter. Ruvola makes a couple more runs at the drogue, and on his last attempt he comes in too fast, over-shoots the wing, and by the time he's realigned himself the tanker has disappeared. They've lost an entire C-130 in the clouds. They are at 4,000 feet in zero visibility with roughly twenty minutes of fuel left; after that they will just fall out of the sky. Ruvola can either keep trying to hit the drogue, or he can try to make it down to sea level while they still have fuel.

We're going to set up for a planned ditching, he tells his crew. *We're going to ditch while we still can.* And then Dave Ruvola drops the nose of the helicopter and starts racing his fuel gauge down to the sea.

John Spillane, watching silently from the spotter's seat, is sure he's just heard his death sentence. "Throughout my career I've always managed—just barely—to keep things in control," says Spillane. "But now, suddenly, the risk is becoming totally uncontrollable. We can't get fuel, we're going to end up in that roaring ocean, and we're not gonna be in control anymore. And I know the chances of being rescued are practically zero. I've been on a lot of rescue missions, and I know they can hardly even *find* someone in these conditions, let alone recover them. We're some of the best in the business—best equipped, best trained. We couldn't do a rescue a little while earlier, and now we're in the same situation. It looks real bleak. It's not going to happen."

While Ruvola is flying blindly downward through the clouds, co-pilot Buschor issues a mayday on an Air National Guard emergency frequency and then contacts the *Tamaroa*, fifteen miles to the northeast. He tells them they are out of fuel and about to set up for a planned ditching. Captain Brudnicki orders the *Tam's* searchlights turned up into the sky so the helicopter can give them a bearing, but Buschor says he can't see a thing. *Okay, just start heading towards us,* the radio dispatcher on the *Tam* says. *We don't have time, we're going down right now,* Buschor replies. Jim McDougall, handling the radios at the ODC in Suffolk, receives—simultaneously—the ditching alert and a phone call from Spillane's wife, who wants to know where her husband is. She'd had no idea there was a problem and just happened to call at the wrong moment; McDougall is so panicked by the timing that he hangs up on her. At 9:08, a dispatcher at Coast Guard headquarters in Boston takes a call that an Air National Guard helicopter is going down and scrawls frantically in the incident log: *"Helo [helicopter] & 130 enroute Suffolk. Can't refuel helo due visibility. May have to ditch. Stay airborne how long? 20-25 min. launch!"* He then notifies Cape Cod Air Base, where Karen Stimpson is chatting with one of her rescue crews. The five airmen get up without a word, file into the bathroom, and then report for duty out on the tarmac.

Ruvola finally breaks out of the clouds at 9:28, only 200 feet above the ocean. He goes into a hover and immediately calls for the ditching checklist, which prepares the crew to abandon the aircraft. They have practiced this dozens of times in training, but things are happening so fast that the routines start to fall apart. Jim Mioli has trouble seeing in the dim cabin lighting used with night-vision gear, so he can't locate the handle of the nine-man life raft. By the time he finds it, he doesn't have time to put on his Mustang survival suit. Ruvola calls three times for Mioli to read him the ditching checklist, but Mioli is too busy to answer him, so Ruvola has to go through it by memory. One of the most important things on the list is for the pilot to reach down and eject his door, but Ruvola is working too hard to remove his hands from the controls. In military terminology he has become "task-saturated," and the door stays on.

While Ruvola is trying to hold the aircraft in a hover, the PJs [pararescue jumpers] scramble to put together the survival gear. Spillane slings a canteen over his shoulder and clips a one-man life raft to the strap. Jim Mioli, who finally manages to extract the nine-man raft, pushes it to the edge of the jump door and waits for the order to deploy. Rick Smith, draped in survival gear, squats at the edge of the other jump door and looks over the side. Below is an ocean so ravaged by wind that they can't even tell the difference between the waves and the troughs; for all they know they are jumping three hundred feet. As horrible as that is, though, the idea of staying where they are is even worse. The helicopter is going to drop into the ocean at any moment, and no one on the crew wants to be anywhere nearby when it does.

Only Dave Ruvola will stay on board; as pilot, it is his job to make sure the aircraft doesn't fall on the rest of his crew. The chances of his escaping with his door still in place are negligible, but that is beside the point. The ditching checklist calls for a certain procedure, a procedure that insures the survival of the greatest number of crew. That Mioli neglects to put on his survival suit is also, in some ways, suicidal, but he has no choice. His duty is to oversee a safe bail-out, and if he stops to put his survival suit on, the nine-man raft won't be ready for deployment. He jumps without his suit.

At 9:30, the number one engine flames out; Spillane can hear the turbine wind down. They've been in a low hover for less than a minute. Ruvola calls out on the intercom: *The number one's out! Bail out! Bail out!* The number two is running on fumes; in theory, they should flame out at the same time. This is it. They are going down.

Mioli shoves the life raft out the right-hand door and watches it fall, in his words, "into the abyss." They are so high up that he doesn't even see it hit the water, and he can't bring himself to jump in after it. Without telling anyone, he decides to take his chances in the helicopter. Ditching protocol calls for copilot Buschor to remain on board as well, but Ruvola orders him out because he decides Buschor's chances of survival will be higher if he jumps. Buschor pulls his door-release lever but the door doesn't pop off the fuselage, so he just holds it open with one hand and steps out onto the footboard. He looks back at the radar altimeter, which is fluctuating between ten feet and eighty, and realized that the timing of his jump will mean the difference between life and death. Ruvola repeats his order to bail out, and Buschor unplugs the intercom wires from his flight helmet and flips his night vision goggles down. Now he can watch the waves roll underneath him in the dim green light of enhanced vision. He spots a huge crest, takes a breath and jumps.

Spillane, meanwhile, is grabbing some last-minute gear. "I wasn't terrified, I was scared," he says. "Forty minutes before I'd been more scared, thinking about the possibilities, but at the end I was totally committed. The pilot had made the decision to ditch, and it was a great decision. How many pilots might have just used up the last twenty minutes of fuel trying to hit the drogue? Then you'd fall out of the sky and everyone would die."

The helicopter is strangely quiet without the number one engine. The ocean below them, in the words of another pilot, looks like a lunar landscape, cratered and gouged and deformed by wind. Spillane spots Rick Smith at the starboard door, poised to jump, and moves towards him. "I'm convinced he was sizing up the waves," Spillane says. "I wanted desperately to stick together with him. I just had time to sit down, put my arm around his shoulders, and he went. We didn't have time to say anything—you want to say goodbye, you want to do a lot of things, but there's no time for that. Rick went, and a split-second later, I did."

According to people who have survived long falls, the acceleration of gravity is so heart-stoppingly fast that it's more like getting shot downward out of a cannon. A body accelerates roughly twenty miles an hour for every second it's in the air; after one second it's falling twenty miles an hour; after two seconds, forty miles an hour, and so on, up to a hundred and thirty. At that point the wind resistance is equal to the force of gravity, and the body is said to have reached terminal velocity. Spillane falls probably sixty or seventy feet, two and a half seconds of acceleration. He plunges through darkness without any idea where the water is or when he is going to hit. He has a dim memory of letting go of his one-man raft, and of his body losing position, and he thinks: My God, what a long way down. And then everything goes blank.

John Spillane has the sort of handsome, regular features that one might expect in a Hollywood actor playing a pararescueman—playing John Spillane, in fact. His eyes are stone-blue, without a trace of hardness or indifference, his hair is short and touched with grey. He comes across as friendly, unguarded, and completely sure of himself. He has a quick smile and an offhand way of talking that seems to progress from detail to detail, angle to angle, until there's nothing more to say on a topic. His humor is delivered casually, almost as an after-thought, and seems to surprise even himself. He's of average height, average build, and once ran 40 miles for the hell of it. He seems to be a man who has long since lost the need to prove things to anyone.

Spillane grew up in New York City and joined the Air Force at seventeen. He trained as a combat diver—infiltrating positions, securing beaches, rescuing other combat divers—and then left at 21 to join the Air National Guard. He "guard-bummed" around the world for a year, returning to Rockaway Beach to lifeguard in the summer, and then signed up for PJ school. After several years of reserve duty he quit, went through the police academy, and became a scuba diver for the New York City Police Department. For three years he pulled bodies out of submerged cars and mucked guns out of the East River, and finally decided to go back to school before his G.I. Bill ran out. He started out majoring in geology—"I wanted to go stomp mountaintops for a while"—but he fell in love instead and ended up moving out to Suffolk to work full-time for the Guard. That was in 1989. He was 32, one of the most widely-experienced PJs in the country.

When John Spillane hits the Atlantic Ocean he is going about fifty miles an hour. Water is the only element that offers more resistance the harder you hit it, and at fifty miles an hour it might as well be concrete. Spillane fractures three bones in his right arm, one bone in his left leg, four ribs in his chest, ruptures a kidney, and bruises his pancreas. The flippers, the one-man raft, and the canteen all are torn off his body. Only the mask, which he wore backward with the strap in his mouth, stays on as it is supposed to. Spillane doesn't remember the moment he first realized he was in the water. His memory goes from falling to swimming, with nothing in be-tween. When he understands that he is swimming, that is *all* he understands—he doesn't know who he is, why he is there, or how he got there. He has no history and no future; he is just a consciousness at night in the middle of the sea.

When Spillane treats injured seamen offshore, one of the first things he evaluates is their degree of consciousness. The highest level, known as "alert and oriented times four," describes almost everyone in an everyday situation. They know who they are, where they are, what time it is, and what's just happened. If someone suffers a blow to the head, the first thing they lose is recent events—"alert and oriented times three"—and the last thing they lose is their identity. A person who has lost all four levels of consciousness, right down to their identity, is said to be "alert and oriented times zero." When John Spillane wakes up in the water, he is alert and oriented times zero. His understanding of the world is reduced to the fact that he exists, nothing more. Almost simultaneously, he understands that he is in excruciating pain. For a long time, that is all he knows. Until he sees the life raft.

Spillane may be alert and oriented times zero, but he knows to swim for a life raft when he sees one. It has been pushed out by Jim Mioli, the flight engineer, and has inflated automatically when it hits the water. Now it is scudding along on the wave crests, the sea anchors barely holding it down in the 70-knot wind. "I lined up on it, intercepted it, and hung off the side," says Spillane. "I knew I was in the ocean, in a desperate situation, and I was hurt. I didn't know anything else. It was while I was hanging onto the raft that it all started coming back to me. We were on a mission. We ran out of fuel. I bailed out. I'm not alone."

While Spillane is hanging off the raft, a gust of wind catches it and flips it over. One moment Spillane is in the water trying to figure out who he is, the next moment he is high and dry. Instantly he feels better. He is lying on the wobbly nylon floor, evaluating the stabbing pain in his chest—he thinks he's punctured his lungs—when he hears people shouting in the distance. He kneels and points his diver's light in their direction, and just as he is wondering how to help them—whoever they are—the storm gods flip the raft over again. Spillane is dumped back into the sea. He clings to the safety line, gasping and throwing up sea water, and almost immediately the wind flips the raft over a third time. He has now gone one-and-a-half revolutions. Spillane is back inside, lying spread-eagle on the floor, when the raft is flipped a fourth and final time. Spillane is tossed back into the water, this time clinging to a rubberized nylon bag that later turns out to contain half a dozen wool blankets. It floats, and Spillane hangs off it and watches the raft go cartwheeling off across the wave crests. He is left alone and dying on the sea.

"After I lost contact with the raft I was by myself and I realized my *only* chance of survival was to make it until the storm subsided," he says. "There was no way they could pick us up, I'd just ditched a perfectly good helicopter and I knew our guys would be the ones to come out and get us if they could, but they couldn't. They couldn't refuel. So I'm contemplating this and I know I cannot make it through the storm. They might have somebody on-scene when light breaks, but I'm not going to make it that long. I'm dying inside."

For the first time since the ordeal began, Spillane has the time to contemplate his own death. He isn't panicked so much as saddened by the idea. His wife is five months pregnant with their first child, and he's been home very little recently—he was in paramedic school, and in training for the New York City marathon. He wishes that he'd spent more time at home. He wishes—incredibly—that he'd cut the grass one more time before winter. He wishes there was someone who could tell his wife and family what happened in the end. It bothers him that Dave Ruvola probably died taking the helicopter in. It bothers him they're all going to die for lack of five hundred pounds of jet fuel. The shame of it all, he thinks; we have this eight-million-dollar helicopter, nothing's wrong with it, nobody's shooting at us, we're just out of fuel.

Spillane has regained his full senses by this point, and the circumstances he finds himself in are nightmarish beyond words. It is so dark that he can't see his hand in front of his face, the waves just rumble down on him out of nowhere and bury him for a minute at a time. The wind is so strong it doesn't blow the water so much as fling it; there is no way to keep it out of his stomach. Every few minutes he has to retch it back up. Spillane has lost his one-man life raft, his ribs are broken, and every breath feels like he is being run through with a hot fire poker. He is crying out in pain and dawn isn't for another eight hours.

After an hour of making his farewells and trying to keep the water out of his stomach, Spillane spots two strobes in the distance. The Mustang suits all have strobe lights on them, and it is the first real evidence he has that someone else has survived the ditching. Spillane's immediate reaction is to swim toward them, but he stops himself. There is no way he is going to live out the night, he knows, so he might as well just die on his own. That way he won't inflict his suffering on anyone else. "I didn't want them to see me go," he says. "I didn't want them to see me in pain. It's the same with marathons—don't talk to me, let me just suffer through this by myself. What finally drove me to them was survival training. It emphasizes strength in numbers, and I know that if I'm with them, I'll try harder not to die. But I couldn't let them see me in pain, I told myself. I couldn't let them down."

Believing that their chances will be slightly less negligible in a group. Spillane slowly makes his way toward the lights. He is buoyed up by his life vest and wetsuit and swimming with his broken arm stretched out in front of him, gripping the blanket bag. It takes a long time and the effort exhausts him, but he can see the lights slowly getting closer. They disappear in the wave troughs, appear on the crests, and then disappear again. Finally, after a couple of hours of swimming, he gets close enough to shout and then to make out their faces. It is Dave Ruvola and Jim Mioli, roped together with parachute cord. Ruvola seems fine, but Mioli is nearly incoherent with hypothermia. He only has his Nomex flight suit on, and the chances of him lasting until dawn are even lower that Spillane's.

Ruvola had escaped the helicopter unscathed, but barely. He knew that the rotors would tear him and the helicopter apart if they hit the water at full speed, so he moved the aircraft away from his men, waited for the number two engine to flame out, and then performed what is known as a hovering auto-rotation. As the helicopter fell, its dead rotors started to spin, and Ruvola used that energy to slow the aircraft down. Like downshifting a car on a hill, a hovering auto-rotation is a way of dissipating the force of gravity by feeding it back through the engine. By the time the helicopter hit the water it had slowed to a manageable speed, and all the torque had been bled out of the rotors; they just smacked the face of an oncoming wave and stopped.

Ruvola found himself in a classic training situation, only it was real life: he had to escape from a flooded helicopter upside down in complete darkness. He was a former PJ, though, and a marathon swimmer, so being underwater was something he was used to. The first thing he did was reach for his HEEDS bottle, a three-minute air supply strapped to his left leg, but it had been ripped loose during the ditching; all he had was the air in his lungs. He reached up, pulled the quick-release on his safety belt, and it was then that he realized he'd never kicked the exit door out. He was supposed to do that so it wouldn't get jammed shut on impact, trapping him inside. He found the door handle, turned it, and pushed.

To his amazement, the door fell open; Ruvola kicked his way out from under the fuselage, tripped the CO_2 cartridge on his life vest, and shot ten or fifteen feet to the surface. He popped up into a world of shrieking darkness and landsliding seas. At one point the crest of a wave drove him so far under the surface that the pressure change damaged his inner ear. Ruvola started yelling for the other crew members, and a few minutes later flight engineer Mioli—who'd also managed to escape the sinking helicopter—answered him in the darkness. They started swimming toward each other, and after five or ten minutes Ruvola got close enough to grab Mioli by his survival vest. He took the hood off his survival suit, put it on Mioli's head, and then tied their two bodies together with parachute cord.

They've been in the water for a couple of hours when Spillane finally struggles up, face locked up with pain. The first thing Ruvola sees is a glint of light on a face mask, and he thinks that maybe it's a Navy SEAL who has airlocked out of a U.S. submarine and is coming to save them. It isn't. Spillane swims up, grabs a strap on Ruvola's flotation vest, and clamps his other arm around the blanket bag. What's that? Ruvola screams. I don't know, I'll open it tomorrow! Spillane yells back. Open it now! Ruvola answers. Spillane is in too much pain to argue about it, so he opens the bag and watches several dark shapes—the blankets—go snapping off downwind.

He tosses the bag aside and settles down to face the next few hours as best he can.

One can tell by the very handwriting in the District One incident log that the dispatcher—in this case a Coast Guardsman named Gill—can't quite believe what he's writing down. The words are large and sloppy and salted with exclamation points. At one point he jots down, apropos of nothing: *"They're not alone out there,"* as if to reassure himself that things will turn out all right. That entry comes at 9:30, seconds after Buschor calls in the first engine loss. Five minutes later Gill writes down: *"39-51 North, 72-00 West, Ditching here, 5POB [people on board]."* Seven minutes after that the tanker plane—which will circle the area until their fuel runs low—reports hearing an EPIRB signal for fifteen seconds, then nothing. From Gill's notes:

> *9:30—Tamaroa in area, launched H-65*
> *9:48—Cape Cod 60!*
> *9:53—CAA [Commander of Atlantic Area]/brfd—ANY-THING YOU WANT—NAVY SHIP WOULD BE GREAT—WILL LOOK.*

Within minutes of the ditching, rescue assets from Florida to Massachusetts are being readied for deployment. The response is massive and nearly instantaneous. At 9:48, thirteen minutes into it, Air Station Cape Cod launches a Falcon jet and an H-3 helicopter. Half an hour later a Navy P-3 jet at Brunswick Naval Air Station is requested and readied. The P-3 infrared-equipped to detect heat-emitting objects, like people. The *Tamaroa* has diverted before the helicopter has even gone down. At 10:23, Boston requests a second Coast Guard cutter, the *Spencer.* They even consider diverting an aircraft carrier.

The survivors are drifting fast in mountainous seas and the chances of spotting them are terrible. Helicopters will have minimal time on–scene because they can't refuel, it's unlikely conditions would permit a hoist rescue anyway, and there's no way to determine if the guardmen's radios are even working. That leaves the *Tamaroa* to do the job, but she wasn't even able to save the *Satori* crew, during less severe conditions. The storm is barreling westward, straight toward the ditch point, and wave heights are climbing past anything ever recorded in the area.

If things look bad for Ruvola's crew, they don't look much better for the people trying to rescue them. It's not inconceivable that another helicopter will to have to ditch during the rescue effort, or that a Coast Guardsman will get washed off the *Tamaroa*. (For that matter the *Tamaroa* herself, at 205 feet, is not necessarily immune to disaster. One freak wave could roll her over and put eighty men in the water.) Half a dozen aircraft, two ships, and two hundred rescuers are heading for 39 north, 72 west; the more men out here, the higher the chances are of someone else getting into trouble. A succession of disasters could draw the rescue assets of the entire East Coast of the United States out to sea.

A Falcon jet out of Air Station Cape Cod is the first aircraft on-scene. It arrives 90 minutes after the ditching, and the pilot sets up what is known as an expanding-square search. He moves slightly downsea of the last known position—the "splash point"—and starts flying ever-increasing squares until he has covered an area ten miles across. He flies at 200 feet, just below cloud cover, and estimates the probability of spotting the survivors to be one-in-three. He turns up nothing. Around 11:30 he expands his search to a twenty-mile square and starts all over again, slowly working his way south-west with the direction of drift. The infrared-equipped P-3 is getting ready to launch from Brunswick, and a Coast Guard helicopter is pounding its way southward from Cape Cod.

And then, ten minutes into the second square, he picks up something: a weak signal on 243 megahertz. That's a frequency coded into Air National Guard radios. It means at least one of the airmen is still alive.

The Falcon pilot homes in on the signal and tracks it to a position about twenty miles downsea of the splash point. Whoever it is, they're drifting fast. The pilot comes in low, scanning the sea with night-vision goggles, and finally spots a lone strobe flashing below them in the darkness. It's appearing and disappearing behind the huge swell. Moments later he spots three more strobes half a mile away. All but one of the crew are accounted for. The pilot circles, flashing his lights, and then radios his position in to District One. An H-3 helicopter, equipped with a hoist and rescue swimmer, is only twenty minutes away. The whole ordeal could be over in less than an hour.

The Falcon circles the strobes until the H-3 arrives, and then heads back to base with a rapidly-falling fuel gauge. The H-3 is a huge machine, similar to the combat helicopters used in Vietnam, and has spare fuel tanks installed inside the cabin. It can't refuel in midflight, but it can stay airborne for four or five hours. The pilot, Ed DeWitt, tries to establish a 40-foot hover, but wind shear keeps spiking him downward. The ocean is a ragged white expanse in his searchlights and there are no visual reference points to work off of. At one point he turns downwind and almost gets driven into the sea.

DeWitt edges his helicopter to within 100 yards of the three men and tells his flight engineer to drop the rescue basket. There's no way he's putting his swimmer in the water, but these are experienced rescuemen, and they may be able to extract themselves. It's either that or wait for the storm to calm down. The flight engineer pays out the cable and watches in alarm as the basket is blown straight back toward the tail rotors. It finally reaches the water, swept backward at an angle of 45 degrees, and DeWitt tries to hold a steady hover long enough for the swimmers to reach the basket. He tries for almost an hour, but the waves are so huge that the basket doesn't spend more than a few seconds on each crest before dropping to the end of its cable. Even if the men could get themselves into the basket, a shear pin in the hoist mechanism is designed to fail with loads over 600 pounds, and three men in waterlogged clothing would definitely push that limit. The entire assembly—cable, basket, everything—would let go into the sea.

DeWitt finally gives up trying to save the airmen and goes back up to a hover at two hundred feet. In the distance he can see the *Tamaroa*, searchlights pointed straight up, plunging through the storm. He vectors her in toward the position of the lone strobe in the distance—Graham Buschor—and then drops a flare by the others and starts back for Suffolk. He's only minutes away from "bingo," the point at which an aircraft doesn't have enough fuel to make it back to shore.

Two hundred feet below, John Spillane watches his last hope clatter away toward the north. He hadn't expected to get rescued, but still, it's hard to watch. The only benefit he can see is that his family will know for sure that he died. That might spare them weeks of false hope. In the distance, Spillane can see lights rising and falling in the darkness. He assumes it's a Falcon jet looking for the other airmen, but its lights are moving strangely; it's not moving like an aircraft. It's moving like a ship.

The *Tamaroa* has taken four hours to cover the fifteen miles to the splash point; her screws are turning for twelve knots and making three. Commander Brudnicki doesn't know how strong the wind is because it rips the anemometer off the mast, but pilot Ed DeWitt reports that his airspeed indicator hit 87 knots—a hundred miles an hour—while he was in a stationary hover. The *Tamaroa's* course to the downed airmen puts them in a beam sea, which starts to roll the ship through an arc of 110 degrees; at that angle, bulkheads are easier to walk on than floors. In the wheelhouse, Commander Brudnicki is surprised to find himself looking *up* at the crest of the waves, and when he orders full rudder and full bell, it takes thirty or forty seconds to see any effect at all. Later, after stepping off the ship, he says, "I certainly hope that was the high point of my career."

The first airman they spot is Graham Buschor, swimming alone and relatively unencumbered a half mile from the other three. He's in a Mustang survival suit and has a pen-gun flare and the only functional radio beacon of the entire crew. Brudnicki orders the operations officer, Lieutenant Kristopher Furtney, to maneuver the *Tamaroa* upsea of Buschor and then drift down on him. Large objects drift faster than small ones, and if the ship is upwind of Buschor, the waves won't smash him against the hull. The gunner's mate starts firing flares off from cannons on the flying bridge, and a detail of seamen crouch in the bow with throwing ropes, waiting for their chance. They can hardly keep their feet in the wind.

The engines come to a full stop and the *Tamaroa* wallows beam-to in the huge seas. It's a dangerous position to be in; the *Tamaroa* loses her righting arm at 72 degrees, and she's already heeling to 55. Drifting down on swimmers is standard rescue procedure, but the seas are so violent that Buschor keeps getting flung out of reach. There are times when he's 30 feet higher than the men trying to rescue him. The crew in the bow can't get a throwing rope anywhere near him, and Brudnicki won't order his rescue swimmer overboard because he's afraid he won't get him back. The men on deck finally realize that if the boat's not going to Buschor, Buschor's going to have to go to it. *SWIM!* they scream over the rail. *SWIM!* Buschor rips off his gloves and hood and starts swimming for his life.

He swims as hard as he can; he swims until his arms give out. He claws his way up to the ship, gets swept around the bow, struggles back within reach of it again, and finally catches hold of a cargo net that the crew have dropped over the side. The net looks like a huge rope ladder and is held by six or seven men at the rail. Buschor twists his hands in the mesh and slowly gets hauled up the hull. One good wave at the wrong moment could take them all out. The deck crewmen land Buschor like a big fish and carry him into the deckhouse. He's dry-heaving seawater and can barely stand; his core temperature has dropped to 94 degrees. He's been in the water four hours and twenty-five minutes. Another few hours and he may not have been able to cling to the net.

It's taken half an hour to get one man on board, and they have four more to go, one of whom hasn't even been sighted yet. It's not looking good. Brudnicki is also starting to have misgivings about putting his men on deck. The larger waves are sweeping the bow and completely burying the crew; they keep having to do head counts to make sure no one has been swept overboard. "It was the hardest decision I've ever had to make, to put my people out here and rescue that crew," Brudnicki says. "Because I knew there was a chance I could lose some of my men. If I'd decided not to do the rescue, no one back home would've said a thing—they knew it was almost impossible. But can you really make a conscious decision to say, 'I'm just going to watch those people in the water die?'"

Brudnicki decides to continue the rescue; twenty minutes later he has the *Tamaroa* in a beam sea a hundred yards upwind of the three Guardsmen. Crew members are lighting off flares and aiming searchlights, and the chief quartermaster is on the flying bridge radioing Furtney when to fire the ship's engine. Not only do they have to maneuver the drift, but they have to time the roll of the ship so the gunwale rides down toward the waterline while the men in the water grab for the net. As it is, the gunwales are riding from water-level to twenty feet in the air virtually every wave. Spillane is injured, Mioli is incoherent, and Ruvola is helping to support them both. There's no way they'll be able to swim like Buschor.

Spillane watches the ship heaving through the breaking seas and for the life of him can't imagine how they're going to do this. As far as he's concerned, a perfectly likely outcome is for all three of them to drown within sight of the ship because a pickup is impossible. "My muscles were getting rigid, I was in great pain," he says. "The *Tam* pulled up in front of us and turned broadsides to the waves and I couldn't believe they did that—they were putting themselves in terrible risk. We could hear them all screaming on the deck and we could see the chemical lights coming at us, tied to the ends of the ropes."

The ropes are difficult to catch, so the deck crew throw the cargo net over the side. Lieutenant Furtney again tries to ease his ship over to the swimmers, but the vessel is 1,600 tons and almost impossible to control. Finally, on the third attempt, they snag the net. Their muscles are cramping with cold and Jim Mioli is about to start a final slide into hypothermia. The men on deck give a terrific heave—they're pulling up 600 pounds deadweight—and at the same time a large wave drops out from underneath the swimmers. They're exhausted and desperate and the net is wrenched out of their hands.

The next thing Spillane knows, he's underwater. He fights his way to the surface just as the boat rolls inward toward them and he grabs the net again. This is it; if he can't do it now, he dies. The deck crew heaves again, and Spillane feels himself getting pulled up the steel hull. He climbs up a little higher, feels hands grabbing him, and the next thing he knows he's being pulled over the gunwale onto the deck. He's in such pain he cannot stand. The men pin him against the bulkhead, cut off his survival suit, and then carry him inside, staggering with the roll of the ship. Spillane can't see Ruvola and Mioli. They haven't managed to get back on the net.

The waves wash the two men down the hull toward the ship's stern, where the twelve-foot screw is digging out a cauldron of boiling water. Furtney shuts the engines down and the two men get carried around the stern and then up the port side of the ship. Ruvola catches the net for the second time and gets one hand into the mesh. He clamps the other one around Mioli and screams into his face, You got to do this, Jim! There aren't too many second chances in life! This is gonna take everything you got!

Mioli nods and wraps his hands into the mesh. Ruvola gets a foothold as well as a handhold and grips with all the strength in his cramping muscles. The two men get dragged upward, penduluming in and out with the roll of the ship, until the deck crew at the rail can reach them. They grab Ruvola and Mioli by the hair, the Mustang suit, the combat vest, anything they can get their hands on, and pull them over the steel rail. Like Spillane they're retching seawater and can barely stand. Jim Mioli has been in sixty-degree water for over five hours and is severely hypothermic. His core temperature is 90.4, eight degrees below normal; another couple of hours and he'd be dead.

The two airmen are carried inside, their clothing is cut off, and they're laid in bunks. Spillane is taken to the executive officer's quarters and given an IV and catheter and examined by the ship's paramedic. His blood pressure is 140/90, his pulse is a hundred, and he's running a slight fever. *Eyes pearled, abdomen and chest tenderness, pain to quadriceps,* the paramedic radios SAR OPS [Search-and-Rescue Operations] Boston. *Fractured wrist, possibly ribs, suspect internal injury. Taking Tylenol-3 and seasick patch.* Boston relays the information to an Air National Guard flight surgeon, who says he's worried about internal bleeding and tells them to watch the abdomen carefully. If it gets more and more tender to the touch, he's bleeding inside and has to be evacuated by helicopter. Spillane thinks about dangling in a rescue litter over the ocean and says he'd rather not. At daybreak the executive officer comes in to shave and change his clothes, and Spillane apologizes for bleeding and vomiting all over his bed. Hey, whatever it takes, the officer says. He opens the porthole hatch, and Spillane looks out at the howling grey sky and the ravaged ocean. Ah, could you close that? he says. I can't take it.

Sebastian Junger is a contributing editor of Men's Journal *and a contributor to various other magazines including* Outside *and* American Heritage. *He is the author of the best-selling book* The Perfect Storm *from which this story was excerpted. He lives in New York City.*

ANTHONY BRENNAN

A ZAMBIAN NIGHTMARE

The only problem is, the machetes are real.

GINA HAS, OVER THE YEARS, OCCASIONALLY AWAKENED ME from my normal deep sleep with a nightmare-induced scream. So when this happened in Lusaka within a few days of our arrival in Africa, I reassured her, I told her that we were OK and that she should go back to sleep.

We were staying in a huge, 6,000-square-foot, ranch-style house; it had a 10-foot cement wall topped with broken glass and covered with barbed wire; all windows and doors were covered with bars; the outside area was floodlit; there were two huge guard dogs—a Great Dane and a Rottweiler—and there was a full-time security guard who patrolled within the garden wall all night long.

So when she awoke and said that somebody was outside our bedroom window I assured her that there couldn't possibly be anyone there since the dogs were quiet. She lay back down but she didn't close her eyes. I closed mine. Within a minute she froze again. "There's someone there," she whispered frantically. I shot up and sure enough there were shadows on the drapes.

35

I leapt out of bed and ran to the window; I threw open the drapes and my heart stopped. There was a gang of six to eight men—all armed with clubs, crowbars, and machetes and standing about 2 feet away and looking directly at me. I let out an incoherent shriek, I think it was supposed to be like the audible weapon that the Maoris used in Robert Graves's short story "The Shout," but it didn't work, or it only worked temporarily. The gang fled to the gatehouse about 50 yards away, but then, clearly illuminated by the floodlights, they paused, regrouped, and immediately started back towards us. I knew we were in trouble.

There was no time to think. Immediately the gang attacked the windows and the steel security bars that were welded over them. Glass flew. The noise was terrifying, but even more so was the image of this gang that was determined to smash its way into the bedroom with no thought for the bedlam they were creating or that the occupants might be armed. They could not have known it, but we weren't. I didn't even have my pants on. I was stark naked!

We fled from the bedroom. There was a phone in the hallway with a pad of emergency numbers. Our hostess, before she had left us there alone had explained what each one meant. The first on the list was the universal emergency number 999, this was followed by four police stations, fire department, etc. I began at the top; 999 rang 30-40 times and no one responded. I couldn't believe it. Was I in my frantic state misdialing? I tried again, still no response. I tried the first police station on the list. "Let it ring," I told myself. After about 30 rings I hung up. All the while there was this incredible pandemonium about 3 feet from my head as the attack continued on the adjacent windows. Try the next one, "Oh God, it's busy." Try another, this time the number of our hostess in Zambia, who lived in the city in an apartment. Her phone must have also rung 30-40 times, and again with absolutely no response. All the while total bedlam—they were now attacking every window on that side of the house.

The noise was horrendous and I was standing there naked trying to find one person who could help. I shouted to Gina to get my pants; she returned to our bedroom, grabbed them and locked the door, then locked the corridor door and pulled the keys. When she arrived I was dialing the last number on the list, the Roma District police station.

After an eternity, someone, who was very obviously asleep, answered the phone. He was befuddled and was not responding at all. Over and over I repeated, "There's a gang of robbers breaking into the house at 5557 Magoye Road, there's at least six of them, they're smashing their way in through the windows; the address is 5557 Magoye Road. Do you understand me?"

In film and fiction the policeman is instantly alert, his authoritative voice has a reassurance, you can imagine the radios crackling, patrol cars with lights and sirens speeding to your aid immediately. But in this case our man was still struggling with sleep or perhaps my unfamiliar accent was difficult for him to comprehend. He was my only hope. I kept asking him if he understood, did he have the address and could he send assistance? Finally he said that he thought that there might be a patrol somewhere and he would try! So much for fact and fiction. On that note of positive reassurance I gave up on the phone, the robbers were only a couple of feet from my head and by the level of the bedlam and destruction they must have been almost through the wall—we fled. As we ran down the corridor, Gina rang the servants bell several times to alert Mr. Tembo, but at five foot, three inches and hardly 130 pounds we knew we were on our own.

I mentioned that the house was large; one day for no

particular reason at all, I paced the distance from the master bedroom to the kitchen. It was 55 yards! And the house extended two more rooms beyond the kitchen. On another occasion I looked in every room in the house, seventeen in all, to determine the most secure place in the event of an emergency. I certainly didn't anticipate anything like this but I suppose our being there alone, being so far from anyone we knew, and being generally fairly security-conscious caused me to check it out "just in case." Well, here we were right in the middle of "just in case!"

We ran to the far end of the house, through the kitchen to a guest bedroom. Off that bedroom was a tiny enclosed patio that had a toilet and a shower, primarily for outside use. It was the shower that we'd been using, since for some unknown reason it was the only one of four in the house that had hot water.

As we passed the main door of the house I saw the dogs. They were right outside the door, totally oblivious to the bedlam that was happening on the other side! I couldn't believe what I was seeing! In the mythology of guard dogs, Rottweilers are second only to lions in their ferocity and aggressive natures. Ours was standing there with that glazed look that tourists get; he generally seemed to be looking at the stars, as was his Dane companion.

I screamed at them to try and get them excited, I screamed "kill, kill," over and over as loud as I could. They both stood and looked at me as though I was silly, not a trace of guard-dogedness, just a canine blank stare.

When we reached the guest bedroom I asked Gina to wait there for me. I had decided that regardless, it would be better to have the dogs in the house with us, so I was going back to get them. I had to unlock the main door and then unlock the two padlocks on the steel grill, which enclosed a tiny entrance patio. I seized the Dane by the collar and tried to pull him into the house. Years of conditioning had brainwashed him into believing that he wasn't a house dog, he wasn't even allowed into the house. So when I tried to drag him he just dug his heels in and it was an impasse. It was like trying to drag a donkey through a door that he didn't want to enter, but finally I prevailed. I then seized the Rottweiler and dragged him, also protesting, into the house. I started to re-padlock the grill, but at that instant the gang of robbers came running around the house. They came straight for me swinging their clubs and machetes at my hands as I fumbled with the padlocks.

For the first time I saw them very clearly. There was a crazy frantic quality in their eyes. I retreated into the house and locked the door, why I'm not sure since it was surrounded by two floor-to-ceiling plate glass windows, which were all that now stood between us and them. I grabbed the Rottweiler and ran, dragging him back to where I'd left Gina. She was now hiding in a cupboard above the clothes closet. It must have seemed like an ideal hiding place except we couldn't lock the bedroom door because the key wasn't in the lock. I screamed at her to come down, but she was terrified and not about to vacate her hiding place; she pleaded with me to come up where she was. There must have been something in my voice that clinched it because she very unwillingly came down.

We exited the bedroom with the Rottweiler into the shower/toilet area and I locked the final door behind us. When I looked around, the area we were in was only 6 feet wide by 3 feet deep with a padlocked steel security grill between us and the garden. I suddenly realized that we were alone, the dog was gone! There was nowhere he could go but he certainly wasn't there! He must have squeezed through the bars! He weighed about 150 pounds but he went through that grill as easily and quickly as a cat.

I knew that the size of the house and the endless rooms would give us a degree of security. The place was so large that we kept discovering "new" rooms even after we had been there a few days. We were being extremely quiet, speaking only in whispers. If any of the robbers were close by we didn't want to reveal our location. But at that instant I saw over the garden wall, about 25 yards away, the neighbor. He was standing on his patio looking directly towards us. I threw caution to the wind and shouted to him, as loud as I could, "Help, call the police, we're being attacked by robbers." I repeated this at the top of my lungs over and over for at least two minutes, but he stood in the shadows of his patio and just stared at us, with no reaction. Finally he turned, walked into his house and the door closed behind him. It was a very depressing moment, his total neutrality left me feeling very alone, and now the robbers were in no doubt that we were still in the house and they must have known exactly where we were.

The shower stall was a typical one with a shower at one end and a small area behind the door. The door was a flimsy wooden affair and wasn't lockable, but if I sat on the floor with my back braced against it I could wedge my feet against a step up to the shower. Gina sat at that end silently terrified. She had the foresight to grab two knives from the kitchen as we ran through, nothing that you'd want to stake your life on, but they were all we had, and better than nothing. I took them both, one in my hand and the other tucked into my belt behind my back. I knew that the robbers had 3-foot-long steel bars and 2-foot machetes. If it came to it, our only advantage, if you can call it that, was that we were in an enclosure, in darkness, and they could only attack one person at a time. Our kitchen knives wouldn't be much use against someone thrusting at us with either machetes or steel bars. Prayer might have been appropriate but I'd never thought in those terms prior to then, so it didn't occur to me. The only thing that did was how to react when the time came, which I was sure it would, and how to defend ourselves in that situation. I had visions of them attacking the door with me braced against it. They would realize immediately that it wasn't locked and that the resistance was me. Therefore the logical thing to do would be to smash through the lower door with machetes and crowbars. I didn't reach any conclusions on how to deal with that reality.

The night was silent; I could hear my breathing and thought that anyone else close by would also. There was no indication of anything happening, no sounds. I assumed that it must be because they were at the far end of the house and were being very quiet. With the door closed in that tiny space it became suffocatingly hot. During the day it was in the 90s, at night, probably in the 75–80s. I remember that we had been sleeping with only a sheet and a mosquito net. The air in the shower stall was stifling, I couldn't breathe, the humidity was horrendous. Sweat trickled down my back. I decided that I must open the door to get some air; I told Gina what I was going to do.

"Please, please don't open the door, please," she beseeched in a frantic whisper. I felt that I had to open it so I moved my position slightly and cracked the door about two inches; the cool draft of air was wonderful, delicious. In an effort to waft some air back to where Gina was, I tried to open and close the door gently but rapidly a couple of times. The silence was shattered when I misjudged it and accidentally banged it closed with a loud noise. We were rigid, the noise sounded as though it must have reverberated through the entire house; now they must know where we were! But they still didn't come. I remember trying to estimate the passage of time; I didn't know what time it was or what time this nightmare had started. I realized that when your senses are deprived it's almost impossible to estimate time. We remained totally silent, only our breathing was audible. In the beginning we could hear the robbers when they were smashing in, but now that end of the house had also fallen silent. Maybe they'd left? I wondered how long until dawn. There were no clues, no lightness of the sky, no bird chorus, just our breathing.

At some point, after what seemed like an eternity, I began to think that perhaps we were going to be OK, that perhaps the robbers would take what they could find and leave. We couldn't hear a sound, maybe they'd already left? Then I started to think about the bedroom. It contained everything we had with us, all of our money (close to $3,000 in cash and unsigned travelers' checks); our camera gear—three Nikons with motor drives plus half a dozen lenses and all of the miscellaneous gear; our passports, plane tickets, clothes. Everything that we owned was in that room, and that was the room that they were smashing their way into when we fled.

I began to think that we might escape alive, but I realized that we would emerge with only what we wore at that moment, Gina had on a pair of pants and a sweater, I had a pair of cotton pants, that was it, that was all we had between us in the middle of Africa! I foresaw the nightmare of dealing with the Zambian Government, Zambian Airlines, American Express, U.S. Embassy, et. al. The regular daytime phone system in Zambia would drive most Westerners who take such things for granted into hysterics, and as I began to think that we might escape this nightmare ordeal, I realized that it might, on the morrow, seem like "out of the frying pan and into the fire," but for that moment we still had to deal with our current set of problems.

After what seemed like an eternity I heard voices outside in the garden. I peered past the edge of the shower door and saw the silhouette of a figure against the first light of dawn as it walked past the grill. I didn't recognize him and thought for sure that it must be one of the robbers now coming to look for us.

Two or three seconds later another figure walked past. It was Mr. Tembo, our housekeeper. My most immediate thought was that they were holding him and forcing him to show them the house. I was reluctant to reveal our location but on impulse and perhaps without thinking I called his name and he came back towards where we were. He couldn't see us in the shadows inside the shower stall, but he said, "You can come out now, the police have arrived."

I remember asking him to bring a policeman to the grill so that we could see him. He said something and a man with an automatic rifle walked back towards us and stood there. It was just beginning to get light; it was 5:30 a.m.

Mr. Tembo unlocked the grill and we walked out; as we walked around the house towards the rear door, the one where I'd struggled with the dogs, I saw a plainclothes white man and another uniformed officer with an automatic rifle. They were standing ankle-deep in broken glass just inside the front door. We were both barefoot; I gave the plainclothes man the various keys that I had in my pockets and asked him to fetch us some shoes from the second bedroom down the corridor on the right. He returned a couple of minutes later with two pair of shoes, both Gina's. She went to get me a pair and came running back a few seconds later shouting, "They haven't taken anything, everything is intact!"

We couldn't believe it. They had stripped the center section of the house of everything removable, furniture, TVs, VCR, drapes, food, utensils, everything. But because we had locked the doors behind us as we had fled, they hadn't gone to that end of the house. My opening the main door grill to get the dogs gave them easy access, they only had to smash the large plate glass windows at the front door and they were in. At that point they must have given up on trying to break in through our bedroom, though they came very close. Two of the bars welded to the window frame were broken, and it wouldn't have taken very much to break one more.

It turned out that the "plainclothes man" was a professor of geology at the University of Lusaka. Apparently there had been so much of this happening that he and a group of locals had formed, what he called a "vigilante" group. The problem was that the police didn't have cars, so the "vigilantes" would use their personal cars to transport the police. They would patrol the neighborhoods at night and communicate by walkie-talkie. Our "police dispatcher" had the address totally wrong. It turned out that there was no such address; they knew that something was happening somewhere but they didn't know where. While we were standing in the yard talking about all of this I noticed that the Great Dane was throwing up. I looked at the vomit and saw that it contained large chunks of what looked like pork fat, it didn't look like anything that he was fed. Then the Rottweiler also began to vomit. The dogs had been poisoned, which accounted for their unusual behavior. Apparently it was a common practice for thieves to throw poisoned meat over the wall an hour or so before they came over. Both dogs were rushed to the vet. The Rottweiler almost died but finally pulled through three days later; the Dane was OK.

We had to go to the police station to make a report at 9 a.m. Our new-found geologist friend said that he would return and drive us there. We spent the intervening couple of hours packing our things and talking through the events of the night. We talked to the "security guard," a man about five foot, two inches, 110 pounds. His job (for which he was paid almost nothing) was to walk around the property all night long and keep us safe from attack. To protect us he carried a stick, a fairly short stick. His story was that the robbers came over the wall, overpowered him by throwing a coat over his head and tying his hands. He said that he heard them talk about killing him, but one of them said "not now, later." He was left tied up in the guard shack. They took his keys to open the gate for their departure. They were laden down with large "sacks," actually the drapes from each room were torn down and used to create "swag sacks."

When Vaughn, the geologist, returned he commented that "everything would be dispersed throughout the compound by now."

"What do you mean?" I asked. "Which compound, in fact, what is a compound?"

"You haven't seen the compound," he said. "Let me show you."

Whenever we had left the house to go into Lusaka during the week that we'd been there we had turned right outside the gate and walked to the highway, about a mile, and thence into the city.

That morning as we left in Vaughn's car, we made a left out of the gate. There was a bend in the road and as soon as we were around the curve I realized that we were in the midst of the most poverty-ridden shantytown you could imagine. Rusty tin shacks, cardboard "houses," open sewers, not a trace of green anywhere, just dusty brown dirt. There are shantytowns of the world's poor in every country, but this was worse than anything I'd ever seen. There were cardboard shacks, with no water, no electricity, no paths, no gardens, nothing, just poverty.

Suddenly it made sense, "our" 6,000-square-foot mansion on the edge of this ghetto was too much, it was there every time they had to walk into town, every day they had to pass it with its lights, TV, music, gardens, everything. "They" decided to share the wealth. Unfortunately for us they chose to do it the week that we were there.

Anthony Brennan, a photographer and filmmaker, had been invited to Zambia to present a display of photographs of Jamaican reggae musicians. He wrote this piece the day after the incident in order to get all of the details down while they were still clear in his mind. He has traveled throughout the western United States, the Caribbean, Central America and Europe. Born in England, he emigrated to Southern California in 1958, where he has lived and worked until his recent retirement.

THE "FRIENDLY" BEAR

*There are lessons to be learned in
the animal kingdom.*

I USED TO HAVE NIGHTMARES ABOUT BEARS. THEY ENTERED my dreamworld in the mid-1970s shortly after I came to Alaska. A geologist then, just out of graduate school, I spent my first summers in some of the state's wildest, most remote grizzly country. And each summer, usually toward the end of the field season, phantom grizzlies would invade my dreams, stalking, chasing, and attacking me. They lurked in the shadows of my mind, ominous and haunting. I now sometimes wonder if those imaginary bears were omens. Perhaps they spoke of things to come, of a July afternoon in Shuyak Island State Park at the northern end of Alaska's Kodiak Archipelago.

Five of us had spent the morning in kayaks; now it was time to stretch muscles and explore one of the many small islands that border Shuyak's northern coast. The islet we chose was inhabited by Sitka black-tailed deer; from the water we saw several animals feeding in open meadows. It was also home to a brown bear female with three tiny cubs. We'd spotted them earlier in the day, though the bear family had since disappeared into the forest.

I'd seen many grizzlies, but that was my first sighting of brown bears, coastal cousins of the grizzly. Alaska's brown bears tend to be more chocolate in color and have smaller humps and shorter claws than their interior relatives. On the average, they're much larger animals, mainly because they have access to more plentiful, energy-rich foods, especially salmon. A large male grizzly may weigh 600 to 700 pounds in fall, when it is fattened for hibernation. But the largest brown bears are twice that size. And nowhere do brown bears grow larger than on the Kodiak Archipelago, home to the subspecies *Ursus arctos middendorffi*. Even here, researchers say, adult females only reach 700 pounds, though this mother bear appeared much bigger.

We beached our kayaks, then split up. I went with Sam, one of the expedition's guides, following a game trail that began in a meadow but soon bordered a thick stand of spruce. Sam called out to announce our presence: "HOOYAH... HOOYAH." Eventually, the trail petered out where the forest reached the island's edge. We had a simple choice: return down the trail or cut through the woods. Sam chose the trees and I followed, despite some misgivings. He was the guide, after all.

The spruce were twenty to thirty feet high, spindly, and densely packed. We couldn't see more than ten to fifteen feet ahead, sometimes less. We were walking slowly, talking loudly, when suddenly my worst nightmare came true: a bear charged out of the forest's shadows.

She must have tried to hide her family in the stand to avoid the strange two-legged invaders of her island. But we'd entered her sanctuary, and threatened, however innocently, her offspring. Retreat hadn't worked, so her only option was to defend her cubs by force.

Things began to speed up and, simultaneously, to move in

slow motion around me. Less than twenty feet away, the bear was a blur of terrible speed, size, and power—a dark image of unstoppable rage. Her face was indistinct, and I sensed more than I saw her teeth and claws.

Two giant bounds were all it took for the bear to reach Sam, who was five feet in front of me. Somewhere amid the roaring that filled my head, I heard a cry: "Oh no!" I was certain Sam was about to die, or be seriously mauled, and feared that I would be, too.

The last thing I saw was the bear engulfing Sam. Then, despite everything I've learned, I turned and ran, breaking one of the cardinal rules of bear encounters. But my instincts were strong, telling me to get out of sight, out of the woods. Climbing one of the slender trees wasn't an option, and without any weapon there was nothing I could do to help Sam. The only question was whether the bear would come after me next.

I ran out of the forest onto a narrow stretch of beach. My thoughts were on finding the other three members of our party and getting Sam's rifle from his kayak.

Back in the forest, Sam was doing what he had to in order to survive. As the bear charged, Sam told us later, he ducked his head and fell backwards. Falling, he saw the bear's open mouth, its teeth and claws. Hitting the ground, he curled into a fetal position to protect his head and vital organs. With the bear breathing in his face, Sam played dead.

The bear grabbed him in a "hug," woofed loudly, and batted him a few times like a kitten playing with a mouse, but she struck him with her paws, not her claws. There was no sound of tearing flesh. When there was no response from her victim, the bear ended the attack as suddenly as she began it. The threat removed, she left with her cubs.

I remained standing on the beach, listening and looking for

any sign of the bear, when incredibly, I heard Sam shout, "The bear's gone. I'm all right."

Miraculously, he was uninjured except for a small scratch on the back of his hand, which he got falling back into a small spruce. For someone who had just been attacked by a bear, Sam was taking the incident much more calmly than I. Perhaps, I'd learn later, this was because he'd been "false charged" by bears three times previously.

Sam quickly recounted the story, then said, "Thank goodness it was a friendly bear. It wasn't looking for a fight. It was just trying to make a point: 'Leave me alone.'"

Hours later, when we were rehashing the attack, he added, "I felt no sense of aggression or panic. I believe animals can sense a person's energy. If you're projecting aggression or if the adrenaline is flowing, they know it. I was very calculating as to what I should do." It turned out he did everything right once the bear attacked. Listening to Sam's story, still pumped with adrenaline, I could only shake my head and marvel at our escape.

Heading across the meadow to warn the others, we saw the sow one hundred yards away, still greatly agitated. She stood up, then fell back on all fours and ran around in circles. She stood up again and looked down the island, and we guessed she sensed or smelled our companions. The bear stood one final time, then turned sharply and loped into another, larger stand of spruce. She was followed by her cubs, three teddy bear-size creatures strung out in a line, running hard to keep up with mom.

We rendezvoused with the others, quickly retold our story, and left the bear's island. Back in camp, we talked for hours about the encounter and second-guessed ourselves. We agreed it had been foolish to visit the island, given our earlier bear sighting, and even more foolhardy to cut through the woods. I was reminded, again, to trust my own judgment.

The encounter also raised questions about firearms, which

can be carried in all Alaska state parks. I've never carried a gun into Alaska's backcountry. I'm not a firearms expert, have no desire to be, and believe guns cause more trouble than bears. Like Sam, I also believe that guns change a person's "energy," and the way you relate to wild places, wild creatures. They offer security, but they also prompt people to take chances they ordinarily wouldn't, sometimes resulting in confrontations that might have been avoided. The usual result is injury or death, often for the bear.

For a while after the Shuyak attack, I questioned my philosophy. It's often said that bears, like people, are individuals. Each one is different, unpredictable. Richard Nelson, an Alaskan writer and naturalist whose philosophy I greatly respect, always carries a gun in bear country. In his book *The Island Within* he writes, "All it takes is once in a lifetime, the wrong bear in the wrong place. Without a rifle (and the knowledge of when and how to use it), the rest of the story would be entirely up to the bear…It's my way of self-preservation, as the hawk has its talons, the heron its piercing beak, the bear its claws."

But, as time passed I grew more convinced than ever that it's right for me, to walk unarmed through Alaska's backcountry. In a sense, my choice is a symbolic gesture of respect to the animal and its world. I'm only a visitor in the bear's realm, passing through and intending no harm.

On Shuyak, we provoked the attack. A mother bear was being crowded. She wanted to eliminate what she perceived as a very real threat. She was protecting cubs, no more, no less. Playing dead removed the threat, and proved the best thing to do. Shooting the bear would have been a tragedy.

Bill Sherwonit is a nature writer and the author of Alaska's Bears. *He lives in Anchorage, Alaska.*

BULGARIAN STRUGGLE

On a bicycle trip across four continents,
the author encounters her worst fear.

ENTERING BULGARIA THROUGH RUSE ENTAILED CROSSING
the Danube by way of the three-kilometre span of the ugly yet
impressive Friendship Bridge. The queues of cars and jugger-
nauts stretched as far as the eye could see. This was even worse
than waiting in line for up to twelve hours for petrol. It could
take as much as three days for a car to cross the bridge and five
days for a truck.

It would have taken me little more than ten minutes had I
not been continuously stopped by holidaying Czechs, Poles
and Russians (on their way to and from the Black Sea coast)
who eagerly invited me to participate in their kerbside pic-
nics. I was amazed at the good nature of the people in such
chaotic circumstances. Had this been a bank holiday traffic
jam in Britain, tempers would have been boiling over like the
radiators. If it had been in America, people would no doubt
have been shooting each other. Here, however, everyone
calmly resigned themselves to continuous problems and the

atmosphere in this stationary and endless traffic was almost that of a carnival.

I had been led to believe that Bulgaria had a far higher standard of living than Romania. Generally I think this was true but the country was on its knees when I was there. Parliament was in turmoil, in the process of electing a new government.

Food was frighteningly scarce for a ravenous cyclist, even more so than in Romania. I once managed to find some rancid sheep's cheese and a rusty tin of sardines, which I succeeded in rationing out for nearly a week. Water was in short supply as well: it was usually turned on for only two hours a day at the most—sometimes not at all—and I would invariably arrive to fill up my water bottles just after it had been turned off.

The people, although slightly more solemn-faced and reserved than the Romanians, were nearly all most generous and fun. One hot afternoon I rode past a group of full-skirted women who were hoeing a field by hand. They glanced up, spotted me and charged across the road to offer me their water. Then they sat on my bike, sang me songs and jigged in the road.

It was shortly after passing a massive billboard which paradoxically proclaimed TOURISM IS THE PASSPORT TO PEACE that things began to go wrong for me. I had not eaten properly for two weeks, nor had I drunk nearly enough to replace the fluid I sweated out daily as I rode in the mountains. On this unfortunate day, I realized I was in a bad way. The sun beat down inexorably and my head ached and thumped in pain. I was hungry and thirsty but I could not stop to rest as I was desperate to find some water.

At intervals I came across small, rusty pipes from which mountain spring-water should have flowed but they were all dry. At last I came to one that dribbled pathetically but a queue of cars, snaking forever down the mountainside, was as long as the Romanian queues for petrol as people waited to fill up their giant plastic containers, beakers, buckets, bottles, jars—any receptacle they could find.

One man had almost finished loading his containers into his boot when he saw me and insisted on filling up one of my bottles. I gulped it down. He wanted to refill it but I would not let him: I already felt guilty, having deprived him of even half a litre of the water for which he probably queued all day. I thanked him and went on my way, hoping to find water in a village fifteen miles further on.

When I arrived, the water was off. The café was closed; dirty plates and glasses were piled high on the tables. I looked at my map—it was about another twelve miles to the next village. Maybe I would strike it lucky there.

Just as I was about to leave, a fisherman in a blue van pulled alongside. In disjointed French, he said he was heading back to Bourgas and asked if I would like a lift. He saw that I was not very well and said I was welcome to come back to his apartment for a rest, to meet his family and to have as much water as I wanted.

In every country through which I cycled, people would stop to offer me a lift—they could not seem to understand that I was cycling for fun (nor could I, sometimes). I always refused, never wanting to take the risk, but the fisherman's offer was very tempting. I had never felt so much in need of a lift and I almost accepted. Instead I thanked him and lied that I was fine.

Feeling on my last legs after riding into a strong, oven-hot headwind, I arrived in the next village to the same old story. No water. I knocked on a door and an old woman gave me half a bottle of water from an urn on the floor. When I pointed to her tap, asking when the water would next be turned on, she just shrugged in resignation and looked heavenwards. Like the man in the mountains, she wanted to give me more water but my guilt prevented me from accepting and I said I had enough.

As I wilted on a bench in the shade, feeling sorry for myself and wondering how I was going to muster the energy for the final twenty-mile burst to Bourgas, the blue-vanned fisherman appeared again and repeated his offer. I was hesitant, but desperate. When I saw a photograph of his wife and two children on the dashboard, I felt that he would be a safe bet. I decided to take the chance.

We bundled my bike into the back; I climbed into the tattered passenger seat and, with a splutter of the engine, we were off. At my feet was a big bagful of tiny grey lobster-like creatures. Their eyes flopped around on stalks and their serrated pincers, although small, looked as ferocious as sharks' teeth. The fisherman said they were delicious.

"Yes, I'm sure," I said, not at all confident, and kept a very wary eye on the bag in case any decided to use my legs as a handy escape route....

Fortunately the fisherman's catch remained well behaved and the blue van arrived in Bourgas without incident. He lived in the suburbs, five storeys up in a grey and shoddy block of concrete flats. I helped him upstairs with his bags to his apartment, where be brought me a big jug of cool water—the best I had ever tasted. But my head still pounded; I felt shaky and exhausted. The fisherman told me to sit down and have a rest; his wife and children would be home soon, he said, as he showed me photographs of them on the mantelpiece. Then he left me alone while he had a shower and busied himself in the kitchen.

A little later he appeared with more food than I had seen in weeks. There were the miniature lobsters (dead), cold liver, hard-boiled eggs, bread, peaches and sour milk. He had gone to a lot of trouble and I said he was a *chef magnifique*. We ate together, communicating with the help of a French/Bulgarian dictionary, while the television in the background droned on about the presidential elections. He poured himself beer from a container that looked like a petrol can and I promptly declined when he offered me some. It did not look like a good remedy for my thumping headache.

Having been fed and watered, I felt much revived and far more like myself. For the first time in days, I could actually think about things other than water or food and I started to take stock of the situation with a clear head. I thought: what *am* I doing? At last it had dawned on me that I was taking a bit of a risk. It was only a passing thought, though. I trusted the fisherman. He seemed a good-humoured and generous man, and anyway his family would soon be home. When the time had ticked well past the hour he had expected them back, I was not in the least concerned—I just started getting a bit itchy to move on. His cigarette smoke was not improving my headache and I wanted to find a place to camp before dark.

The fisherman said I was welcome to stay the night. I thanked him but said I wanted to cycle down the coast to make Turkey by tomorrow. I cleared the table and took the plates out to the kitchen. When I returned, he was standing in the doorway and I remember thinking how big he looked. He repeated his invitation for me to stay the night and meet his family—they would be home soon. Again I thanked him but said I must be going.

"*Non!*" he bellowed suddenly, so fiercely that his angry eyes almost popped out of his head.

It was an awful moment. My stomach dropped a mile. I felt very frightened, but also cross.

"What do you mean, no?" I said in English. "Yes! I'm going, thanks."

As I stepped forward to push past him, he thrust me backwards forcefully, kicked me to the ground and jumped on top of my sprawled form. As I was pinned to the ground beneath his massive hulk, he tried to burn my face with his cigarette. I managed to protect my face and fend it off so that he only burnt my wrist.

I wriggled my other arm free and hit the cigarette aside. Then he grabbed my wrist and pushed it back so far that I thought it was going to snap. I screamed at him, calling him every name under the sun, and thrashed around wildly trying to push him off.

I had been pinned on the ground in that position many times before but usually laughing my head off beneath Mel in our self-defence classes. Any movements I had been taught, however, now went to pot. Reality was different and I just kicked out willy-nilly, desperate to escape.

I managed to squirm myself from beneath him and made a hasty dash for the front door which, of course, had no handle and needed a key to open it. Luckily I had previously noticed the key on the table and I swept it up as I shot past. I plunged it into the lock. But this was a Bulgarian lock. When I turned the key, it just kept turning. Nothing happened. I tried frantically. The door would not open. It was like a bad dream, or a scene from the movies—so nearly free but not near enough.

Within moments he had lunged upon me and hurled me back across the floor. He kicked me viciously, dragged me and yelled at me, then threw me on to his bed, trying to rip off my clothes. Struggling wildly, I lashed out for all I was worth, but he was bigger and he was stronger and he picked me up and threw me around the room like a ragdoll. He punched and whacked me in the face and kicked me in the back and stomach.

I had always wondered what it felt like to be beaten up—and now I knew. It did not hurt at all. I did not feel that I was part of my own body. It was an unreal experience; I was very aware of what was going on and yet I felt alienated from it. Through an intangible haze, all I could feel were dull thuds as he hit me about the head. I remember thinking: I mustn't get knocked out, I mustn't get knocked out. I knew that anything might happen if I lost consciousness.

My only advantage seemed to be that, being fairly supple from cycling, I managed to keep bouncing back up on my feet again whenever he hurled me to the ground, instead of lying in a crumpled heap of broken bones. Locked into the flat, with nowhere to run, the only thing I could try to do was immobilize him, knock him out or even kill him. I was desperate enough to do that.

At one stage he grabbed me from behind and, with all my might, I thrust my head back into his face. The noise of our two heads crashing together was awful. He howled, and let me go—but I had only succeeded in making him more furious. With bloodshot eyes bulging like those of an enraged bull, he picked up something hard and heavy and whacked it over my head. I saw stars and things went black momentarily, but it did not knock me flat.

Dazed, I found myself flung into the kitchen. I managed to kick him where it hurt most but it was not hard enough. Like a crazed psychopath, he grabbed a carving knife, pressed it to my throat and dragged me across the floor to the balcony.

Well, I thought that was it. My time had come. I could not believe this was happening, but thoughts like that were not particularly useful for self-preservation. I did not want to die—or be hurled over a balcony five storeys up. I had to do something. I had about five seconds to devise a plan.

The more I had retaliated with hits and kicks, the wilder he became. So I tried the opposite. I went limp, floppy, defenceless, to calm him down. It worked. He dropped the knife and let me go. I started doing stupid things; I started laughing, trying to make him believe that a nasty joke had just got out of hand. I tried to make a joke about our injuries by comparing wounds—bloody gashes, bumps and bruises. We were both in a terrible state, with ripped clothes, blood and sweat. I made an effort to clean his wounds and he started to relax. I was desperate to keep busy. I did silly things like straightening the rugs and the furniture and washing up the dishes.

Then he pulled me on to the sofa with him. I sat in the corner, rigid, legs tightly together but half-heartedly smiling. I was terrified of making him angry again because I knew it would be curtains for me if I did. He poured himself more beer from the petrol can and tried to force me to drink some. He was now pretty jubilant; he thought I had resigned myself to being his, that he had me for the night.

I realized that I would be safe as long as I did what he wanted. On the outside, I gave the appearance of being completely calm and relaxed, slapping his hand playfully (though I would have gladly shot a bullet through it) as it started to work its way up my thigh. But on the inside my head was in turmoil, I was petrified, screaming in my head and frantically repeating to myself, "What can I *do?* What can I do?"

He was practically sitting on top of me now, one arm around me, the other trying to feel all over. Drunkenly, he kept trying to kiss me. I kept my mouth tightly shut. But he did not like that; he started to get agitated and annoyed. With a gruesome grin, he indicated the balcony. I knew only too well what he meant: if I did not comply with his wishes, then over I would go. I knew I was playing a dangerous game; he appeared relaxed but he was hovering on the brink of anger and violence. I had to be careful—one wrong move from me and his brutal rage would be triggered off again. I had to bide my time. I had to be careful. The television flickered on in the background.

He forced his slimy tongue into my mouth. I felt sick, disgusted. I wanted to bite it off, like in *Midnight Express,* but that idea was even more revolting. Anyway, it would not knock him flat. He tried to push me down to his nether region. I managed to distract him: there was a documentary on the television showing a pig giving birth. He thought this very funny. I did not care what he thought, as long as his focus was not on me.

The position did not look promising. I was trapped in a locked flat five floors up with a drunken, sex-crazed madman. No one knew where I was. I could not believe I had got myself into such a ridiculous mess. I became very aware of the shouts and laughter of children playing in the street below; of the women hanging out their washing and happily chattering in the block of flats across the road; of the airplane going over, its passengers sipping drinks or reading newspapers. I was deeply envious of all these people. I wanted desperately to be in their shoes; to be free; to be away from this hell-hole. I wanted to run out on to the balcony and scream to them all—the people opposite—the people in the street. I wanted *help.* I longed to yell to the world for help.

But what good would it do? They would just see a girl having a fit and before anything could be done I would be tossed over the balcony. If I wanted to survive, I could not act rashly.

Most of all, I wanted to be safe—I wanted to be home. Instead, I sat squashed up on the corner of that horrible sofa, fending off sexual advances as good-humouredly as possible, and racking my brains as to what I could do.

Communication with him was not easy. Not only was he drunk but he had also given up all attempts at French. It was

down to murmuring the odd Bulgarian word and gesticulat-
ing—something that was made even more difficult by the fact
that the custom of shaking and nodding one's head has quite
the opposite interpretation in Bulgaria. A nod means no, a
shake means yes. This is muddling at the best of times but
many Bulgarians have adopted the more familiar connotation
when talking to foreigners: nod—yes; shake—no. The result
was utter confusion all round which, under any other circumstances, could have been decidedly comical. Now it was
deadly serious. I did not know if my head was inadvertently
saying yes! yes! when he was asking if he should throw me
over the balcony. To play safe, I neither shook nor nodded but
went round in circles.

The sun started to set. I had been imprisoned for over five
hours. He was now completely and drunkenly relaxed. He
kept hold of me, stroked my legs and occasionally kissed me,
but he was in no hurry. He knew he had me for the night. He
knew he could do whatever he wanted to do to me. And I
knew that if I remained his captive for the night I would be
raped. And that, even if I survived, there was no guarantee he
would then let me go. He had proved he was violent and for
all I knew he would have his fun, use me and abuse me, and
dispose of me. That way there would be no way I could report him to the police.

There was one thing of which I was certain: I would never
let him rape me. I would rather jump off the balcony than submit to his repugnant desires. And I can now understand how,
when desperate, people will do rash things. The thought of
falling five flights did not scare me in the least—quite the opposite, in fact: the idea of flying free through the air away from
him was preferable by far to remaining in the rapist's den.

And I almost did it. I almost jumped. But I stopped myself.
I thought of Mum—how her worst fears would come true;

how her regular supply of postcards would dry up; I thought of her ever growing and sickening worry. Then I thought of the money I was raising for the Guide Dogs for the Blind Association and I felt a surge of determination that I was going to buy that guide dog, no matter what. And I thought of my cycling, how important it was to me, how much I loved it and how much more I wanted to do. All these thoughts combined to stop me from taking a death-leap over the balcony. I was not going to kill myself for this one lunatic. There had to be another way and I had to find it. But soon.

Sweating profusely, I suddenly realized how thirsty I was. I said I wanted a drink and walked into the kitchen. He was like a limpet—he did not leave my side for a moment. I gulped down glassfuls of water, which he found most amusing and patted my stomach as though it was about to explode. I smiled and chuckled back, but all the time I was scanning the kitchen for potential weapons. There were empty wine bottles by the sink; there was a heavy pot; and there were knives. But trying to knock someone out or launch a life-or-death attack is incredibly difficult when they are constantly on top of you. If I had lunged for the wine bottle, his arm would be upon mine and his fury roused. That would be it—my chances ruined. If only he had turned his back for a second, it might have given me the opportunity to knock a pot on his head. But he never turned away and I was too frightened to risk my attack backfiring. I could end up with a bottle in my face, or worse.

The kitchen had a tiny balcony and I sauntered out, pretending to admire the sunset but really to see if it offered any possible means of escape. There was nothing—just a dead drop to the street down below.

There was a small bar across the road and he pointed towards it. He kept repeating, "Whisky? Whisky?" He seemed to be suggesting that we go down there together for a drink. Had he run out of beer, or was he too drunk to realize that if we did go down there I would be free and he would not? A fantastic surge of hope flooded through me. but I tried not to look too enthusiastic. We went back inside, where he made it clear that if we were to go for a drink I had first to have a shower and change from my cycling shorts and ripped, bloody t-shirt into a dress. A dress! I did not have one. Pedalling around with a party frock in my panniers was not something I did. I had a clean pair of longjohns and a fairly respectable shirt, but that was all.

That would not do, he said. It had to be a dress. I thought of his wife, but of course there was no wife. No, he said, we were not going to the bar. Maybe he had not intended to go at all—the whole thing was just a cruel ploy to raise and then crush my spirits. I felt desperately depressed. But there was one last chance: the balcony off the living room.

Standing out there, I could just glimpse the sea through a gap between the flats opposite. I managed to get him to ramble on about something to do with the sea while I took the opportunity to size up my chances of escape. I saw a crowbar propped up on the corner and I toyed with the idea of attacking him with it. But all I could envisage was an ugly struggle and me being the one to end up over the balcony.

Then I saw that there was a neighbouring balcony on the other side of a thick concrete partition. The only way I could get into it was to jump a good four feet up on to the front of his balcony, balance there and, without toppling off, swing out and over to the other side. And I would have to do it quickly, before he realized what was happening and pushed me off. It looked practically impossible and I doubted whether I was even tall enough to jump on to the front rail. I did not think I had the guts. But the more I cast furtive glances at it, the more I knew that it was my only chance of escape.

He gestured for me to move back inside—it was now almost dark and he wanted to close the door to stop the insects from getting into the room. If I was going to make my jump, I had to make sure he went inside first. As we moved towards the door, I suddenly lost my courage.

There was a flowering plant just by the door and I stopped him, exclaiming some rubbish about how lovely it was. He moved towards it and was now in front of me. I had given myself one last chance. While he drunkenly drivelled on about the plant, I knew it was now or never. Inwardly I was worked up into a frenzy—my mouth was dry, my heart was pounding, my head was exploding with "I've got to do it! I've got to do it!"

We could not gabble on about a flowering plant all night and I gestured that I was ready to head in. He took one step inside and as soon as I saw his back turn on me my head screamed "NOW!" I hurled my water glass at him and sprang up on to the balcony railing.

I felt some dangling wires, which I grabbed with my left hand and then kicked myself off and swung round the wall, landing on the floor of the neighbouring balcony. I had done it—I was free! It was the most incredible feeling I have ever had.

I screamed for help and crashed my hand against the window of the flat.

But there was no one in. Suddenly I was terrified that he was going to come round after me. With the adrenalin pumping furiously, I swung myself out like a demented Tarzan and round another three balconies. At last a woman saw me and rushed out. I have never been so relieved to see anyone in all my life. I then knew for sure that I was safe.

My immediate reaction was to hug her. The family looked rather shocked, which was hardly surprising—they were probably not used to having a blabbering, bruised and bloodied alien landing on their balcony halfway through supper. I tried to explain that there was a madman on their floor who had beaten me up and I scampered to the telephone, crying, *"Militsia! Militsia!"* They did nothing, for which afterwards I was grateful. Everything would have got too complicated if the police had become involved—I could not speak the language and how could I explain my case? For a start, most people could not understand how a girl could want to travel alone in foreign countries. For all they knew, maybe I had been looking for a good time which had gone a bit wrong.

Men and boys from the street had seen me leaping from balcony to balcony and now raced up the stairs. Some were armed with rough cuts of wood. I felt as if I had an army on my side. One boy, Yancho, the only one who could speak English, said, "Please, please—what has happened?"

Briefly I told him, but while we were all clustered in commotion round the stairs the door of the fisherman's flat opened. He had groomed himself, put on a shirt and then entered into a heated argument with the crowd. The sight of him sickened me and I was filled with nothing more than contemptuous hate. Had someone handed me a gun at that moment, I could quite easily have shot him in the goolies.

I ran past him down the stairs. Yancho followed and I told him that my money, my shoes and my belongings were still in the flat. With reinforcements, Yancho went and retrieved everything for me and then we all went outside.

They led me to some wooden tables where men were drinking, smoking and playing cards. Yancho, concerned and caring, was beside me all the time. For a moment I just sat with my head in my hands as the clamouring crowds gathered. I wanted to get away from everything—to wake up in my own bed knowing that the whole thing had been a hideous nightmare. Then I felt Yancho gently touching my arm.

"Please," he said, "what are you going to do?"

"I don't know," I said, "just get away from here as far as possible—find a hotel or somewhere to camp."

"You cannot," he said. "It is late—all hotels expensive and full in Bourgas. And you have many hurts. This man, he says you are very welcome to stay with him."

"Whoa!" I said, and cowered into the corner.

"It's no problem," said Yancho, "he has family."

"I've heard that one before!" I replied with a teetering smile.

"No, it is okay. He is my friend."

I said I would only trust that man if I saw his family on parade in front of me. A few minutes later the man, Valcloo, appeared with his wife, Rilka, who spoke excellent English and worked for Balkan Airlines, and two lovely young daughters, Jenia and Polina (who was clutching a hamster). When I discovered that they lived on the ground floor, I decided they were a safe bet and said I would love to stay with them. Yancho came with me and helped me with my bike. As we walked, he told me the fisherman was renowned for getting drunk.

"No one really knows him," he said. "He was married once, but he had much problem."

Rilka tenderly administered first aid to me as I sat on the toilet seat. That was when I started shaking—the most uncontrollable jitters I have ever had. I went into a spasm of violently quivering trembles. But my hands were the worst: they were jumping and bouncing all over the place in such a ridiculous fashion that we both burst out laughing. I was not really in a laughing mood—I felt terribly sick; my head, with a protruding lump like a unicorn's horn, ached more than ever and my whole body felt an agonized wreck. All I wanted to do was to curl up in a dark room and go to sleep. I was totally shattered.

Rilka had other plans. Although it was well after midnight, she had whipped up a meal and said how honoured she felt to have me to stay—she had never had a foreigner in her home before. How then could I say I would rather go to bed?

At last Rilka made up a bed for me on the sofa and left me to lie in the dark with only the insane wheel-spinning hamster and blood-whining mosquitoes for company. As I shut my eyes, the room spun and my head whirred and I was back in "his" flat—back in the nightmare.

In one way I wanted desperately to catch the first flight home and forget this lark of gallivanting round countries alone. People had always told me that the world was a dangerous place and I now realized that perhaps they were right. But the more I thought about it, the more I thought no, why should I give up what I loved doing most just because of one drunken goofhead? Through all the years I had spent saddle-bound, all the wonderful places I had seen and people I had met, this was my only bad experience. I may have escaped his clutches but if I gave in, went home, found a sensible job and threw my bike in the shed, it would be like surrendering, and he would have won in the long run.

After a restless few hours, I arose at dawn and crept out of the house with Rilka, who was going to work. We walked along the back streets together and met Yancho. They joined the bus queue and then both gave me a huge hug and told me to write. Then I cycled south out of the city and kept going, riding in a sort of frenzied daze, ignoring the pain and noticing nothing around me. I was just intent on putting as large a distance as possible between me and Bourgas. The further I left that doomed city behind, the more my spirits rose.

After escaping alive from a car crash in China, Paul Theroux had said: "There is something about the very fact of survival that produces a greater vitality." I now know exactly what he meant. As I soared south along the coast I felt as though I was bursting with a sense of elated energy and I did not stop riding until I reached the patrolled watchtowers and grim, high barbed-wire fences which heralded the border with Turkey. I was back in the saddle again, grateful to be still alive, and with the reassuring and familiar sound of the wind in my wheels.

At a tender age, Josie Dew fell out of a fast-moving vehicle and developed a life-long aversion to cars. Then she got her first bicycle and never looked back. She has cycled through 36 countries on four continents. This story was excerpted from her book The Wind in My Wheels: Travel Tales from the Saddle.

PYTHON!

A snake hunter in Africa is caught off guard.

AN ADULT PYTHON MAY BE MORE THAN TWENTY FEET LONG, weigh up to a hundred pounds and have a girth as great as a man's waist. Pythons either lie in wait underwater, or in ambush along a well-used game trail, from where they make lightning strikes with a formidable array of curved teeth, then anchor onto their prey, constricting it to death. The strike is usually a seizing movement, but the blow of such a muscular head lands with sledgehammer force and is quite capable of laying out a fairly large animal. A normal diet consists of hares, monkeys, small antelope, and wild pigs, but there is no reason why a fully grown snake should not consume an unwary novice herpetologist.

The first time Adrian Boshier saw a python, it was so big that he almost failed to recognize it. Then he noticed that the tree trunk in his path was moving. He stood entranced as yard after yard flowed by. It was unbelievable; somewhere was a head and, at some stage still to come, a tail. And in between, more snake than he would have thought possible.

When he plunged into the undergrowth in search of its head, the python began to coil its body. This seemed an undesirable situation, so he put his stick across its back and made a grab for its head. It was then that Boshier learned the difference between the strength of a snake that relies on poison, and one that depends on its muscle for a living. He was jerked right off his feet and forced to cling to its neck with both hands, whereupon it promptly behaved like a python and began to engulf him in its coils.

Boshier released one hand and tried to pull free, but could not even get a grip on the broad body. Then he tried unwinding the snake and found to his relief that this worked. Pythons seem to be unable to resist a strong centripetal force. As fast as it threw its coils around him, he unwound them. And there they remained in an animated embrace.

"We became acquainted," he said later. "We really did!"

After an hour of action, the python began to relax and Boshier released the pressure on its neck. He watched carefully for any sly maneuvers, but the snake lay without resistance. Boshier felt so certain of this change in attitude that he even stroked it. And it seemed to settle itself more comfortably, half of its enormous length cradled in his arms.

He wondered what to do next. The bags he had with him were far too small. He decided that he needed help, but the nearest village was more than a mile away. Stroking it for reassurance (his own as much as the snake's), he began to gather up its coils, draping the python's body about his own—doing deliberately that which he had so recently fought to prevent.

The python seemed to like it! They set off together, in this odd embrace, and Boshier soon discovered that the snake was extremely heavy. By the time they reached the village, he was exhausted. But help was a little hard to find. A fourteen-foot python is very thick and when draped around a skinny human, not much of the latter is visible. The sight was more than even the strongest hearts in the village could stand. Evacuation was virtually instantaneous.

Standing there in the empty village, Boshier realized the futility of trying to hold on to his prize. So he staggered off into the bush again and, at a safe distance from the settlement, unwrapped his acquiescent burden. It slipped quietly away, but a legend had been born.

Lyall Watson, a self-proclaimed "scientific nomad," travels the world in pursuit of the paranormal. Born in Africa, educated in Holland, Germany, and London, he now lives in Ireland. He is the author of Supernature, Gifts of Unknown Things, *and* Lightning Bird: The Story of One Man's Journey into Africa's Past, *from which this story was excerpted.*

DANGEROUS LIAISONS

*The biggest challenge on this climbing expedition
in Pakistan was not the mountain.*

THE GUNS POINTED AT ME WERE NOT TOYS AND THE SOLDIERS
holding them, despite their mismatched uniforms, were not
clowns. I hadn't expected AK–47s to be the biggest danger on
the Baltoro, but then nothing on this expedition happened as
I expected. When our liaison officer finished screaming at me
and the soldiers finally left, I sat down and held my head in
my hands. The expedition had gone down the drain, I was
going to jail, and we hadn't even reached basecamp.

Suneeb, one of our porters, sat down next to me. "This
liaison officer," he said, "is a crazy man, very bad man." I nodded. "You," he continued in a different tone, "are a good leader
for us, care for the Balti people. He has insulted you, so
tonight, *Inshallah*, we shall kill him. We will slit his pig throat."

I can pinpoint exactly when the mess that became our expedition to Chogolisa began: October 24, 1993. I was sitting
below the west face of Cholatse, having just made the second
ascent of the peak's Southwest Ridge. I was feeling pretty

good about myself, a little too good in fact. I wished in my journal for a bigger, harder version of what we'd just done, something like Chogolisa.

Eighteen months later Andrew Brash and I were in Rawalpindi sitting face to face with the man who over the next two months would turn my wish into a nightmare: Captain Mohammed Ayub, our liaison officer. Ayub immediately informed me that in Pakistan his army rank meant great status, something I could not possibly have as a civilian. "You," he said with an extravagant wave of his hand, "are nothing here." Captain Ayub had just returned from six months duty on the Siachen Glacier, the front line in the border war with India, the highest battleground in history. It is not what military men consider a choice posting, and I had to wonder privately about Ayub's real status. He made no secret of his displeasure about returning to the "God-forsaken hell of the North," as he called the Karakoram Range.

"Many peoples have died in these snows," he explained while Andrew and I unpacked the $2000 of kit the regulations required we buy for him. "They are having parts of their bodies chopped off due from cold. This, I think should not be happening to me." Reasonable enough. "So these," he continued as he pushed away a pair of brand-new plastic boots, "are substandard. I will not go to the mountains in these. And this," he held aloft a new down jacket, "have you not brought another color? I am captain in Pakistan army. This is not smart looking." Andrew rolled his eyes. Though we'd only known the captain for ten minutes, things already looked bleak. Then, dismissing our carefully thought out schedule, Ayub announced, "We cannot possibly rush up into the mountains tomorrow. I must have perhaps one week to buy the proper equipment, which you will pay for. Then, perhaps we shall move from this place."

As Ayub stood there with his scrawny arms akimbo, I felt the Italian temper that has caused so much trouble in the past welling up inside me. With a conscious effort of will I controlled a feeling I would come to know well in the weeks ahead: the desire to throttle Captain Ayub. Instead I pleaded that the current good weather would enable us to fly to Skardu and thus avoid the death-trap Karakoram Highway. I suggested that the extra cost of the hotel, food, and of course the captain's extra salary during the delay was more than we could afford. "Rule and regulation clearly tell expedition to come prepared to stay in Rawalpindi for two weeks," barked Ayub. "Two weeks! If you have not brought sufficient funds, then the expedition must be canceled immediately." I shut up.

I for one was not spending even one week in the sweltering hell-hole of Rawalpindi and I had only to glance at Andrew's widening eyes to know how he felt about the matter. We mentioned to the captain that we wanted to go to Peshawar and play tourists. He replied that we could not leave the hotel without his permission, and that visiting Peshawar, about four hours west toward the Afghan border, was totally out of the question. Again came the urge to throttle. I said nothing until the next morning when I asked permission to go shopping. After noting his benevolence, Captain Ayub gave his blessing; we promptly left the hotel and went shopping...in Peshawar.

Andrew was nervous about Peshawar from the beginning. A worker at the U.S. consulate there had recently been held at gunpoint for an hour in broad daylight and was only saved when her captor, still holding the gun to her head, was shot by a USDEA sniper. In Peshawar, the conduit for weaponry heading to the Afghan freedom fighters, every type of artillery and ammunition known to man is freely available on the streets. I thought it would be exciting, though I had second thoughts as we passed signs at the entrance to the city announcing, "You are now leaving the area where the Government of Pakistan can guarantee your safety."

Smoggy, crowded, and even hotter than Rawalpindi, the city itself turned out to be dull. The taxi ride home was not. Our driver was fluent in English and we took the opportunity to whine about the asshole ruining our trip. "I hate the army, the police, the ISI [Pakistan's KGB]—all those hooligans," the driver announced. "They killed my brother because he refused to pay their bribes. Would you like to see a photo of him?"

As we pulled into the police checkpoint, and the machine-gun-toting officer approached the car to demand his bribe, the driver handed back a photo. His brother, lying on a steel table, was missing the back half of his head, his eyes and much of his chest. We didn't leave Rawalpindi again.

About a week later Captain Ayub finally exhausted his last excuse to delay us. Of course, the stable high pressure that had been parked over Pakistan since our arrival was also exhausted. As the rain poured down in sheets, flights to Skardu were grounded, which meant only one thing: the Karakoram Highway.

Careening through rain-slick turns 500 feet above the Indus River, I thought over all I'd read about the highway. Some have written it is the most beautiful road in the world, winding as it does past Nanga Parbat. Others have said it's the most exciting, entertaining part of an expedition to Pakistan. Those people are idiots. In many places the "highway" is nothing more than a shelf blasted into the sheer wall of the gorge. More than once a timely deceleration saved us from being crushed under a falling bolder. This I can only attribute to divine intervention, since in his hash-induced trance our driver seemed unable to locate the brake pedal. It appeared at times as though he was trying to physically outrun Death up the highway. I suppose in a race like that, the speed limit is simply as fast as whatever grossly overloaded vehicle you're unlucky enough to be in can go. As it turned out Death must have taken a rest day during our 24-hour heat. Judging by the number of burnt buses scattered below the highway, it was well earned.

Arrival in Skardu was hardly a release from our troubles. On a bed at the K2 motel we spread out what was left of the expedition finances. Thanks in large part to Captain Ayub and his at-our-expense account, our once Himalayan pile of rupees was down to a molehill. We'd been informed that the road to Askole—dubious in the best conditions—had been wiped out in fourteen landslides triggered by the continuing rain. With Jeeps trapped between some of the slides, it was conceivable that we could shuttle loads over the debris. We figured we could afford two extra porter stages and still get back from basecamp. The porters, now camped outside the gates of the motel, would be our responsibility as soon as we started walking and we had to pay them every day whether we covered any ground or not.

When to leave Skardu thus became a critical decision. Captain Ayub, interested only in lounging about the motel as long as possible, was of no help. After conferring with Phil Powers, leader of an expedition to Hidden Peak, and Issaq, our cook, we agreed to caravan the two expeditions together and make a dash for Askole the moment the rain stopped.

About the time it seemed we'd be taking an ark to Chogolisa, the rain finally turned to drizzle. Two hours later eight climbers, ninety porters, three cooks, two liaison officers, and 2,250 kilos of stuff were on their way to Askole.

"Have you any dynamite?" Captain Butt asked me during a fuel stop.

"Why?" I asked.

"To blow up the road, of course," he laughed as he walked away to buy some. Captain Monte Butt, the Hidden Peak liaison officer, was the antithesis of Captain Ayub. Monte, who spoke flawless English, became our source for advice on everything from handling the porters to fixing the road. As the five Jeeps rumbled along, Monte kicked back on the roof of one, grooving to London techno on his Walkman, while Ayub sat in the cab barking orders at the driver.

Caravanning worked well. The extra manpower allowed us to quickly fix bits of the road and keep moving. Our only significant delay was at the final police checkpost at Dasso, a windblasted cluster of police barracks sitting next to the last road bridge over the Braldu River. "This is bogus!" the officer yelled as he thrust my peak permit for Chogolisa back at me. "You have made this up on your typewriter in America. You must go back to Islamabad and get another." I thought I was about to have a seizure and Andrew looked like he was ready to slit his wrists before following that order. It was, of course, a subtle way of requesting compensation for his plight, stuck guarding Dasso Bridge. Captain Ayub spotted this amateur quickly and stepped in to settle the matter. If any money was to be bled out of Chogolisa expedition, it was going into his pocket, not some bridge guard's.

Shortly after Dasso we came to a landslide that no amount of effort was going to fix. Monte surveyed the scene and walked away in defeat, holding his dynamite like a child with a broken toy. We'd made excellent progress in the Jeeps, but it was still three-and-a-half extra porter stages to Askole, one-and-a-half more than we could afford. That was a problem. Fortunately, it was one we wouldn't have to deal with until later. We started walking the next day in steady rain and pounded our way to Askole. Along the way we crossed paths with a soaking wet Alan Hinkes, just returning from the summit of K2. "You should bloody well turn around now, lads," he said bitterly. "There's nothing up there worth this fucking walk." It was the best advice anyone could have given us. Of course, we ignored it.

The first few days of the approach proper turned out to be beautiful. We'd split off from the Hidden Peak expedition at Korophon, wishing them well and promising to visit them at their basecamp. The rain had finally abated and as we followed the Braldu River toward its source at the Baltoro Glacier, we actually began to feel as though our luck had changed. Of course, we were still in Pakistan, so when a porter carrying kerosene burned all the skin off his back, I was up all night cleaning what was left of his skin, dressing up his wounds and trying to explain to him that if he carried his load the next day he would die. Ultimately, only the threat of arrest from the irredoubtable Captain Ayub sent this man and his son packing toward the hospital, four days down valley. Still, this and other ongoing catastrophes—like the fixing rope some soldiers relieved us of at the Drumordu River crossing—failed to dampen our new enthusiasm.

"This is a disgrace to Pakistan army," Ayub announced when we reported the rope incident to him. "Why have they not come with rope of their own? And this bridge man; he has no right to charge a toll whatsoever. I will write each one of these men in my report and *Inshallah* they will be hanged for this." Capital punishment seemed a bit stern to me but who was I to question Pakistani justice. After all, Captain Ayub for once seemed to be on *our* side.

Two days later we reached the campsite of rDukus, where the view across the Baltoro toward the Trango group is surely one of the most impressive in the mountain world. Unfortunately, we couldn't sit outside and enjoy it because of the flies attracted by the stinking heaps of excrement and garbage dumped there. As we camped in what amounted to an open-air toilet, the phrase "Throne Room of the Mountain Gods" took on new meaning.

rDukus is important for another reason. When you step off the grassy moraine onto the ice and rock of the Baltoro, it is likely the last step you'll take on solid ground until you return. This is especially significant to the porters, who usually insist on a cash payment in lieu of foam pads, shoes, or other equipment. They march onto the glacier unequipped to live on the ice, though large numbers suffer hypothermia or trench foot. It is not surprising then that the porters prefer to spend as few nights camped on the Baltoro as possible, which was fine with us. We decided to follow their pace to basecamp, having no idea when we left rDukus how much this choice would affect us.

On the six-hour walk from rDukus to Gore II, an army camp on the glacier and our destination for day eight of the approach, we were awestruck. Masherbrum, Gasherbrum IV, Broad Peak, and Mustagh Tower all came into view. The weather was brilliant and Andrew and I lagged behind the porters and Captain Ayub, absorbed in a photographic orgy. After about four hours of the walk we met one of our porters coming down the glacier from Gore II. He proudly announced that all the loads had reached Gore II and, as it was still early in the day and they were running low on food, the porters requested permission to continue on to Concordia. We sent him back to deliver our permission; this would mean reaching basecamp a day early and that would save the porters an extra night on the ice and, we hoped, prevent them from going hungry. It seemed like a great idea, so we were surprised to find all the porters sitting next to their loads when we reached Gore II.

The mystery cleared itself up when I saw Captain Ayub's feet sticking out of his tent, the only one set up. Gore II is at 14,000 feet and he was totally spent from the walk. Whatever bullshit he was about to offer, this was the real reason for not moving on. Captain Ayub rose from the tent and announced, "We will only be doing whatsoever-absolutely it states in Rule and Regulation. You have said we will be camping at this Gore II and this is where we will camp."

"Yes, but the porters have said they are running out of food and need to get back home quickly," I offered in response.

"This is not *my* fuck up!" Ayub snarled. "This is *your* fuck up." Of course the one English phrase we'd added to his lexicon was "fuck up." How appropriate, I thought. "Who are you? I have told you, and told you that you are nothing." I felt my violent urges returning. "These Johnnies"—he waved toward the porters—"they do not know what is good for themselves." Beating his chest, he said, "I know what is good for them…and if I have to beat them to make them do what is best then I will beat each and every one of them."

After an hour-long harangue, I finally managed to slip my copy of the dreaded Rule and Regulation book in front of the captain, wherein he read that if I, as leader, put my reasons for disagreeing with him in writing, my decision was final. We were going to Concordia.

Or so I thought. I walked back to the porters and announced my victory. "Now it is too late John," Issaq told me. "It will be dark soon and there are crevasses. We will go tomorrow." I threw up my hands, and turned around to go tell the Captain. He was busy supervising the disassembly of his tent when I told him we'd be staying at Gore II.

For a moment, there was silence. He stood up, turned around, and stared hard at me. In that instant my whole world collapsed to the small space in between us. Then he started to shake; they were small tremors at first, but soon his whole body vibrated. His eyes bulged, his teeth started to gnash, and he seemed to transform into pure hate. I was scared.

"You-are-*joking*-with-*me!*" he screamed. He was beating his chest. "I am captain in Pakistan Army. Government of Pakistan has given me three stars. You do not treat me like slave!"

Spit and foam flew from his mouth as he continued screaming and beating his chest. Captain Ayub had gone insane. I tried to explain that I was only doing what the porters wanted. "It does not matter what they want. Why have you not asked me?" he spat his response. "Always asking this cook or Butt, never *me*. I am Liaison Officer. I am in command."

His screaming was so loud that our audience of porters was soon joined by a group of soldiers, from the nearby army camp. They hadn't left their guns behind. Ayub saw them before I did and after a quick order they surrounded us and those guns were leveled in my direction.

Suddenly I had no desire to argue. I felt sick. My mind was filled with images of a taxi driver with half his head blown off. Was Ayub angry enough to kill us? There was no one for a hundred miles in any direction to stop him. I apologized but it was too late. The soldiers stood by as he continued his tirade. "You will not be allowed to leave Pakistan until the ISI has interrogated you about your crimes."

"Crimes?" I asked.

"You have called Pakistan Army a disgrace at the Drumordu River. You have photographed army camps and this is a treason, a violation of Official Secrets Act. This-is-punishable-by-death."

It was Ayub who'd called the rope-theft incident at the Drumordo River disgraceful, and the photos I'd taken were of mountains near various army camps. That was the truth, but we stood in a world where truth didn't matter. "I will now write your confession and you will surrender all of your film to Pakistan Army," Ayub said.

While I waited for my "confession" to be drafted, I returned to my tent and spooled up some unexposed film. I might have been terrified but I wasn't stupid: somewhere in the 50 rolls I'd exposed there was sure to be something objectionable and I couldn't take any chances. When I returned, the captain was still quivering with anger and he handed me the most bizarre document I had ever seen. Written in the first person in my name was a confession of several crimes against Pakistan. I was supposedly admitting to photographing military installations, bridges, and aircraft. I had repeatedly insulted the Pakistani Army, the Government of Pakistan, and Islam. I had disobeyed direct orders from a Pakistani Army officer. At the bottom was a space for my signature. It was tantamount to a death certificate.

"I can't sign this," I said shakily. "It's not true."

"It is true," Ayub replied. "I have said it is true, so it is true. You will sign!"

"No, I will not!"

During the tense hour that followed we went back and forth repeatedly. Finally, when the soldier's guns began to droop and Captain Ayub felt he was losing face, he snatched the paper and announced he would sign it for me. I watched in stunned silence as he put my name to the paper, folded it up and walked away toward the army camp to have tea.

I sat down and tried to clear my spinning head. What had just happened? How had a simple misunderstanding spiraled into a confession of *treason*? What was going to happen next? It wasn't long before Suneeb sat down to answer my last question. *Murder* was what was going to happen next, because the expedition was completely out of control.

I'd been thinking it might come to this from the moment the guns came out. Ayub was serious, and seriously deranged. If he chose to, he could kill Andrew and me and the only thing our families would ever know was that we disappeared while attempting Chogolisa. It wasn't so far-fetched. People disappear every season in the Himalayas. It would have been easy for him to kill us.

Or, I began to think, for us to kill him. The thought scared me. I was seriously considering killing Captain Ayub. It was insane: the whole place, the whole situation, and I had absorbed some of it. Ayub must have sensed this. He came back over and tried to make me sign a contract taking full responsibility for anything that might happen to him, including accident or poisoning. He knew we couldn't stay camped next to his soldiers forever. I thought I recognized some of my fear in his eyes. Again I refused to sign.

The expedition, as far as I was concerned, was over. The only way to solve our problems was to return to Islamabad and get inside the U.S. Embassy as soon as possible. Andrew was disappointed but he understood: it wasn't his name on the confession.

"We're going back to Islamabad tomorrow," I announced.

Ayub looked surprised. "No, we must continue. Fuck up is finished. ISI will deal with you when you return."

Why was he arguing to continue the same expedition he'd done so much to destroy? Andrew figured it out: Ayub was being paid by the day. Inadvertently, I called his bluff and now had a bargaining chip.

"Tear up the confession," I said, "and we continue."

"Not today," Ayub answered, "but if you behave on the climb I will return your film and rip up your confession." It was a bizarre blackmail deal, but it defused a situation where violence still hung in the air. It is disturbing to admit now, but I wasn't thinking of killing Ayub as right or wrong. It was a purely practical decision. There was a chance that we could get out of our mess peacefully, and a dead liaison officer would mean a lot of questions. I decided, at least for the time being that it wouldn't help. "Please don't kill him tonight," I told Suneeb later. "Wait."

The next day we reached Concordia, where we ran into some trekkers on their way out of the mountains. I decided to dispatch a letter with them. I didn't want to alarm my family but at the same time I wanted them to take some precautions for me. If I was tossed in jail when we returned from the mountains, I didn't want to spend one extra minute there. Captain Ayub was suspicious of everything, so I waited until dark before quietly slipping the letter to a beautiful Swiss woman named Maria, and told her to mail it from Geneva. It was ridiculous; I felt like a B-movie James Bond.

The following morning the laziest of the porters started suggesting locations for basecamp only 30 minutes out of Concordia. Andrew and I used every bit of charm we had to coax six hours of walking out of them. When they finally refused to go any further without pay for a full extra stage, we established basecamp. Of course, this meant it was time to face up to an old problem: money, or more specifically, the lack thereof. At Concordia we confirmed our earlier suspicions that after paying these porters we wouldn't have enough cash left to pay for the return trip to Skardu. The concept of credit does not exist on the Baltoro, and if even one of our porters found out how broke we were, no one in Baltistan would come and retrieve us and our gear.

The payoff went smoothly except for the moment when I saw Ayub stuff a wad of our rupees into his pocket. He just didn't quit. When questioned he insisted it was his money, but offered no explanation of how it came to be in *our* pile of porter wages. As soon as the porters were paid off, they took off down the glacier, apparently unsuspecting that they had our last rupees.

I woke up early the next morning to have a look at the spot

that would be home for the next month. Though I couldn't see the northern face—our proposed route—Chogolisa's summit was clearly visible 9,000 feet above. I started daydreaming about walking across that perfect flat summit ridge at 25,000 feet.

Issaq was soon standing next to me and brought me back to reality by handing in his resignation. I had never heard of a cook *quitting* an expedition, throwing away what might be his only opportunity all year to earn hard currency. Issaq claimed he was ill but it was clear that he just couldn't take another minute of Captain Ayub. When Ayub heard of the resignation he realized he would soon be in camp alone with Andrew and me, and immediately announced that it was his duty to leave and find another cook. An hour later, Andrew and I were alone.

That afternoon Andrew also decided to leave, but only to visit the Hidden Peak team for a couple of days. I stayed behind to start a recon and to carry gear up to the base of the climb. When I reached the bottom of the face the next morning it looked huge, and totally different from the ten-year-old photos we had. It looked suicidal. Andrew came to the same conclusion at Hidden Peak basecamp, and both of us started looking at the Northeast Ridge, an elegant line that had only seen one ascent, a huge siege that used 10,000 feet of fixed rope. An alpine-style ascent would be incredible.

Andrew returned two days later, as did Captain Ayub with our new cook, Gulham. I was a bit suspicious of Gulham, whom Ayub had found just hanging around Concordia. When I went to shake Gulham's hand, he thrust out a page from Jim Curran's book *K2: Triumph and Tragedy* that had his picture on it. The caption read, "Gulham: film porter impossible, opportunist." I'd had Curran to my house for dinner years before and remembered a story of a porter in 1986 who'd tried to slip out of K2 basecamp with Kurt Diemberger's tent and personal belongings after it was assumed, wrongly of course, that Kurt was dead. It can't be the same guy, I thought.

A week later, when Gulham's kitchen contained, among other things, one of my sleeping bags, a pack, my spare boots, Andrew's ski poles, spare hat, socks, gloves, and down jacket, I revised my thinking. Of all the men in Baltistan Captain Ayub could have possibly found to replace Issaq, he picked the only one documented in mountaineering literature as a kleptomaniac.

Despite Gulham's best efforts, Andrew and I were able to scrape together enough of our equipment for our first attempt on August 13. The unlucky date lived up to its reputation. At our bivy at the bottom of the route the stove refused to light. After four hours of effort Andrew booted it across the ice and we returned to fetch the spare. We spent the 14th in basecamp under crystal-blue skies. It was the best weather of the trip and, looking at the summit of K2, we were sure that people were going for it. What we didn't know was that seven people would die for it that day, among them one of Andrew's good friends, Jeff Lakes.

The spare stove also refused to work and so on the 16th we were back at the bottom of the route with a fire-spitting conglomeration of every working stove part we had. It was dangerous as hell but at least it burned. We'd planned to climb at night, so just as the sun set we started through the icefall. It was such a chaotic mess that there was no way we could reach the clean northern branch of the ridge taken by the Spanish in '86. We opted instead for the southern branch and its 6,000 feet of virgin terrain.

The initial climbing was easy and straightforward. We found a great bivy on the ridge proper and spent the day looking up at what we figured would be the crux of the route.

Three thousand feet above, at about 20,000 feet, the ridge rose dramatically to a vertical ice cliff. There seemed to be a way around it, by threading through a narrow slot between an ice cliff and a huge serac hanging off the ridge. Barring that, it would be a direct attack.

The next night, as we set out, the moon was a little smaller, the air a little colder, and we found some of the scariest terrain either of us had ever encountered. Somehow the ridge itself was split by crevasses every hundred meters. We'd never seen anything like it. Climbing along a 60-degree arête of rotten snow we'd suddenly find our tools and feet popping through into space. The view through the holes to the glacier below was sickening. At one point I had to tunnel more than a body length into the slope to find ice for a screw. All Andrew could see from 50 meters below was the weak glow of my headlamp coming out of my little mineshaft. The pitch after that, he tried a similar belay excavation, and tunneled right through the ridge into thin air.

It was 2 a.m. before we reached the bottom of the ice cliff. We reckoned it was near vertical for close to 400 feet without any appreciable breaks. Andrew leads Grade 6 water ice, so when he said forget it, I forgot it. The alternative didn't look much better. We headed for a slot we'd seen from below, a huge partly-filled crevasse formed by a serac that had calved from the ice cliff. Andrew led a brilliant pitch across a gaping crevasse which split the ridge with a hundred-foot deep gash. He swung his way over stacked blocks and an overhanging snow mushroom to gain the slot. I led across the floor of the slot next, expecting every step in the deep snow to collapse. At the end of the rope I saw a small gap in the ice cliff and began to head toward it. The snow was terrible and we were moving at a crawl. Soon it became apparent that in order to reach the gap we would have to spend an hour or more wallowing away under some enormous overhanging seracs perched above the ice cliff. It was too dangerous, but it was also too late. It was 3:45 a.m., we'd been climbing for 11 hours, and we had to find a bivy. As we couldn't get out of the slot and onto the ridge above, the only option was to bivy on the serac. We climbed up, chopped out a platform, and crashed until 10 a.m. When we awoke we had a whole day ahead to sit on our little perch. Looking around, we realized we occupied the only island of safety on the entire slope below the ridge.

After a nerve-wrecking day waiting for *something* bad to happen, we finally started climbing at about 6 p.m. The plan was to regain the ridge via a diagonal end-run around the ice cliff and the serac. After eight steep pitches, we regained the ridge—and the crevasses. Andrew stepped through the ridge crest into a gaping hole. The hard work of slithering across the slot was followed by the even more tiring climb up the steep, sugar-snow arête on the opposite side. We continued upward on the ridge for another three or four pitches of terrible snow to a small, filled-in crevasse, where we prepared a bivouac without discussion.

When we woke later in the morning it was snowing, and clearly had been since we'd gone to bed. If there was one thing the Northeast Ridge of Chogolisa didn't need, it was more snow. The following morning, August 18th, it was still snowing and a thick fog had rolled in from Kondus Saddle. Was this the same fog that engulfed the Duke of Abruzzi in 1909, the same fog in which Herman Buhl disappeared in 1957? It sure was the same mountain in damn near the same spot. We were getting scared.

At 2 p.m., we tuned in our radio and caught Phil Powers' end of a call to Broad Peak. I heard Phil's voice crackling, "can you tell us about the accident." We jumped into the conversation. Seven people were dead. Jeff Lakes was dead. It was the final blow.

Jeff had really wanted to go to the Karakoram that year and asked Andrew if he could join us. We'd politely turned him down: we wanted to try as a team of two. So Jeff found his way onto a K2 expedition.

It didn't take a lot of talking to decide our climb was over. Descending what we'd climbed was impossible with our three screws and three pickets, forcing us onto the concave face between our line and the Spanish route. It took two days to get down, and the day after we reached basecamp the entire face slid, scouring clean all of our tracks.

During the six days we were gone, Ayub and Ghulam had been falling over each other to see who could steal the most. The shortwave radio, a camera, medicines, boots—they'd grabbed it all. We had to politely ask for individual items back as we discovered them missing. The only thing we really wanted now was to get the hell out of the mountains, and we sent Ghulam to find some porters. Not wanting to be alone with us, Ayub also took off for Concordia, promising to return with porters.

Ten days later the porters arrived, and two days after that I was again walking past Gore II, revisiting all the bad memories of that place. I couldn't wait to reach a shower and a bed, but I wondered if I'd be enjoying those amenities in a jail cell. As I passed by the last of the rag-tag army tents, a lone porter, coming up the valley, stopped me.

"Mr. John, from Chogolisa expedition?"

"Yes?"

"I have Federal Express for you." He pulled a large red, white and blue box from his pack. It was probably the highest and most remote delivery in the company's history, and certainly the most important package I'd ever received. Beside *Playboy* and *Penthouse* magazines was a letter from my father.

My letter had reached him from Geneva just the week before, and per my instructions he'd contacted my friend Eshun Khan, son of retired Admiral Sahid Khan, former Chief of Staff of the Pakistan Navy and currently Pakistan's Ambassador to the Hague.

According to the letter, Admiral Khan was mad as hell that we'd been treated so disrespectfully. He expected a phone call as soon as possible. I was laughing like a lunatic before I'd finished reading.

We broke the news to Captain Ayub that evening by asking him if he could help us arrange a trip to Karachi, where the Admiral lived. "It is much too dangerous there," he told us. "You cannot go."

"I think my friend can ensure our safety," I responded, handing him the letter. I watched the color drain from Ayub's face as he scanned the page.

"Admiral...Sahid Khan?" His voice quivered.

"Yes," I explained, "his son and I were great friends at university."

Ayub looked ill. He retired to his tent and we didn't hear from him until the next morning when he woke us with breakfast in bed. It was pathetic. The entire journey back to Skardu became one attempt after another by Ayub to make up to us.

When we reached the road, we told the porters we were broke. They took it surprisingly well; Ayub appointed one porter as representative to go with us to the bank in Skardu for the porters' money. The day after we arrived in Skardu, one seat opened on a flight out. Andrew and I agreed that I should take it and call the ambassador. I walked out onto the tarmac, leaving Ayub screaming at airport security to stop the plane.

"What would you like me to do to this man?" These were

the first words I heard through the phone receiver after I finished my story. The casual power in Ambassador Sahid's voice stopped me cold. As soon as he'd answered my phone call, I had felt safe. The passion and urgency of the days on the Baltoro evaporated. On the verge of winning the game of Pakistani justice that I'd been preparing for two months to lose, I hesitated. Captain Ayub had stolen from me, threatened me, and in many ways he'd ruined our expedition. But was that reason enough to do to him what I suspected the ambassador could do? The silence on the line began to be uncomfortable.

"I just don't think that he should be allowed to do this again." That was all I could say, and as the words came out of my mouth I felt sorry for Captain Ayub.

Seven months to the day after leaving Pakistan, I was tromping down from Point Five Gully on Ben Nevis, Scotland, and ran into an English climber I'd met at Concordia at the end of our expedition. He filled me in on what happened to Captain Ayub.

"It was in all the papers after you left. Dishonorable discharge, lost his pension, court martial. Probably in jail by now."

I shook my head and kept walking. So that was it, the end of the story. It wasn't the way I'd have chosen to win.

John Climaco has been a climber for 20 of his 30 years. In that time he has traveled extensively throughout North and South America, Europe, and Asia. His writing has appeared in several climbing-related publications. He currently lives in San Francisco.

JIM NOLLMAN

INCIDENT AT BOAT BAY

Whose wilderness is it?

I WAS FEELING SICK, STOLE AWAY FROM OUR BUSY WHALE CAMP to spend the afternoon sleeping it off in the comfort of the research boat anchored just offshore. Awakening refreshed, I was rowing the dinghy back to the beach when I heard the first scream. My first thought was that one of the three little girls in camp had been stung by a yellowjacket. Then a second scream. This one much louder, much more urgent, announcing more pain than any single yellowjacket could cause. I still believed it was a child, perhaps my five-year-old daughter Sasha who had lately started screaming like a banshee to express even minimal discontentment. Maybe someone stepped on a hive. That would be worth screaming about.

A third scream arose with such wrenching substance that it caused all other sounds in my world to vanish; a veritable monster of a shriek, materializing out of the woods with so much gut-wrenching power that I turned pale from the very sound of it. Now I understood the scream's location, and message. A woman was crying for her life at the edge of the forest that faced the little saltwater cove.

I saw my wife Katy motioning for me to row harder, faster towards the little cove. "It's Jill," she shouted across a hundred yards of water. "She's hurt...she's bleeding...there's a mountain lion...it's just standing there on the trail watching her. We can't get past it...see if you can pick her up by boat." I rowed with all my might around the point and into the little cove. Jill emerged from the forest, bleeding from her shoulder, her leg, her head. A moment later, Linda ran out of the woods, put an arm around Jill's waist. The two of them stepped into the frigid British Columbia seawater up to their waists. As I approached, Linda blurted out that she had it under control, then added, "you've got to get that mountain lion out of camp before it attacks someone else!" Linda guided Jill around the point towards the camp kitchen.

I brought the dinghy to shore in front of the place the two women had emerged from the forest. Gene stood at the tideline with a driftwood club held up like a baseball bat. "Do you see it crouching there?" he asked, pointing at an indistinct light spot amidst the salal and fern undergrowth. "Look, right there, where the trail touches the beach...that's where the cougar got Jill." Gene sighed, a sign that he felt unsure of the next step. He thrust the caveman's club into my hands which unwittingly propelled me forward. I looked at the trail, looked backwards into Gene's tense face, then back to the trail again. Took a few more steps forward. Still didn't see anything I could identify as a cougar. "Be careful," Gene beckoned, "It's crouching right there in front of you!" I wondered how Linda had gotten past the cat to assist Jill. I backed off, silently motioned Gene into the dinghy. The two of us quickly rowed around the rocky point to the camp kitchen.

Katy and Linda stood over Jill, washing the deep puncture wounds on her shoulder, back, and thigh. "That's where he grabbed me with his teeth," remarked Jill in a surprisingly analytical voice as she stared at her left upper arm. It was then I noticed her bloody, torn, t-shirt. Silkscreened onto the back of it was a huge cat's face representing her own bike shop business, Wildlife Cycles of Orcas Island. I noticed the bleeding was already diminishing, and concluded she was not in any grave danger. But her scalp needed suturing. She certainly needed a tetanus shot, probably something to keep her from getting rabies. Our first aid kit was chock full of things like bee-sting remedies and ace bandages. No one had stocked it to provide for anything of this magnitude. There was simply no precedent. I'd camped on this island every summer for the past ten years studying the wild orcas that reside off this east coast of Vancouver Island. No one, either in our party or, in any other of the many research groups along the coast had ever mentioned sighting a cougar.

The three little girls huddled together watching their mothers tend to Jill. I walked over to them, hugged all three of them to me at once. "Someone needs to call the Coast Guard," Katy announced, staring at me. My initial thought was that Joseph was the skipper of the boat we were using to conduct our research. It was his radio; he had the most experience at dealing with the Coast Guard, knew the lingo of *roger* and *10-4*. "Where's Joseph?" I asked. "He should do that."

"Here I am," a voice whispered directly behind me. I turned to face him. Joseph was holding a rifle in his hands. His first mate, Keith, stood beside him cradling a shotgun. I have never been comfortable around guns. They seem the icon of a culture I do not wish to live in, the accessory of nature "lovers" who feel a need to kill animals to bond with them. I had not known Joseph kept guns on the boat.

"Did you call the Coast Guard yet?" I asked.

"No I didn't. Do we need to?"

"Yes, of course we do. Please, go back to the boat and call them. Tell them there's an emergency. We need to get Jill to a hospital."

"I'm probably the best shot here." He answered flatly. "I need to deal with that cougar."

My face tensed. For some reason, the image of Gene carrying his big caveman stick came flashing back to me. "Listen, Joseph. I'm pleading with you not to shoot that cat. If you see it, fire over its head. That should scare it away. But please, do not shoot the cougar."

Jill piped up. "Don't shoot it. This is the cougar's land. You're asking it to pay a pretty big price for some human being's two week summer vacation."

I stood for a brief second searching from Jill's wounds to Joseph's rifle to the dark woods where an invisible cougar still prowled. My point had been made. I rowed the dinghy back to the boat, feeling apprehensive over taking myself out of the loop of potential events. No more than ten minutes had passed since I'd left the boat the first time.

I was on the radio to the Coast Guard emergency officer, discussing the quickest way to transport Jill across fifty miles of water and forest land to the nearest hospital, when I heard the boom of a gunshot. My face drained. I somehow knew instinctively that Joseph hadn't fired over the cat's head. He'd shot it. Katy would later tell me that at that moment Jill, Linda, herself, and the three girls all started weeping.

Writer, musician, and whale communicator Jim Nollman lives with his family in Friday Harbor, Washington.

SANYIKA SHAKUR, A.K.A. MONSTER
KODY SCOTT

THE WAR

*For L.A. gangs, protecting the local turf
is a deadly business.*

WHEN I TURNED ONTO MY BLOCK AND HAD GONE ABOUT four houses, a purple Duster sped toward me and fired one shot. Either the driver or the shooter—or perhaps both—were inexperienced in the technique of doing a drive-by, because I didn't even feel the closeness of the bullet. My forward motion and their speed in the opposite direction had obviously thrown the shooter's aim off. He probably aimed directly at me—a moving target—causing his shot to go somewhere behind me, no doubt into one of the houses I was passing. The car kept straight but picked up speed, probably thinking they had actually done something. My pace had been momentarily broken, but I never dismounted my bike.

When I got to my house my sister was standing out front. Though she had heard the shot, she had not known what had happened. Surprisingly, she was not accosted and asked to identify herself. Had the shooters found out that she was my sister, she would have been shot or kidnapped. Though our war had not yet reached the level of kidnapping and executing

family members, it was being talked about as an inevitable con-
sequence in our headlong escalation.

This, too, pointed up the inexperience of these shooters. If
they were on Sixty-ninth Street, that meant they knew I lived
there, and their intentions were to try to catch me or one of
my homies coming from or going to my house. My combat
mentality was still at its peak from the brush with death
around the corner, so when I got to where my sister was
standing I yelled at her to "take her ass in the house," and that
"didn't she know there was a goddamn war going on out
here?" She stared for a moment then ran inside.

Putting up Li'l Monster's bike, I had a thousand thoughts
running through my head. Once in my room I sat down on
the end of my bed to devise a plan in the midst of this latest
attack. Usually we'd respond right away, but tonight there
seemed to be a lull in our communication—the drums
weren't beating. I phoned Sidewinder in an attempt to consolidate a riding party of able soldiers and was shocked at what
I heard. The very same car that shot up Sleepy's car had also
rode on Sidewinder and some other homies up in the Eighties
hood: their initial attack had taken place on Seventy-first
Street. But this wasn't the shocker, for it was common for one
car to make a full sweep of an entire neighborhood. The surprising news was that in their attempt to shoot one of our
homies, they had shot and critically wounded a member of the
Inglewood Family Bloods, who had been creeping into our
hood to shoot Sidewinder and the homies. The shooter car
met a righteous resistance in the Eighties and didn't get the
chance to do any damage, although shots were exchanged.
When asked what they did with the Blood, Sidewinder responded, "We sent him to his Maker."

It seemed then that we were in totally occupied territory.
Hanging up the phone I lay back on my bed and looked over

at the empty bed beside mine. My younger brother, Li'l Monster, had been captured for an armed robbery along with Li'l Harv and a woman named Speedy—a close associate of the hood and a firm supporter of the criminal class. He had been given six months in camp. I wished he was there because he'd be down to launch an attack from right here. But Bro was not there and Crazy De was still in the Hall. Shit. I felt trapped. I had to do *something*.

I retrieved my double-barrel from beneath the dresser and checked it for munition. Then I went out and got back on Bro's bike. Holding the shotgun—which had been sawed off for stealth—across the handlebars, I peddled west toward the borderline that separated our hood from the Sixties

Wearing my combat black I crossed Western Avenue and entered their hood on the left flank, in what today we call the first parallel. I made my way cautiously up Sixty-ninth Street to Horace Mann Junior High School. Rumor had it that they had been using Horace Mann as a meeting place, for they had still failed to procure a park for their meeting and mounting place.

I circumvented the school on its left side, which was on Seventy-first. There I parked my bike and traveled on foot. I hopped the school fence with the shotgun in my waistband, landing on the other side with a thud. When I got to the lunch area I was disappointed to find no one there. Had they been at the school, this is where they would be found, because the lunch area was covered with a roof.

Moving now on instinct, I continued through the lunch area and out to the makeshift bungalows, which had been constructed to allow school to continue while the administration building was being renovated. I began to hear music in the distance. The closer I came to the north side of the school, the louder the music got. "Finally," I said to myself, "someone to shoot."

Creeping slowly toward the area I believed the music—and now loud talking—was coming from, I kept a vigilant eye out for sentries or stragglers who might announce my presence and blow my surprise attack. And, of course, the very real possibility existed that if I did not strike swiftly, causing much damage and confusion, they could mount a response and trap me in the school. I had brought only two shells, both 00. At each corner I crouched and peeked from a low position—combat training I had learned from old war movies. But as I negotiated each corner I found no one there. Where were they? Then a terrifying thought occurred to me—the roof. These muthafuckas were on the roof. This gave them a vantage point far superior to my ground-level position.

But the sound disproved my theory: it was an even-level sound and not, as I had surmised, an above-level sound. My second thought was confirmed as I made my way around the next set of bungalows. They were not even in the schoolyard, but outside its gate, parked on Sixty-eighth Street, talking as they played the car radio, beer bottles on the hood and roof of the car. Luckily for me, they were on my side of the street, for had they been on the other side I would not have been able to maximize my damage.

Not only did I have to shoot through the fence, but my targets were in the street. This put about seventeen feet between us. I had 00 buckshot, which would compensate for the distance; but my weapon was sawed off. This meant that my shot would be more of a spray than a solid impact.

Realizing that my transportation was clear across the school, I debated whether I should expend one or both barrels. Expend one and use one to secure my escape, or pull both triggers at once, using the tremendous sound as a diversionary tactic and hoping to realize my intent, which was a funeral or two.

Making my decision, I stepped to the gate, stuck the barrels through and shouted, "Gangsta!"

BLOOM, BLOOM!

I let loose one and then the other in rapid succession, then turned and ran back through the bungalows and the lunch area and finally reached the fence on Seventy-first. Stopping to put the shotgun in my waistband, I saw a car bend the corner. I held the shotgun out instead and ducked behind a trash bin to let the car pass. It was occupied by two older civilians. When I got back up and shoved the gun in my waistband, I jumped. "Ahhh!" The barrels were still hot and burned my private parts. Holding the gun in my hands, I scaled the fence.

I ran back to where I had left the bike and, goddamn, someone had stolen it! Now I began to panic, because Western Avenue, the first parallel, was over a block away. Surely, I thought, the survivors would be in the vehicle looking for their assailants—and they'd be armed. Besides, I had no shells.

I turned on my heels and trotted down Seventy-first, trying to stay as close as possible to the lawns in case I had to run through a yard. Once I got to the first parallel I felt better, but no safer. The barrels had cooled down enough now to put the gun in my waistband, so I hid the weapon. Finally I made my way down our driveway and into the house.

I reloaded the shotgun and laid it against the stereo speaker. I then turned on the TV and watched the "Benny Hill Show." I felt much better.

Kody Scott was born in 1963 and grew up in South Central Los Angeles. In sixth grade he joined the Crips and soon earned the name "Monster" for his many acts of depravity. He is confined to the California Correctional Institute at Tehachapi, where he has transformed himself into black nationalist Sanyika Shakur. This story was excerpted from his book Monster: The Autobiography of an L.A. Gang Member.

ERIC HANSEN

THE SEASON OF FEAR

Strange creatures walk the Borneo forest.

THE LAST SOUNDS I REMEMBERED HEARING BEFORE FALLING asleep were the rhythmic tones of the *gampang* (hardwood xylophone), the wind, and the pattering of rain on the leaf roof of the longhouse. It was uncomfortable sleeping on the plank floor, but whenever I woke up I could hear the *gampang* being played softly. By dawn the music had stopped and drops of water were falling from the eaves and nearby branches. Through my mosquito net I could see a rooster, perched on a low windowsill, crowing small puffs of steam into the crisp morning air. My feet felt cold on the smooth hardwood floor-boards as I tied my sarong and wrapped a blue-and-white checked bedsheet around my shoulders. Walking down the longhouse porch, I came upon the familiar wrinkled and smil-ing faces of two old men, Pa Bit and Pa Ulay. From beneath a shared blanket they invited me to sit with them at their morn-ing fire burning neatly in the bottom half of a dirt filled tin trunk that had once been painted bright blue with red flow-ers. The men thumped a huddled mass of dogs with pieces of

101

firewood in order to make room for me. Yelping and whining, the dogs disappeared into the heavy mist that billowed down the 200-foot covered porch. As we sat talking, Pa Bit's daughter appeared with a breakfast of boiled rice, smoked deer meat, and black tea. Tiny shafts of sunlight gradually began to appear, slanting down weakly through gaps in the roof as the fog lifted and the morning air began to warm.

Here in the village of Long Sungai Anai I was above the impassable Ambun Rapids of the Kayan River. *Ambun* is an Indonesian word meaning mercy. From Long Belun Alim, on the Bahau River, I had walked for two days, thirty miles, with a group of rattan cutters through the jungle to avoid that boulder-filled gorge of waterfalls and perpetually rising mist. The Ambun Rapids were the last major obstacle blocking my way to the Apo Kayan—the highland plateau of central Borneo. From the highlands six major rivers flow down to the Celebes, Java, and South China seas. The Apo Kayan is part of the large white patch on my map bordered by comments such as "Unsurveyed," and "Limits of Reliable Relief of Information." Few Westerners had come this far. Over the next two months I would discover and map a network of trails that spread throughout the rainforest—linking rivers, garden plots, and villages.

I wanted to leave for the village of Long Nawang in the morning. It was a nine-hour walk through the jungle, and I was told that I needed a guide because the trail was difficult to follow. I asked Pa Bit and Pa Ulay if they could come with me, but they were busy splitting lengths of rattan with their long-handled knives. I continued down the longhouse porch looking for a guide, but after half the morning searching in vain, I decided to go by myself. I had survived my travels through the interior for more than four months, and since it was only "one more day's walk" to the main Kenyah villages at the headwaters of the Kayan River, I felt comfortable trying to find the way alone. Pa Bit helped me sketch a crude map of the rivers and mountains, but suggested that it would be foolish to go without a companion. Other people in the village were much more adamant. They went to great lengths to warn me of the confusing trails, the long distance, and the dangers of walking alone in that particular part of the jungle. The hand-drawn map looked simple enough, so I couldn't understand their attitude. There was an urgency to their voices that seemed exaggerated, an apprehensive tone that I couldn't quite identify. For a moment I thought I could detect a note of fear. Still unfamiliar with how the Kenyah expressed themselves, I assumed they were simply being overly cautious. I left the village late that morning, keeping in mind that I could return if the trail was too difficult to follow.

Within an hour I was beyond the last shimmering green fields of hill rice and had entered the deep jungle. Enormous hardwood trees blocked out the sun and created a diffuse light that filtered down through the tangle of vegetation into the depths of the rainforest. There was cool shade along the narrow dirt footpath, but the humidity and the weight of my woven rattan backpack soon had me streaming with perspiration. I had just replaced the plaited carrying straps, and they were still stiff and uncomfortable. They soon began cutting into my skin, so I removed my shirt and used it as a shoulder pad. The occasional breeze that blew across my bare midriff helped to keep me cool. I followed a good trail through stands of giant bamboo, some of it eight inches wide and ninety feet tall. I encountered a now-familiar landscape pattern of knee-deep exposed tree roots, hanging-moss forests, and single-log bridges that provided slippery passage over mud-and-vine choked waterways. The walking was slow, but I was in no hurry.

At times the jungle closed in, and I had to follow tunnels cut through the interwoven mass of barbed vines, aerial roots, fallen branches, and dense shrubbery. These tunnels were cut for the local people, so I was forced constantly to duck. Sometimes I crawled on my stomach. Massive dead tree trunks covered in blue-green moss that appeared to have been caught in mid-fall by the tangle of vines and branches leaned at fantastic angles. Glittering armies of black ants filed across the trail, disappeared into a mat of twigs and rotting leaves, and reappeared a few yards farther on as they marched over a fallen tree and out of sight. Enormous heart-shaped leaves, three feet across, curtained either side of the trail, and I felt as if I were a small bug crawling through some fantastic garden. The staccato bursts of insect sounds, rasping and vibrating, filled the thick, moist air until I couldn't hear my footsteps. I recognized the lilting call of the bulbul and the distinctive leathery wingflap of the hornbill. I called to the birds, and sometimes I could get one to follow me. They would stay with me for a mile or so, keeping just out of sight. When one bird lost interest, I would try to attract another. I found myself imitating nearly every sound that I heard. I was trying to talk with the jungle.

Gibbon monkeys, with their "whoop-whoop" cries, swung hand over hand through the canopy. I stood behind a buttressed tree root watching two wild pigs dig up a creekbed with their powerful snouts. A slight gust of wind brought clusters of fragrant white flowers down from the treetops. The five-petaled flowers spun like little propellers, slowly descending to the jungle floor. I stopped walking and filled my lungs with the thick perfume that hung in the air.

The light, the temperature, the sounds, and the smells of the rainforest were in a perpetual state of change. Walking through patches of warm aromatic air, I would suddenly encounter the stench of putrefying flesh or feces. Everywhere I looked there were signs of decay and regrowth. Sprays of purple orchids sprouted from dead branches, and wherever one of the giant trees had crashed to earth, ripping a hole in the roof of the jungle, young saplings had sprung up, competing for the narrow patch of sunlight.

I crossed many rivers that day, but the water was never more than waist deep. Clear and cool, it ran slowly enough to be crossed safely. With my *parang* I would cut a six-foot sapling for balance, heave my pack high onto my shoulder, and slowly make my way to the opposite bank. I kept my shoes on to protect my recently healed feet from the painful river rocks, and the cold water felt wonderful rushing past my bare legs. On the far bank the trail would sometimes invisibly follow the river for a few hundred feet before reentering the thick foliage. To pick up the trail again I walked up and down the edge of the forest, looking carefully for footsteps or the telltale sign of where a *parang* had slashed the undergrowth. When the trail narrowed and disappeared, I knew I had gone the wrong way. I would retrace my steps to the last trail junction and continue on. I carefully marked each fork in the trail with a blaze in case I became lost and had to return to Long Sungai Anai. By midafternoon I was beyond the point of being able to return, but I still felt confident I was making good time and that I would be able to reach Long Nawang before dark. Pa Bit's map and directions were excellent.

I sat in the sun at the edge of a clearing in the jungle to enjoy the sight of sun on the long grass and unfolded my banana-leaf lunch packet of boiled rice, dried meat, steamed vegetables, and chillies. Grasshoppers made short energetic flights across the shoulder-high buffalo grass; swarms of brightly-colored butterflies clustered on the jungle floor. It was a perfect day for walking: dry, few leeches, a reasonable trail, and no sense of urgency. I hadn't seen a soul all day and had completely forgotten about the warnings from the people in Long Sungai Anai. I wiped my fingers on the banana leaf and let it drop at my feet where it would soon be reclaimed by the jungle. Pushing my way through the buffalo grass, I reentered the green darkness of the rainforest. Within minutes I realized the grass must have had sharp serrated edges because my face, hands, and legs were covered with a crisscross of shallow, stinging cuts.

An hour later, at the crest of a densely forested mountain trail, I was looking up at a towering wall of vines and branches when I noticed a flurry of movement at the base of the trees. Obscured by shadows, I could see women and children fleeing towards the undergrowth. Within moments the jungle had swallowed them up, leaving a small group of men standing at the edge of the clearing. One of them instinctively reached for his *parang*. The men were apprehensive, but I had no idea why. To reassure them, I approached nonchalantly as possible, smiled, and slowly removed my pack and *parang*. In spite of the awkwardness of the situation, I let them see I was unarmed. We exchanged greetings mechanically. The men, dressed in rag shorts or loincloths, were carrying blowpipes and spears. Their earlobes had been distended, and intricate blue tattoos covered their throats, chest, and arms. The men had been squatting on the ground, leaning against their heavy cargo packs. Woven out of shiny golden brown rattan, the packs contained rice and sections of green bamboo filled with wild bee honey. One of the loads was a dead deer trussed securely on a stake. Long strips of fibrous bark had been passed through slits in the hide and fashioned into shoulder straps. It was easy to spot the man who had carried the pig: his buttocks and legs were smeared with blood and covered with flies.

I spoke with the group in Indonesian for about five minutes.

I told them where I had come from, what I was doing in the jungle, and why I was by myself. These people were Kenyah and were fluent only in their own language, so I got the feeling that they didn't understand much of what I said. I wanted to let them know there was no reason to be afraid. They seemed to relax slightly, but no real conversation developed. We never sat down. The uncertainty of the situation made it too awkward to linger, so we all put on our packs and said goodby. I felt confused about their reaction to me, as we quietly walked off in our own directions, I glanced back and saw the last two men standing at the edge of the forest with their blowpipes. The looks of suspicion and terror on their faces made me catch my breath. I managed a friendly wave before we lost sight of each other. The women and children never reappeared.

Minutes later I stopped at the end of a narrow ridge. Peering through a gap in the vines and branches, I caught a glimpse of the Kayan River valley. Below me the expanse of distant treetops stretched far away into a blue-gray haze. I see faint wisps of smoke filtering through the branches into the afternoon sky. Beneath that immense green canopy were eight major Kenyah villages. The only knowledge I had about the people in the villages came from obscure museum journals, a World War II account by Tom Harrison, and stories from missionaries who had made infrequent visits through the years. Although a token form of Christianity was practiced here, I knew this tribal area had retained strong ties with animistic traditions. It was still a world of supernaturalism, omens, and black magic.

As I stood there, I remembered the group of Kenyahs I had just met. The startled expressions on their faces haunted me. I couldn't understand why the women and children had fled at the first sight of me. The incident made me reflect on the rumors and warnings I had heard about the Apo Kayan. I recalled a night in the three weeks earlier in the mission station of Long Bia when Nyonya Nam Sun had cautioned me not to walk by myself in the farm clearings, or to go out at night. "People are afraid," she had warned. She had also mentioned the words *bali saleng*. Back in my room at the trading station I found the definition in my dictionary: *bali saleng* meant the black ghost. Still standing on the trail, fragments of overheard conversations drifted back to me: "…jungle spirits…blood sacrifice…spring-powered shoes for jumping over trees… pregnant women abducted…selling blood to oil companies."

Superstition, I reassured myself, folk history, part of their oral traditions. I started walking again, but my mind was no longer focused on the trail. I began searching my memory for more recollections.

There is an established Kenyah tradition of making blood offerings before starting any new longhouse construction. On previous occasions I had seen the blood of a rooster or pig poured into a posthole before the first post was placed; prior to Colonial times a proper sacrifice would have been a young girl, a slave, or a captive. With this offering the power of *bali tanab*, the spirit of the earth, would have been invoked to bless the project and protect the men during construction.

On the east and south coasts of Borneo, near the towns of Samarinda, Tanjung Selor, and Balikpapan, as well as to the north in Sarawak, huge construction projects are underway: bridges, high rise buildings, roads and hydroelectric schemes. Each project is associated with a different spirit. There is *bali minyak*, the spirit of oil; *bali jambatan*, the spirit of the vehicle bridge; and *bali rumbad tinggi*, the spirit of the high-rise. All of these spirits require blood offerings, and shamans known as *dayungs* are hired to perform ceremonies. No construction project could be started without first calling in a *dayung* to appease the appropriate spirits; otherwise the local labor force would refuse to begin work for fear of spirit retribution. There are many well-documented cases of major projects that experienced endless difficulties until the proper ceremonies were observed. Company reports tell of equipment failures, unseasonably bad weather, widespread illness, and absenteeism. Vehicles have been known to disappear into muddy roads overnight. Even PERTAMINA, the national oil company of Indonesia, hires a *dayung* to help launch a project. The company had learned from experience.

Officially, animal blood has been substituted for human blood, but few, if any, inland people believe in this. From the central highlands all coastal development plans are viewed with suspicion and fear. The villagers reason that if one longhouse pole traditionally required the blood of one human being, then how much blood from how many people is needed to construct a 30-story concrete building? I had heard people from the highlands refer to construction projects in terms of their cost in human blood. By village estimates there are "200 person" hydroelectric schemes and "100 person" bridges. Development projects are rarely seen as employment opportunities.

The role of a *bali saleng* is to collect the blood. He is half-man, half-spirit; he lives in the forest; he is believed to be employed by large companies. I had heard that the standard price for five pints of blood was one million rupiahs ($1,500 U.S. at the time). For a big project, many *bali salengs* are employed. As I continued walking, I realized that among the inland people I might be mistaken for a *bali saleng,* but feeling confident in my ability to speak Indonesian, I assumed I would have no trouble explaining who I was.

What I did not know was that the description of *bali saleng* changed regularly, and that he came only at a very specific time of the year. At the time I happened to be traveling through the Apo Kayan, the description was "a tall white skinny man with brownish hair who walks through the jungle. He will come over the mountains from Sarawak during the season of grass cutting."

My long day's walk came to an abrupt and welcome end when I arrived in Long Nawang just before dark. People were in the fields cutting grass, and because of the omen, they had been expecting me for the last two months. I received a noticeably cool reception. Usually when I entered the village in Sarawak or Kalimantan, the children would get very excited, following me closely. As they jumped up and down, their delighted voices would rise above the usual din of barking dogs and crowing roosters. The first evening many people would come to the headman's room to greet me. We would drink rice wine, laugh, tell stories, and, if people were in the mood, dance to the music of three-stringed *sapeh* until late at night. After being in the jungle for even a short time, it was a thrill to be included in the clamor and excitement of the longhouse.

That first night in Long Nawang was different. I sat alone with the headman, Pa Biah Leng, and his wife. There were no visitors, and the longhouse was unusually silent. After dinner, Pa Biah rolled himself a large conical cheroot with a scrap of used notebook paper and some of the tobacco I had given him. He was dressed comfortably in a checked sarong and white singlet. His jet black hair was glistening from his evening bath in the river. He was a well-preserved 63-year-old. As the match flared, I could see the carefully penciled school lessons illuminated along the length of his cheroot.

Without looking at me Pa Biah asked, "*Tuan*, why have you come to the Apo Kayan?"

"I wanted to come here because few white men have traveled through these jungles. I have shotgun shells I want to trade for gold and for *gaharu* (the aromatic hardwood)."

He seemed skeptical that anyone would come from so far away for the reasons I gave. That evening, after I spoke to Pa Biah about my encounter in the jungle, he told me the story of *musium takoot*, the season of fear. He explained that every year during October and November people are isolated in their fields, weeding the rice fields and constructing small farm huts in preparation for the harvest. This period of the year used to be one of the traditional headhunting seasons because it was relatively easy to ambush individuals who were working far from the villages. Headhunting no longer occurs, but the seasonal fear has been sustained by the belief in *bali saleng*.

"The people are afraid," Pa Biah warned me. "Don't travel by yourself; it is not safe. The people know you have come to the valley. They may hurt you if they see you alone in the jungle."

The red glow from Pa Biah's cheroot gradually faded, and as he coaxed the fire back to life with his foot, we sipped hot bitter tea from chipped enamel mugs. Ibu Iting, his wife, sat nearby. She was making thread by pulling strands of cotton from the edge of an old piece of fabric. While holding the ends of two strands in her left hand, she twisted them together by rubbing them between her right hand and thigh. She threaded her needle and continued to listen to our conversation as she patched a well-worn pair of trousers.

"Last year," Pa Biah continued, "*bali saleng* was described as a brown-skinned man with long black hair and pointed teeth. He wore powder blue, short-sleeved, military-type shirt with matching shorts. He had a special set of spring-powered shoes that enabled him to jump four meters in the air and ten meters away in a single bound. He could spring through the air to cover long distances quickly and capture people by surprise. After tying up his victim with strips of rattan, he would take the blood from the wrist or the foot with a small knife and a rubber pump. The corpse would then be hoisted with vines up into the jungle canopy so that searchers could not find it."

Listening attentively, I tried to imagine a police department's composite sketch of such an individual. The image of *bali saleng* was still too farfetched for me to take seriously.

"A *bali saleng* cannot be killed by man," Pa Biah continued. "Bullets bounce off him, spears cannot pierce his body, and when he gets old he will take on a young man without family and train him."

Pa Biah went on to tell me that the year before a pregnant woman was reported to have been killed by a *bali saleng* near the village of Long Ampung. Pregnant women are considered prime targets because they contain the blood of two people.

That night the people of Long Nawang locked themselves into their family quarters and did not open their doors until daybreak.

I listened to Pa Biah's stories with interest, but I failed to recognize my own imminent danger. I was placing too much confidence in my knowledge of the language and too little importance on the power of fear. Instead of accepting the people's beliefs as something real and adjusting my behavior accordingly, I was relying on a false sense of security. With nearly eighteen hundred jungle miles behind me, I had become careless.

The next morning I got up and left at dawn—alone. I didn't get far. Four hours up the valley, as I followed the Kayan River southeast from Long Nawang, I was attacked in the village of Long Uro. The first thing I heard was the frantic pounding of children's feet along hardwood planks of the longhouse porch. There were a few startled cries from the women then the sound of men's voices. It all happened very quickly. It took me a moment to realize that I was the cause of the commotion.

A group of about two dozen men, some armed with spears, came down to the trail where I was standing. After some excited questioning and gesturing (not all of which I understood), I felt their hands on me. I was stripped of my pack and forced to the ground. I didn't resist. I sat in the dirt with my back to a drainage ditch as the men formed a tight semicircle in front of me. For the next two hours they fired accusations at me in Indonesian. I was repeatedly questioned and cross-examined. My mind became alert, and I was careful not to show any fear. They wanted to know why I was by myself, why I didn't have a cooking pot, what I was doing in the Kayan River valley, and how I had come over the mountains from Sarawak. My answers didn't sound very convincing, and I soon realized how vulnerable I was. The experience of facing so many frightened people was intimidating. My belongings were ransacked; shotgun shells, diaries, salt, clothing, and half-finished letters to friends littered the ground. I was repeatedly asked about the contents of my pack. After two men had gone through everything, I realized that they had been looking for spring-powered shoes, the small blood knife, and the rubber pump.

Over and over they repeat two questions: "Why do you walk by yourself?" and "Why aren't you afraid of *bali saleng*?"

The fact is that no one in Borneo walks by himself in the jungle. It is too easy to fall down or to get lost or sick. Every year people disappear in the rainforest without a trace. Solo travel isn't done except by the spirits. It was difficult to explain to these villagers why I had no fear. By now hours had passed, and I felt my energy fading. These frightened, angry people, with their excited sing-song manner of speaking, were exhausting me. Here in a village of practicing animists was a middle-class Westerner arguing about evil spirits in their jungle. By consistently basing my answers on logic and reasoning,

I was only making the situation worse. It would have merely increased their suspicions if I had claimed not to believe in spirits. How could I possibly be convincing? I asked myself. It became irrelevant and unimportant to me whether they understood who I really was. By this time I wanted only one thing: to be able to leave the village safely. I realized that I had to accept their fear and deal with it on their terms. It was absurd for me to try to convince them that one of their greatest fears was unfounded. A solution came to me unexpectedly.

The Kenyah, as do all the inland people, have a tradition of amulets, charms, and spell-breakers. The collective term for these items is *jeemat*. A *jeemet* can be made from a wide assortment of materials; the most common are seedpods, bones, wood shavings, crushed insects, beeswax, cowrie shells, and odd-shaped black pebbles known as hook stones. A *jeemat* can be made by man or found, but the most powerful ones (the hook stones) are given by a spirit or ghost. Directions for their use are revealed during a dream. It is very bad luck to lose or give away a charm that has come from the spirits. *Jeemats* are usually worn around the neck or wrist and are an important part of one's personal adornment. They are visible proof of one's faith in the power of the spirit world.

With this in mind. I remembered I was wearing a small, stuffed fabric banana pin that a friend had given me before I started my trip. The pin was about three inches long and had a bright yellow, polka-dot peel. The banana was removable. It could be dangled at the end of a short safety string. Until that moment in Long Uro, I had used the pin only to amuse people.

"This," I said, gesturing to the pin, "is my *jeemat*. It protects me from *bali saleng*." It caught them off guard; it also aroused their interest. One of the men came forward to touch the banana, but I cautioned him not to. He stopped three feet away from me.

"It had very strong *obat*," I said. *Obat* has many definitions: magic, power, or medicine. "Be careful, this charm was made especially for me by a spirit. That is why I'm not afraid to walk alone in the jungle." The mood of the interrogation changed as interest shifted to my banana pin.

"Where did it come from?" "What is it made of?" "Do you have more?" "How much would one cost?" they wanted to know.

I did not concoct my banana-pin story because I thought my tormentors were simple-minded or childish. Quite the opposite. The Kenyah have a highly developed relationship with the spirit world. I couldn't think of any other story they might believe. From generations of experience, they know how to coexist with both good and bad spirits. Firmly rooted in the twentieth century, I certainly didn't have anything to teach them. I was the outsider, the ignorant one. I had great respect for all the inland people. With their unique forms of architecture, social organization, and sophisticated farming techniques, they have established themselves in an incredibly difficult environment. The decision to present the banana pin as a powerful charm not only helped save me in this situation, but also forced me to reconsider how I was responding to the people. I stopped being the observer and began to accept their supernatural world, and my journey was never the same. In that single moment I grew much closer to my experiences.

The tension eased after I had revealed the power of the banana-pin charm. A few obstinate older men insisted on going over the fine points of my story, but the rest seemed to think I was probably harmless. I was flushed with relief. The blood and adrenaline pounded through my body and made my fingertips and toes ache. I felt light-headed and blessed to have survived this incident unharmed.

I was free to go, but it was too late to continue up the valley to my original destination—Long Sungai Barang. I had to spend the night in Long Uro. Dozens of eyes stared at me through knotholes and cracks in the rough wooden walls as I ate a miserable and lonely dinner. I was served half-rotten fish pounded in a mortar, bones and all. Having finished my meal, I strung my mosquito net in a filthy corner, unrolled my mat, and escaped into an exhausted sleep.

During the night there must have been more discussion because in the morning, just after I left the village, I came upon a young man standing at the side of the pathway. He was barefoot, well muscled, and dressed in blue shorts. He wore white gloves and held a large unsheathed *parang* at his side. He didn't respond to my greeting as I approached, but as I passed he fell into step a few feet behind me. I continued on for a short while then decided it would be better to confront him. I turned to speak, but he had vanished into the undergrowth. I knew that he could be no more than fifty feet from where I stood, but I couldn't see him. For months this jungle had seemed so benign and giving. How quickly it had become frightening. It was clear to me that at any moment I might be ambushed and killed.

Farther up the valley I passed abandoned farm huts and stopped briefly in the village of Lidung Payau to ask directions to the village of Long Sungai Barang. On the far side of Lidung Payau, I saw what I soon realized was a cage fashioned out of logs six inches in diameter. The structure was raised off the ground and had a slat floor that let excrement out and the flies in. The cage measured six feet by five feet by four feet and had a shingled roof. It was "home" not to an animal, but to a man. There were no doors or windows. I later learned that the inhabitant, barely visible between the gaps in the horizontal logs, had lived in the cage for more than two years. I don't know what his crime was. The cloud of furiously buzzing blackflies must have driven him mad. I looked upon this wretched man as a fellow sufferer, but when I tried to speak with him, he moved to the far side of his cage, and I could sense his fear of my presence.

I no longer had my sense of security and self-confidence. I lost track of time. As my anxiety mounted, a few hundred yards began to seem like miles. My thinking became erratic and unsound. There was no turning back, and for the first time since leaving Long Sungai Anai three days earlier, I began to panic. I sensed that I was being watched. Soaked in perspiration, I paused frequently to look over my shoulder and listen for the sound of human voices or of jungle knives slashing through the undergrowth. I scanned the surrounding walls of impenetrable green and brown foliage, but I could detect nothing. There were only the normal sounds of the jungle: the wind, the flutter of leaves, dripping water, and rubbing branches. I could see black hornbills perched nearby, so I called to them. I wanted to hear something friendly and reassuring, but their calls came back to me sounding like strangled pleas.

I hurried on to Long Sungai Barang, hoping that word of the incident in Long Uro hadn't preceded me. I wanted a fresh start. I now realized the full extent of my naiveté, my incredible stupidity. I was completely alone and vulnerable. I didn't know what else to do except to keep walking and to try to relax. I stopped frequently, considered going back, couldn't decide, then continued on. Whenever I sat down to rest and clear my mind, a new wave of anxiety would engulf me.

I knew that Long Sungai Barang was the last village in the upper Kayan River valley. If the people there weren't friendly,

I would be trapped. Four hundred miles of primary rainforest separated me from the most accessible coast.

It was late afternoon by the time I entered the longhouse at Sungai Barang. I was disoriented and confused, and my legs were bleeding freely from the leeches and barbed vines. I was surrounded by about a dozen Kenyah men. I could feel the deep, painful grooves that the straps of the rattan pack had cut into my shoulders. My shirt was pasted to my back from the heat of the day. The men seemed relaxed and curious, but I felt they looked right through me and sensed my uncertainty.

We talked about the approaching rice harvest for perhaps ten minutes; then to my left I heard the familiar creak and slam of a sapling-powered hardwood door. In midsentence I looked up, expecting to see the headman, but there before me stood a young, white-skinned woman with golden hair. She was dressed in a flowered sarong and a blouse. She was barefoot, pretty, and smiling. I was completely unnerved. It just wasn't possible for her to be there. I became incredulous and even more confused. Finally I just smiled back and felt my pent-up fears and anxieties begin to dissolve.

The first thing I noticed as she stood there was the fragrance of her skin. It wasn't the scent of soap or perfume; it was the scent of another culture, another world, a fresh, wonderful smell that made me question my attraction to smoky jungle campfires and eating wild animals. We spoke Indonesian. There was no urgency to our voices. In Kenyah fashion we began with trivial matters in order to mask the real intent of our conversation, and gradually we led up to the important questions. More people came to the room. They sat quietly, watched, and listened. I Eventually the temptation to speak our own language was overwhelming. The woman smiled again and in perfect English said, "I'm Cynthia. I live next door. The headman won't be back until late tonight. Would you like to come over to my place for a visit?"

Eric Hansen has worked as a goldsmith, a buffalo catcher, a pig farmer, a wild dog hunter, and a barber in Mother Teresa's Home for the Destitute and Dying in Calcutta. He is the author of Motoring with Mohammed: Journeys to Yemen and the Red Sea *and* Stranger in the Forest: On Foot Across Borneo, *from which this story was excerpted.*

ANDREW BILL

JUST DESERT

The author learns one of life's great lessons.

AT THE TYPICAL MANHATTAN COCKTAIL PARTY, AS THE SUITS
mingle and admire, as kisses are exchanged and ambitious eyes
flutter around the room, the conversation curves around to the
inevitable question: what do you do? I realize it's a position-
ing tactic, a modern substitute for sniffing and howling. In this
spirit, I answer that I am a traveler. If pressed further, I tell
them that since the age of 17, from the first moment I had the
finances, freedom, or both, I have traveled. First around my native Britain, then across the Channel on short "vacation" sor-
ties into France. Then, like a child that's interested only in its
outer boundaries, I ventured further and longer away from
home. Until, at the age of 37, I have lived on three continents
and left my footprints in over 100 countries. As a travel writer,
I have made it my career, my passion, my character. Traveling
is what I am.

The next question—if there is one—is either "where's your
favorite place?" or "what was your worst moment?" The first
I just brush aside. The heart of the true traveler is fickle,

promiscuous. How can there be favorites when the whole motivation for travel is shunning the familiar for the excitement of newness? In response to the second question, I have many stories to tell.

Especially in the course of my early travels—when a lack of money and a lot of time necessitated hitchhiking through the night, sleeping in city parks or on lonely beaches—I have gathered a store of tales enough to fill a thousand cocktail parties. I have been cornered in the solid 2 a.m. shadows of the Greyhound Bus Station in Boston by a knife-wielding Irishman who, fired by the strong spirits of his homeland, was convinced "the only good Englishman was a dead Englishman." I have been shot at in the bright-red poppy fields of the Golden Triangle where Burma, Laos, and Thailand converge to form the opium capital of the world; framed and arrested in a small tropical "prawn" town in the north of Australia where just being a foreigner was tantamount to a confession of guilt. I have been given a death sentence by a doctor high in the Himalayas, and attacked by a wave of rats on a black night in Mexico. Yet among all these experiences there is one moment in the Sinai that stays lodged in the forefront of my memory like a bone in the throat. Remarkable not for its drama but for what it taught me about myself, it remains as fresh as the day it happened over fifteen years ago.

"*Masari?*"

I shrug my shoulders to tell him I don't understand. Not that word. Not any word. I can't even look it up in my dictionary. It probably isn't Egyptian at all, but one of the many Bedouin dialects.

"*Masari?*" he says again, spitting out the word like an olive pit.

I look back at him, reading his face for clues. A dusty red-and-white checked headdress obscures all but the small oval from forehead to chin. Dirt has been ironed into a thousand lines by the desert and the sun. His eyes, even in the shadow of the room, are burnt into thin rheumy slits. Untamed jet-black eyebrows hint at the color of his hair. The lips are set in what can only be impatience, rapidly dissolving into anger. I can't tell what age he is, still less what he is saying.

"*Masari?*" he almost shouts it this time, "*Masari? Felous? Felous?*" It's obviously a question. Fumbling in the folds of his tunic, he extracts a disheveled Egyptian pound and waves it in my face.

Here it is. The moment I have been expecting for the last hour. Dreading. One thing I have learned from my few years on the road is that nothing is for nothing. It's exactly proportionate: the more foreign the country, the more I am regarded as a one-man walking business opportunity. The postcard that costs 5¢ to a local, costs $1 to me. The "set price" for the taxi ride from the airport magically inflates out of control as soon as I hit an open stretch of road. I'm perpetually on guard, seeing the rip-offs as obstacles to be avoided by the savvy traveler. The few times I get badly caught, I rationalize the loss. What does a dollar mean to me, after all, compared with its power in local currency. My simple camera is worth a year's worth of meals to a starving family. I have spent more on having a tooth capped than many Third World-ers will ever mass over a lifetime of grueling labor. And yet I feel a mounting indignation swelling inside, from a sense of my own gullibility, from allowing myself to be fooled like a common tourist.

But today I have committed the cardinal blunder. My caution overpowered by two days of aching hunger, I have accepted food and hospitality from a total stranger. Worse, he is a nomad, a desert dweller, dealing from a completely different deck of customs and values. For him "taking" is the same as "earning." And I followed him home, ate everything that was offered, and never agreed on a price in advance. Stupid! Stupid! Stupid! Now he is going to levy an enormous price—somewhere between my money and my life—on a few pieces of dehydrated bread, rubbery meat, and a tomato sucked dry by the sun. And the spirit in the sheep-bladder bottle would strip paint. Considering my choices, I look around the room.

We are sitting in what had been, just four months before, the living room of a modern, luxury condo. The place has been stripped to the bare walls leaving only a few hints of its former style. Chrome light fixtures in the shape of medieval torcheres hang upside down from wires as though someone had ripped them down in a hurry and given up half-way through. There is no electricity anyway. The broken-in door swings awkwardly on its hinges. The window panes are all broken and, caught by the late afternoon breeze off the sea, floral curtains wave out like flags. Dust covers everything in a softening film. In the middle of the green wall-to-wall shag carpet burns an open campfire made of broken drawers and paneling. Around its edge, the nylon weave is curling, sending up a black-smoke stench.

Around its edge lounge five other Bedouin men, all dressed in the same robes as my host, with traditional *okal* headdresses and the *khangars* at their belts. Clearly these half-swords are not just for show. Throughout the meal these men have looked over at me with dirty, gold-toothed smiles, obviously enjoying the game of ripping off the white-skinned foreigner. It occurs to me this is a familiar situation and I am probably not the first Westerner to be sharing this room and their food. If I run for the door, surely one of them will be there to block my exit. If not, I have no doubt, they will catch up with me in the streets below. The smiles will then be gone and who knows what will follow.

Seeing no alternative, I loosen the tails of my shirt, uncover and unzip my money belt. All my valuables are now on show. My watch, passport, the few traveler's checks I have, and the thick soiled wad of local currency. Glancing quickly at my host, I see his eyes widen. With my heart in my mouth I try to offset the inevitable. I say the one Egyptian word I know, "*bekam?*" (how much?).

The Sinai Peninsula is the huge triangle of desert dividing the two outstretched arms of the Red Sea. Above it teeters Israel; to the left, the great sprawl of Egypt. Its harsh, unforgiving lunar landscape is burnt as hard as a pot in a kiln. From a rugged mountainous interior, a boulder and scrub strewn terrain spills down to an unremarkable coast. One hue—beige. Until you dip one inch below the surface of the sea. As if all the color had drained into the water, there lies a marine world of unimaginable beauty.

In 1982 the Sinai was on the front page of every newspaper. After two years of "preparation," Israel had honored the terms of Begin and Sadat's Camp David accord and handed back the region to Egypt. Along with the desert, Egypt inherited all the buildings and infrastructure that had sprung up over the previous decade when the coasts along the Gulfs of Aqaba and Suez had blossomed as the Riviera of the Middle East.

Naturally there was chaos. When the Israelis left they took everything with them. Everything that could be moved, unscrewed, dismantled or otherwise heaved on to flat-bed trucks and driven north. The pans and cookers from the hotel kitchens, the sinks and door knobs from the luxury apartments, the tiles from the walls, the contents of the luxury beach-front boutiques. And, of course they took all the food.

If I knew this at the time, I paid little attention. As a university student, my needs were simple and my tolerance for discomfort, high. Besides, my interest was far more Old Testament than media front page. For me the Sinai was the romantic bridge between Africa and Asia. It was birthplace of the alphabet, the stage-set of *Exodus*, where the seas had miraculously parted for the escaping Israelites, where God had spoken from the flames of a burning bush, where Moses had found and dropped the Ten Commandments, that summary of divine law. On another, more immediate level, the Sinai was also the site of the best scuba diving in the world. Compared with this, what could possibly be so bad?

Well, there *was* the temperature. In retrospect, August was probably not the best time to be carrying a 50-pound backpack through a desert described even by the guidebooks as "intensely hot." And there *was* the lack of any predictable transport. As I left the air-conditioned bars of Eilat, Israel, at my back and made my way on foot along the dusty road to the Egyptian border, the heat bore down on my head like a broiler, flooding the world with white heat, melting the horizon in a watery wash of quivering snakes.

At the border there were no crowds of flag-waving well-wishers, no congratulations, nothing of significance to mark my historic crossing but a few strands of barbed wire half-heartedly stretched across the road and curling off into the scrubby desert on either side. At the end of the hundred yards of no-man's land I came to the Egyptian line. To the left a soldier in a ragged uniform was sleeping off his lunch in the shade of the only tree. To the right, the border post—a banged-up shed like a Porta-Cabin.

Inside, another soldier barked a single word, "*felous*," then remembering a few words of English, he repeated, "money, money." An official-looking sheet was thrust in my hands explaining in a collection of languages that everyone who passed across the border had to change an amount of dollars proportionate to the length of stay. No exceptions. Four days? Two hundred dollars—an incredible amount which to me translated into at least 20 days of travel under normal circumstances. I handed over all the currency I had—around 40 dollars—with a shrug. After a few minutes of furious tapping on a decrepit addition machine, the soldier handed back to me an inch thick wad of notes, so soiled I could hardly make out their denominations. Doubtless, there had been a small commission for the officer's time.

I soon found out that in the Sinai it didn't matter how much money you had because there was nowhere to spend it. When the bus finally arrived a few hours later, the fare to Nuwaybi cost the smallest note in my wad. For the next few hours I sat, crammed in with a sweating mass of humanity and sundry livestock, as the bus creaked and groaned through a flat, unchanging landscape. The image of a cold beer and a good meal swam through my half-waking mind like a mantra.

But when I finally arrived in Nuwaybi, the once glamorous resort on the Gulf of Aqaba, I found that it was shut. Closed. Not open. The neat grid of streets was lined with boarded-up stores, weeds were growing rampant through the sidewalk. Eventually I managed to pick up some *falafel* (deep-fried chick pea balls) and some bread, as dehydrated as the desert itself. That night I slept on the beach, underneath the boardwalk, burrowing deep inside my oppressively-hot down sleeping bag to escape the clouds of mosquitoes.

As the days followed a similar course, I began to associate more and more with the plight of the Israelites. It may not have been 40 years of privation and hunger but, as I made my

way south, it certainly felt like it. The towns of Dhahab and
Nabq were empty shells, all the more melancholy for what
they had been so recently. At least the Israelites had manna
from heaven, whereas I was reduced to eating whatever I
could find. A jar of jam for lunch, crackers for dinner, and one
day—oh the luxury—some canned sardines. There wasn't
even any diving to be had. The few dive shops that deserved
the name were cobwebbed and dark, waiting for their equipment to arrive.

But it didn't matter because I had set my sights on the
southernmost town of Sharm ash-Shaykh. Things would be
different there, I was told. According to the guidebook, it was
an oasis of civilization, studded with bars and restaurants.
Furthermore it was the jumping-off point for the greatest dive
site in the world. Under the surface at Ra's Muhammad, the
very peak of the Sinai, the fish—hammerheads, black-tips, rays
as big as bed quilts—were so plentiful, they blocked out the
sun as the schools swam overhead.

Like any other mirage, the oasis of Sharm faded before my
eyes, its promise evaporating into the dry sand as soon as I
climbed from the bus one late afternoon. Like the towns that
had gone before, an eerie vacancy haunted its main streets and
beach-front, as if it was a film-set waiting for the extras to arrive. Gone were the tanned couples promenading, the tables
spilling out of cafés onto the street, the bikini-ed beauties, the
cool palm-decked lobbies of the big hotels. Gone were the
expensive boats, the bars heaving with the après-sun crowd.
The only movement came from a few enduring old Mercedes
kicking up clouds of dust and the occasional Bedouin leading
camels on a tether. In the hollowed-out cavern of a store, I
found a bearded German who told me, in broken English, he
had come to start a scuba business but was now going back to
Berlin to wait until the situation here improved. "Here there

is no customers," he explained dejectedly. "If they come, they can stay nowhere, and eat nothing."

No food. I was so hungry by this stage, I was even ready to break my vow and choke down another *falafel* ball. So I started combing the back streets looking for a restaurant. The locals had to eat somewhere, didn't they? I approached a few people, but they only shook their heads or pointed off in a vague direction. It was then that I saw my Bedouin and asked him in polyglot—raising my hand to my mouth and shrugging my shoulders—if he knew of any food.

To my surprise he beckoned to me to follow. Staying thirty yards ahead of me with his long strides and flowing robes, he set off through a white maze of alleys. After each corner I became more disoriented, more and more concerned I was being led into some sort of trap. What was stopping this desert savage pulling me into a doorway and sliding his knife across my white throat? In my backpack there were surely items of clothing that would be of use or amusement. At each turn my guide turned and beckoned me on again as if anxious I would lose interest and turn around.

After fifteen minutes I was so lost, I had to keep going. Then suddenly he stopped and, without a smile, imitated my gesture of eating and pointed up some exterior stairs to an upstairs apartment in a block of luxury condos. I hesitated. He repeated the gesture and urged me on. On the second landing he pushed open a door that hung loose on its hinges; clearly it had been jimmied open. Walking into the room I smelt first the stench of singeing carpet, then, as my eyes grew accustomed to the smoke and darkness, I saw the group crouched around the fire. They looked up at us. Our friend explained and smiles broke out. Obviously they liked his plan.

For the next hour I sat aside from the main group, leaning against one of the walls. There was no attempt at conversation.

Nobody spoke. In silence—as slowly and deliberately as if they always cooked their food on a fire in the middle of a carpet—the Bedouin pieced hunks of fresh meat on the end of their knives, roasted them over the embers, then slid them off onto clean slabs of paneling that one of them ripped off the wall. After adding fresh salad and bread, my host passed a mounded plate over to me. I was too hungry to wonder where the fresh food came from, what the meat was, or what my new friends were expecting in return. Only when the meal was over and the food had cleared my head, did I realize the bad situation I was in.

"*Bekam?*" I say again, fully expecting my host to dispense with formalities, reach in and empty my money belt.

After a long minute he repeats the word at the others as if it's the biggest joke he has heard in ages. He says it again, pointing at me. The Bedouin around the fire sit up to enjoy the scene. Gold-teeth glint in wide grins.

Nervously I take out one of the bigger bills and hold it out. But it's not enough. My host shakes his head. I take out more bills. Still he shakes his head. It happens a third time. Just when I'm about to hand over the entire wad, he leaps up and goes over to the air-conditioning unit below one of the windows. He struggles with it, twisting it from side to side, until it comes clear of the wall. Rummaging in the exposed insulation, he pulls out a simple black metal box and brings it over to me, placing it as gently as an egg in my hands. He signals me to open it, which I do, fearfully, bracing for a trick. It's full of money. I pick some up and look up inquiringly at the man's face. Seeing my confusion, he leans over and closes my fist around the pound notes I have drawn from the box. I look around at the others. They are smiling encouragement.

Suddenly I understand what's going on. The realization hits me like a slap. The blood rushes to my face as the great temple of my Westernized preconceptions and prejudices collapses in a heap around me. To them I am not a condescending rich kid on vacation or a gullible traveler ripe for exploitation. They simply see another nomad who is in need. They see a beggar. They are not trying to take my money. They are trying to give me theirs.

To maintain his life-long travel habit, Andrew Bill has answered a variety of callings, including river guide, road sweeper, painter, waiter, farm hand, and construction laborer. As a journalist and editor he has scoured the globe for many of the world's most prominent magazines and guidebooks. Today he runs a custom publishing company based in New York. This story was excerpted from The Intentional Traveler, *a work-in-progress edited by Thomas C. Wilmer.*

PART TWO

Going
to the Edge

CHIMNEY ROCK

Climbing in the Cascades, the author falls—
and begins a journey he will
never forget.

IT WAS A BAD MOMENT BUT I HAD TO REALIZE IT COULD BE worse—I could have been way above Doug and have faced taking a long leader fall. As it was I expected a short fall before the rope, passing through the sling above, stopped my fall when Doug locked the rope in his belay device.

When I peeled, the attitude of my body was sideways—my head way out to my right where I had reached for the hold, my left hand coming off the one hold above, my feet sticking to the left. The face here was quite steep, and I just launched off, pretty clean, straight down. Below, the face steepened to overhanging, so I did not bounce or tumble. But the rope kept running through the 'biner above me as I sailed through space with only minor, scraping contact with the rock. I prepared for the jerk that would come when the rope caught me. But it didn't come, and I wondered why it was taking so long.

Then I smashed against the rock face. The blow knocked the breath out of me and completely turned me around. I heard bones break. The violence of the impact was unbelievable, the pain spectacular. Another impact followed in rapid succession, worse than the first. I felt more bones break in my shoulder, heard them crunch and felt my body give. It was nightmarish. So this is what it's like, I thought. After the second collision, I started tumbling down the steep face. My sensations were of cannon-loud explosions as my helmet crashed against the rock, and sledgehammer body blows as impact after impact jarred and tossed my body. I saw nothing after those last desperate moments looking for holds. I ultimately lost my sense of orientation as I hurtled downward, smashing against the south face as I fell.

I knew I was dying, and felt intense sorrow about that. My life did not flash before me, but I thought of Anne, the dark-eyed beauty who shared my life. I felt sorry that I would spend no more time with her and the eccentric fox terrier that made up our family. I felt anger that my good life would end this terrible way, being pummeled and broken by the fall down the mountain.

The fall seemed to take a long time. A big surge of fear swept through me, blocking thought, but as the fall progressed the shock of dread replaced fear. I hated getting beat up like that, dying like that. The thing was, it wouldn't stop, and I knew no one could take that kind of abuse and live. The impacts continued, they racked and tossed my body, but strangely did not impair my lucidity or stop my stream of consciousness. I kept thinking about Anne, kept coming back to her, and how I wished this thing was not really happening to me. Could this be a dream, a hallucination? No, but it took time for me to admit that I was in the process of being killed by falling off a mountain. Just another dead climber, I thought, nobody's fault but mine. A paragraph in the *Seattle Times*, I read them all the time.

I registered the pain and altered attitude of my body after

each collision. Some were worse than others, I could tell, some breaking bones, some not. I began to feel somewhat separate from my body, but I was absolutely aware: it was as if my body were being killed while I watched and listened.

There was a shape to it, starting with the slip and free fall, and then the endless, terrifying rag-doll impacts accompanied by explosive blows to my helmet. Those were, by far, the worst, then there were more painless freefall—pure air time—and then *wham!* Suddenly my fall was arrested. I had arrived at a tiny ledge just as the rope jerked me up short.

A shattering, unnerving quiet replaced the cacophonous noise of my helmet banging against the rock face. It happened fast. One nanosecond I was falling and dying, the next I was suddenly looking out over the valley, suspended from the climbing rope like a puppet, feet barely touching the small ledge on the sheer rock face. I could hardly believe it. I felt overwhelmed, not ready to believe what had happened. Waves of pain rolled over me. I got a funny, shocking feeling. My field of vision began to shrink noticeably and rapidly. The world appeared unnaturally blurry and bright, but it was getting smaller. I felt ineffably strange, as if I were hardly there at all. Then, I noticed a change: the pain became extraneous, and my attention shifted to my diminishing consciousness and shrinking field of vision. I felt neutral, separate, and thought perhaps this might be death. I was not surprised. I hung there in a peaceful, sunlit silence. There was no hurry.

I don't remember how long I was in that state of suspended reality. I may have passed out. At some point, however, the scope of my world began to expand, slowly, definitely. A familiar feeling—that accustomed, essential sense of self—slowly reemerged. Squinting into the brightness, I realized that my prescription sunglasses had come off in the fall. But I was not dead. As if to reinforce that fact, the pain returned with a vengeance, shutting out thoughts of other matters. The pain was exacerbated by my awkward bouncing around at the end of the climbing rope.

I knew I must be badly hurt, but had no idea what the inventory of injuries might be. My left arm hung at a bizarre angle. My left leg was twisted outward and throbbing. My pelvis radiated a deep pain where it met my left hip. Each dangling movement registered in multiple points of pain on a scale I had never experienced. I was sufficiently loony that I was unable to truly grasp what had happened, barely able to take in the fact I was not dead. I kept thinking, Man, I am actually here on this little ledge, still breathing. Unbelievable.

Everything about my body was racked with pain and seemed oddly displaced or rearranged. I felt woozy and weird. Right then, more than anything else, I wanted to take a load off, to sit down on that little ledge. But there was too much tension on the taut rope, which ran like a steel cable from my harness up and out of sight beyond an overhang back to Doug. My line of sight above was restricted to about 50 feet of steep rock face, the blue rope running upward plumb-line straight. I could not unclip. I hung there exactly like a doll on a string.

I tried to move my left arm to take weight off the rope so that with my right hand I could unclip the big harness carabiner from the knot in the rope. With that attempt, an explosion of pain ripped along my left arm. The limb literally flapped in the breeze. I reeled and moaned and I feared I would pass out. So this is what they mean by writhing in pain, I thought. I hung there limp, helpless, my full weight on the harness. Turning slowly at the end of the rope, first one way, then another, I stupidly looked out over the valley and felt a more lucid consciousness gradually return. My situation became clear: busted up and possibly dying after a bad mountaineering fall.

"Slack! Slack!" I cried in a plaintive voice, the loudest I could muster but not one I recognized as my own. "Slack, Doug! I'm hurt bad!" If Doug had me on belay, he could pay out a little rope through the belay device and lower me to the ledge. But no slack came. For a long time in the still of that summer morning, there was no reply. There was no noise at all. I hung there awkwardly. Then Doug's voice, small and disembodied, carried down to me.

"OK, but it might be kind of sudden."

I took that in and realized that I must be at the end of the rope—literally. Somehow the belay must have gone wrong. I must have fallen the full length of the rope, 150 feet. Only the anchors into which the other end of the rope was tied prevented my from plummeting entirely off the mountain, and pulling Doug off with me. Doug had no more rope at his end or he could have simply lowered me to the ledge. With my weight on the rope there was nothing he could do except cut it or untie from the anchors, or maybe rig some kind of prussik arrangement. The prospect of Doug's unfastening the anchors and letting me drop suddenly—even a few feet—really got my attention. Such a move could send me careening beyond the ledge and off the mountain, or at least injure me more by dumping me in a heap on the ledge.

"No, no," I shouted back. "Don't do that!"

I was standing awkwardly on my tiptoes, trying to control the twisting and swaying. I was afraid I might pass out. I started to panic. Frantically, I dug for my pocketknife, thinking I might cut the rope above my harness. But I could not get my right hand into my left pocket. My shorts were pulled up and askew by the harness, which was loaded up with my weight. I was sweating profusely and feeling, by turns, faint and overcome by pain. A panicky thought took me over: if I don't do something real soon I'm going to die right here on the end of this rope.

I looked around. The ledge sloped slightly downward, and so was higher where it joined the mountain than it was at the outer edge. If I were able to back up enough I might gain five or six inches of elevation, enough to unload the rope and get sufficient slack to unclip. But as I began to maneuver on my toes, my weight came on my left leg. That same outrageous pain—I was beginning to know it now—blasted out of my hip and knee. I collapsed once again onto the rope, limp, wasted. I hung on the rope and closed my eyes. I tried to chase the panic, which constantly nipped at the edge of my consciousness and threatened to screw up my thinking.

I either had to do something myself or yell for Doug to chop the anchors and just take my chances. Hanging on the taut rope I mustered my concentration. Keeping some of my weight on the rope I began to perform a sort of one-legged soft shoe on the ledge, moving backwards on my apparently undamaged right leg and foot. Doing so gained me a few inches in distance and altitude and took measurable pressure off my harness. I was learning how to use my damaged body. With two or three more spurts of grisly dancing I achieved enough purchase on the ledge to heel-toe up the sloping rocky shelf a foot or more, as far as the ledge allowed and just enough to put a little slack in the rope. With my good right hand, I reached around my body, opened the big Stubai locking carabiner on my harness, and pulled out the figure-eight knot at the end of the rope. Free at last from the rope, I crumpled slightly, but managed to keep my balance and hold myself upright on my right leg.

Unroped now, I felt a new surge of fear—that I might fall again. I was balanced on my one good foot on the downsloping rocky ramp of the small ledge, without any sort of safety line. A fall here would send me over the lunch-tray-sized ledge down to the glacier hundreds of feet below. To make matters worse, my pack had slipped off my shoulders but was still attached at the waist belt. It flopped around dangerously, my ice axe with its three sharp ends still affixed to it. The ledge was small. The pack might push me off. But it contained essential items. I couldn't just kick it off the mountain.

Slowly, I reached across with my right hand and unfastened the waist belt. The pack fell down behind my legs. I kept it there, behind my body, so it wouldn't tumble off. Thus encumbered, with my useless left leg flopping in front of me, I began to lower myself with infinite care to a sitting position on the ledge. The maneuver was horrendously painful, but the ledge was big enough to accommodate me, back against the rock face, heels hooked on an outstanding little lip that happened to lie exactly at the edge. I had been moaning softly, making little sounds with my exhalations (they came naturally and seemed to help) since my arrival on the ledge, but bending my left knee into the extreme sitting position required by the ledge made me cry out loud for the first time. Panting, I slid my pack from behind me to my left side, one shoulder strap hooked over my left calf to keep it from falling off. There barely was enough room for me, much less my pack. I squirmed around on the uneven ledge. I thought: this will do.

But the perch was, in its own way, a screaming terror, a tiny ledge hanging in space from the sheer expanse of rock. The exposure was spectacular. The big south face of Chimney's South Peak rose vertically above and behind me, and plummeted down 600 or 700 feet below me to the Chimney Glacier, easing in angle as it neared the ice. Unlike the perfectly smooth granite walls of Yosemite, this rock face was broken, faceted like a huge gemstone, in some places overhanging, in others, slightly off vertical. To my right the wall overhung dramatically, to my left a narrow, shallow chute ran from about five feet above to end just at the left side of the ledge. This small depression, perhaps two feet wide and a foot or two deep at the top, was substantial enough to channel water but almost as steep as the rest of the face. I could see the line of footprints Doug and I had made on our climb up this morning. It seemed as if that pleasant morning climb had happened on another planet.

Sitting there on the ledge was a big improvement over dangling on the rope, a much less desperate situation. I was amazed that I was still inside my body looking out at the scene of forest, lakes, and mountains. My shattered arm fascinated me. It seemed to belong to someone else. My breathing was rapid and shallow. I wondered if I were mortally wounded in some way that I had not yet noticed.

I wondered what had gone wrong, why had I taken such a long fall. But, I thought, it really doesn't matter now. I've got to focus. I fought against the adrenaline and fear and disorientation, and tried to concentrate. I looked again at my left arm hanging in the dirt smashed and crooked, my left leg swollen to an alarming size, especially at the knee and hip. I heard bones grinding when I shifted position. But my feet moved, and inside my boots, I wiggled my toes vigorously: my spine must have survived intact. I arched my back, reassured about that. I sat back, feeling better about my chances. If I didn't move or pass out, I thought that I might be able to stay put on the ledge.

That's when I noticed big black blotches all over the rock around me, on my pack and my clothes. Blood was everywhere. My blood. Big swashes, little pools, innocent-looking stains.

I stared at this blood dumbly, then with rising alarm. Where was it coming from? I looked over my body from my sitting position, and saw that the left leg of my shorts was soaked in blood. Feeling around my body, I found it pouring from my left arm. I gingerly examined the smashed limb. Splintered bones protruded from my elbow. Oh God, I thought, I'm going to bleed to death.

"Doug! I'm hurt bad! I'm bleeding bad! Can you get down to me?"

For a long time there was no reply. It occurred to me it had been a while since the fall had happened. Or had it? What time was it? What was going on at Doug's end? Then, his voice reached me, sounding very far away.

"No! No way!" I thought for a few seconds. "Doug! Go for help. I'm hurt bad, I'm bleeding bad. I might not make it. Go fast, Doug."

I was at the very edge of panic. This blood was bad business. My desire to live was overpowering, while my chances of doing so were diminishing. I sat on my south-facing ledge in the hot sun, and a clammy sweat coated me. I had to do something about the bleeding.

My bloody pack was precariously perched, poorly stashed into the little chute beside me, held in place by my immovable left leg. I thought about the first-aid kit I always carried with its manual of emergency medicine. But what I saw with alarm was that the side pocket of the pack, which held my water bottle was pointed downhill, threatening to dump the bottle down the mountain. I needed water to live. Gingerly, careful to keep from falling, I reached across my body and with my good right hand turned the pack around. The water bottle was secure.

"Wait!" I cried back to Doug. "Can you lower some water? Are you still there?"

Obviously he was, for his rope still hung beside me, the figure-eight knot from which I had unclipped dangling in space above my head. He called out to wait a second and I watched the end of the rope rise up and out of sight. Minutes later I heard Doug shout, "Here it comes."

Into view came a water bottle and a blue fleece jacket clipped to the end of the rope with a 'biner. So steep was the face the bottle hung in midair, several feet away from the rock. By rocking the rope back and forth like a pendulum, Doug was able to swing the bottle and jacket to within grasp, and I stashed them in my pack. He would be able to get more water on the way down—assuming he could manage the technical part of the descent alone. It wouldn't be easy.

"I'll send up the other rope," I shouted back, thinking that with both ropes he might be able to make long rappels and thereby get past the most difficult parts of his upcoming solitary descent. I pulled my red rope from my pack, clipped it to the 'biner and watched as he pulled it out of sight.

"Go fast, Doug," I urged. It felt strange to bid him goodbye. We had never before split up on a climb. Shortly thereafter my calls went unanswered. He was gone.

Alone and bleeding, I looked around. The ledge was unnervingly small. Save for the rock face I leaned against there was nothing but airy space in all directions. I sat vertiginously exposed in full sunlight at more than 7,000 feet on the south face of the mountain. The rock and air were heating up fast. My physical efforts of the past few minutes—stashing gear in the pack, shouting to Doug, squirming around on the sharp stones of the ledge—had left me light-headed and enervated. I gritted my teeth and concentrated on not passing out.

I was shattered by the fall and terrified of falling again. The pain from my leg, pelvis, and arm began to coalesce into a kind of bombardment, which may have helped me stay conscious but also kept me from thinking straight. I was determined to seize control. Blood was everywhere, still pouring from my left elbow and pooling around the little green succulents that grew in a shallow layer of dirt on my ledge. It looked like arterial bleeding to me. I stared incredulously at the smashed bone sticking out from the skin.

I didn't know what to do about the bleeding. But in my first-aid kit—a comfort kit really, with Band-Aids and aspirin and moleskin and antacids and tweezers—was a little booklet bound in survival orange I had been carrying around for a decade. I dug around in my pack, unzipped the little case, and pulled it out: *The Hip Pocket Emergency Handbook.* Sitting there on the ledge with my knees bent, I opened the book on my lap and began to read beneath the hot summer sun.

The table of contents was right on the cover. In the chapter entitled "Bleeding," I immediately found what I was looking for: the top priority for injured people who are still breathing is to stop bleeding. The little book put it this way: "Work fast, be careful. Concentrate only on keeping blood in the body!"

Nothing ambiguous there, and it even gave two suggestions on how this might be accomplished: pressure points and compression. The appropriate pressure point for my elbow was clearly illustrated as being in my armpit. I reached around with my right hand and groped for my left armpit. But my shoulder had been so smashed and dislocated I actually could not recognize its architecture to find my armpit. Oh no, I thought. Just how bad off am I? The possibility that some as-yet-undiscovered injury might prove fatal still haunted me. But I managed to shrug it off, say to hell with that, do something else. Just keep yourself from bleeding to death.

The next suggestion was compression, so from my pack I pulled out a thin, foot-square, Ensolite-foam sit pad. This item, a prized possession that comes along on every climbing trip, affords a portable, comfortable place to sit on snow, rock, or wet grass. I folded it in half like a piece of stationery and slowly, ever so gradually, began to wrap my left arm from midtriceps to wrist. I simply took my time and moved carefully. I could hear and feel the bones grinding together and could feel them emerging from skin around my elbow. But the pain was not greatly worse than before. My arm was most compliant, as if it had joints every few inches. I removed the rubber Japanese watch from wrist and let it fall onto the ledge. Soon I had a sort of rude splint fashioned, which wrapped my arm like a hot dog in a bun. A stream of blood flowed out the back.

From the top of my pack, I pulled out the two nylon straps that held my crampons in place. With my one good arm, my teeth, and a lot of contorted wriggling, I managed to wrap both straps around my arm just fore and aft of the elbow. Because the booklet cautioned that a tourniquet could mean loss of the limb, I adjusted the tension just tightly enough to put some pressure against the open wound without cutting off the circulation. It looked to me a decent job: my smashed arm was well protected by the foam pad, and to some extent stabilized. The flow of blood even seemed to slow. The first-aid book also said to never take away compression bandages, just add more—"cloth of any kind." Rummaging around in my pack I found a pair of gloves, which I stuffed inside the makeshift splint. In, too, went some sling material that had been in my first-aid kit for years, finally put to good use, and a spare sock.

I let my head fall back against the rock, and realized my helmet had come off in the fall. It must have been toward the end, for I distinctly remembered my head bouncing off the face. The helmet had saved my life. Looking out over the landscape, focusing into the distance, I could make out hardly any detail. Was my vision damaged as well? Then I remembered my sunglasses had gone their separate way in the fall. What about my regular pair? Deep in the top pocket of my pack, in the black crush-proof case, were my wire-rim glasses. Intact. Slipping them on was a genuine comfort. And what there was to see! My view was outrageous, and under normal circumstances the exposure would have been exhilarating. But instead I felt completely removed from normal sorts of responses. The sun was punishing. I couldn't believe what had happened to me. I was marooned, broken, exposed to the elements. I was scared.

I dug out my water bottle with my good hand and carefully cradled it against my makeshift splint while I unscrewed the lid. Raising it to my lips I took a small sip, then another, then a big, long drink, then another. Drinking the water was restorative, calming, but I knew I'd have to ration carefully in this heat. Screwing back on the lid, I regarded the bottle's half-full state and carefully put it in my pack.

My situation seemed unreal. The ledge was cramped, uncomfortable, and paved with sharp, little points, but it was a resting place. I pondered my luck at having landed on the only ledge in sight. Nobody lasts long at the end of a rope. My soft landing—arriving on the ledge exactly as the rope went taut—smacked of divine interference. A full-speed landing surely would have killed me.

I had no room to move, in fact could hardly shift my weight, but I had water and food and clothing. On the other hand, my injuries were probably serious, the bleeding might get worse. Doug might not make it off the mountain. Was I bleeding inside? Was I in shock? Can a person die of shock? Not much I could do about any of that. But I felt that if I kept myself screwed down pretty tight, I could hang on for—what? A day. A day for sure, maybe more.

How long would I have to hold on? I tried to think soundly. If Doug made it off the mountain, help surely would come within two days. If he didn't, no one would miss us for days, and it would take more days for a search effort to be organized. Too long. I had to believe in Doug's ability to get down safely and move fast. I fixed on that. I felt my resolve coming together. I was going to live if I could. I was going to try not to do anything stupid. I put a name to what I was doing: waiting to be rescued. I said it out loud.

Doug and I had discussed our progress shortly before the accident, so I knew the fall happened at about 9:30 a.m. Tuesday, July 26, 1988. It pleased me to be doing something normal, such as checking the time. But it was going to be many hours, even days, before my situation improved, and I had no stomach for the kind of clock watching I was prone to do. I let the watch fall back into the dirt and reached again for the water bottle.

With the midday summer sun cooking my south-facing ledge, the hot rock around me, like a reflector oven, magnified its efforts. At more than 7,000 feet the sun baked my brains at solstice strength. But there was nowhere to go. I retrieved my yellow baseball hat, ripped and dirty, from the outside of my pack, and put it on. It helped immensely. My dress for the climb turned out to be most appropriate: the thin polypropylene material of my long underwear bottoms and long-sleeved top saved me from getting badly burnt. But I felt myself wilt under the combination of injury and exposure. I felt weak.

I took another drink. From that swallow, and all the others, I extracted maximum benefit: I held the water in my mouth, letting it soothe my parched throat, rolled it around, savored it. Only then did I swallow. I screwed the lid back on: down to the third of a bottle. If only I had more water. Maddeningly, far below me near the entrance to the steep couloir Doug and I had climbed to reach the U Gap, a stream of glacier melt water picked up volume in the hot sun. I remembered climbing past the stream in the morning, thinking it would be a perfect place to tank up the water bottles after a long, hot morning on the rock. Now its trickle and splash, utterly out of reach, tormented me.

In those midday hours, the torment of heat and thirst incited me to plot insane schemes to escape my predicament. Maybe, I thought, there's a way I could get down. On the glacier I would be able to recline, wait for help more comfortably, drink water till I burst. Hell, I thought, I'll just rappel down—with one good arm and one good leg, I might make it. Then I remembered I had given Doug my rope. Then I remembered even if I had the rope it was almost a thousand feet of rock face down to the glacier below. Then I remembered the intense pain from merely shifting around to look over the edge. I remembered I'd fall off if I so much as tried to stand, that I was apt to pass out from pain or shock or loss of blood at any exertion. I kept remembering. I was stuck.

The tumbling fall had put holes in my polypropylene, and I stared in disbelief as the skin under the bigger holes burned so badly that quarter-sized water blisters began to form. Jesus, I thought, that's bad. My whole body was overheating under the dark blue material, exacerbating the wooziness I already felt. I began to fear the sun might kill me. I consciously kept my head turned so that my face was in the shade of my hat bill. But it wasn't enough. I had to find some shelter.

My pack was by now securely stowed by my left side; it wasn't exactly within easy reach because only my right arm worked, but its mere presence was a comfort to me. Its contents already had saved me. The precious water bottles were in the side pockets, my first-aid kit with its medical manual in a top pocket, and a light fleece jacket, windbreaker, and wool hat in the main compartment. My lunch—the remnants of salami, some Fig Newtons, a small piece of cheese, and some cracker crumbs—was in the lower compartment. Strapped to the outside was my red SMC ice ax, apparently no worse for wear after the fast ride down the mountain.

I thought about the ax, and gingerly began the tedious task of undoing its strap with my good hand. It took a long time. Finally freeing the ax, I placed it across my lap and pulled out my ugly orange Early Winters fleece jacket. These simple efforts so taxed me that I allowed myself a medium-sized slug from the water bottle and a long rest before moving again. Then, holding the head of my ax, I began to probe above me with the sharp end of the shaft. I couldn't see properly, but I did make out a small cleft in the rock right above my head. Into that crack I tried to stick the shaft of the ice ax, but it wouldn't stay put; the crack was too wide and shallow. I tried again and again in different parts of the cleft, without success. Finally, I lucked into finding a place where there was enough purchase on the shaft in the shallow crack to wedge immediately above my head. Perfect. I rested for a while. Then I reached sloppily, but created a small awning under which I could get my head and shoulders. I had shade.

It remained unpleasantly hot inside my makeshift parasol, but to be out of the direct rays of the sun was a tremendous relief. To celebrate my improved surroundings, I pulled out the water bottle for a victory slug and was alarmed to see it nearly empty. I rationalized before the onslaught of growing thirst: this heat might weaken me to the point of fainting and send me tumbling off. Better to drink it now and be parched during the cool of the night. But not wanting for some superstitious reason to empty the one bottle, I pulled out the nice, heavy, full bottle Doug had lowered. In the shade of my ridiculous shelter, I carefully unscrewed the bottle and drank deeply. Hallelujah! Lemonade! Doug often added fruit-juice mixes to his water, and thanks to him, I was sitting in the shade drinking lemonade. It tasted great. I think I might have exacerbated my thirst in the long run, but I revelled in the pleasure of those first sips, my head stuck up under my jacket with nothing to see but the labels and the stains, thinking I might just make it.

Peter Potterfield was editor-in-chief of Pacific Northwest *magazine in Seattle for more than a decade, and his work has appeared in numerous publications including* Outside, Reader's Digest, Backpacker, Condé Nast Traveler, *and* Travel & Leisure. *He wrote the climbing sections for Fodor's adventure guide and is the co-author of the best-selling* Selected Climbs in the Cascades. *This story was excerpted from his book* In the Zone: Epic Survival Stories from the Mountaineering World, *where you can also read the acount of his rescue from Chimney Rock.*

CAPITAL OF CHAOS

A country descends into madness.

WEAVING AT HIGH SPEED THROUGH THE SMOLDERING wreckage of Monrovia, our driver, on my left, and the glassy-eyed young Liberian on my right passed a fifth of gin back and forth. Every few blocks our white van screeched to a halt at makeshift barricades of burned-out cars or rusty barrels. War-crazed kids with AK-47s peered menacingly at the six Western journalists inside before letting us pass. The fighting that had shattered this West African nation's thirteenth peace accord two weeks earlier was still raging, and we were carefully skirting the growing column of gun smoke rising from its epicenter at a military barracks. This was our first glimpse of the ravaged city, and our means of seeing it was either bold and resourceful, or incredibly stupid. We weren't yet sure which.

After two days of phone calls, the country's most powerful militia leader, Charles Taylor, had agreed to meet the press, and sent a vanload of young groupies to pick us up at the U.S. Embassy. The American compound was a tense sanctuary.

Two hundred marines stood guard at roofs, doorways and windows, their guns aimed outward. Some of the consular staff wore bulletproof vests when walking from building to building. Before stepping through the embassy's metal door and around a newly added coil of barbed wire, we knew we were in trouble when we had to sign a statement releasing the embassy from any liability for us.

Our drive took a circuitous route through the friendly territory of our guides' faction—the National Patriotic Front of Liberia. Some streets were a post-apocalyptic party scene. Amid the debris and stripped storefronts, hyped-up teenagers celebrated in a drunken euphoria. Looted booze was abundant. Vehicles with doors ripped off and painted with names such as "Colonel Death" provided a Somalia-style display of bravado. Other streets were eerily desolate except for the bodies left where they had fallen.

For our chaperones, the trip was something of a victory drive. Confident of winning, they were eager to show their gains. At one point we drove through the central market area, a once-bustling tangle of buyers and sellers that spilled from sidewalk to street. Now only the merchant's wooden stalls remained. "See, they're still standing," the teen on my right said, as if it were proof of some smart-bomb-like-strategy.

The most frustrating part of covering, and presumably living through, Liberia's civil war was its utter lack of strategy, ideology or purpose. Editors back home asked irritating questions like: What is the war all about? What does each side want? The answers have been lost in an anarchic scramble for power and loot.

The oldest independent republic in Africa, Liberia was founded in 1822 by American slaves, who named their capital after President James Monroe and adopted a variation of the Stars and Stripes as their flag. It was a relatively tranquil

backwater, known less for politics than for its rubber and foreign ship registry, until 1980, when Samuel Doe, an obscure
master sergeant, staged a bloody coup that toppled the
Americo-Liberians who had dominated power for over a century. Dispatching president William Tolbert and his aides with
a series of executions, Doe set the stage for the violence to
come. Taylor returned the favor in 1989, mounting the war
that would end up overthrowing Doe in 1990, but kept going
long after one of his rival factions paraded Doe's tortured
body through the streets.

Since then, more than 150,000 lives have been lost as two
warring factions splintered into five, and the soldiers—most
teenagers and some as young as ten—turned the country into
a *Lord of the Flies* free-for-all. Adolescent commanders, with
nicknames such as General Butt Naked (who goes into battle
wearing only shoes) and generals George Bush and Saddam
Hussein, fight in the streets with everything from grenade
launchers to tennis rackets to butter knives.

There had been hope that a peace accord might put an
end to the fighting. It split power among the three main faction heads, among whom Taylor is the most vocal. The
American-educated, Libyan-trained ex-guerrilla leader lives
in a neat two-story house in Monrovia's most exclusive
neighborhood, replete with manicured lawn and a high,
well-guarded perimeter wall. His quarters are decorated in
red velvet. One love seat features his photo on the backrest
under a gold-scrolled H.E., for "His Excellency." His office
desk faces a floor-to-ceiling, wall-to-wall mirror, so he can
view the arbitrary wielding of power in his impeccable Mao-
style taupe suits.

Interviewing Taylor was an exercise in keeping a straight
face. When asked why he admitted to stockpiling weapons
when he was supposed to be disarming under the peace

accords, he replied that such public knowledge was "healthy for the peace process." When asked if his aggressive pursuit of rival faction leader Roosevelt Johnson on trumped-up charges wasn't, in fact, disproportionate to the crime, Taylor told an American reporter to "remember Waco." He assured us that all such provocative moves were made for the sake of peace and stability.

Average Liberians long ago stopped listening to the rhetoric. More than half of Liberia's 2.5 million people are now homeless. One young family, Bill, Troiphene and their two-year-old daughter, Bilphene, were driven from their small Monrovia home in 1990 to a life of refugee camps in south-eastern Liberia, Guinea and Ivory Coast. Lured by the optimism of a seven-month-old peace accord, they bundled up their belongings once again and returned to Monrovia, just in time for another round of street fighting.

"You can't continue leaving your country," says Troiphene. "If we have to go again we'll probably not come back." The couple was lucky. The bandits who ripped through their modest downtown home left their bed and bureau and a couple of Bill's suits. Troiphene was wearing flip-flops the day the fighting started. They became her only shoes.

Perhaps the most surreal place during all the fighting has been the Mamba Point Hotel, just a block from the U.S. Embassy and less than a mile from the center of battle. On its front porch, overlooking some of the biggest waves produced by the Atlantic Ocean, the hotel's Lebanese owners continued sipping their morning coffee and afternoon beers, keeping tabs on clashes through walkie-talkies dangling from their hips. Just inside, at a dining table in the tiny conference room, an exhausted gaggle of journalists typed away, juggling plugs on a portable generator and discussing whether to have lobster or fried pork with curry sauce for dinner that night.

Despite its temptingly well-stocked kitchen, the hotel was one of the few businesses in town to escape looting and destruction. It wasn't for lack of trying on the part of heavily armed fighters. In the early days of the clashes they demanded and received, the shoes off manager Imad Aoun's feet, as well as the money, jewelry and clothes of 40 hotel guests. Then they wanted the cars in the parking lot.

"We became professionals," owner Chawki Bsaibes admits, explaining that every day he and Aoun would hot-wire two cars to appease the teenage thieves. "Some of them didn't even know how to drive, so we had to put the cars on the road for them."

When the parking lot emptied, Aoun and Bsaibes cut a deal. Fighters became security guards and were paid a daily amount that varied with the number of guests. The scheme worked well until a few days after I arrived, when the security guards were routed from their positions by surprise offensive launched by a rival gang.

I awoke to the pops and whizzes of an early-morning battle down the street. By early afternoon the pops were bangs, and the whizzes were passing in front of the hotel. We were trapped, able to see the whitewashed walls of our only refuge, the embassy, but unable to make the short dash to safety.

Crouched on the floor against the bar, it was easy to appear calm. I'd heard of only one reporter killed in Liberia, a BBC correspondent who had been beaten by faction fighters and later died in London of his injuries. Still, fear boiled in a nauseous knot in my stomach. The first images that flashed through my mind were not of my life, but of those movie scenes of the last chopper leaving Saigon from the roof of the American embassy. I'd never fully appreciated the plight of those sweaty people who ran through the streets to get there. Next came thoughts of loved ones, followed by panic, followed by an intense and strangely pragmatic fear that my computer would be looted. A few TV cameramen had brought bulletproof vests, but I found them unbearably hot and too heavy to run in.

And then it ended as abruptly as it began. The assailants mysteriously retreated, our "security guards" reappeared and I was none the worse for wear, except for a lingering urge to duck at the sound of gunfire and anything else that sounded like it.

Liberians aren't so lucky. After six years, the conflict continues, despite the efforts of West African, American and U.N. negotiators. One reason is that the chaos has become very profitable, at least for the warlords. Natural resources—timber, gold, diamonds—are plundered for arms and cash. The borders with Guinea and Ivory Coast have been flooded with commerce. Every day high-level fighters arrive with truckloads of air conditioners, computers, TVs, furniture and anything else they've been able to strip from abandoned offices and homes. Subsistence farmers with nothing else of value have been forced at gunpoint to hand over the tin roofs and wooden walls of their shacks.

An end to the madness is nowhere in sight. After Somalia and Bosnia, the world has grown weary of interventions. Liberians are on their own now, looking for a miracle in the hard faces of their children.

Jennifer Ludden is the Middle East correspondent for National Public Radio based in Jerusalem.

BAJA BITES BACK

*The desert has a way of erasing trails, and anything
that depends on them.*

Massive cliffs midway between Loreto and La Paz,
exactly where Trudi had triple-underlined her "Good Luck"
on my map, forced me to climb inland. Experience had taught
me that leaving the coast was a dangerous game, but local fish-
ermen assured me that there was a trail leading up the cliffs
that would take me through a maze of mountain canyons back
down the other side.

I began the climb with a gallon and a half of water. Things
went wrong from the start. I couldn't find the trail, and I left
my own trail of blood as I cut and crashed my way up the
cactus-strewn slope, an insignificant speck among the huge
boulders and rock walls.

It was hot and still. I had drunk half my water by the time
I stood on top, and the way down was far from obvious. No
trails, no clues, just a maze of arroyos dropping into sheer-
walled canyons going nowhere, certainly not going back to
the coast. A great block of mountains barred the way.

I had no option but to venture further inland, and my water

bottle seemed like an hour-glass slowly draining. The sweat dripping from my sunburned face and soaking my shirt had to be replaced.

After anxious hours battling the unbelievably rugged terrain, I at last found myself in an arroyo falling towards the coast. In the race to safety, I scrambled down the steeply dropping, dry waterfalls and over stacks of rounded boulders. Descents I wouldn't normally have tried had to be attempted.

My tongue was thick and dry. My head was pounding. Inexplicable aches and pains were spreading through my body. I'd pushed myself too hard and rationed the water too strictly. Collapse now, I thought, and it's *adios.* My only hope was down, down to the sea. No matter what the risk, I had to keep going down.

I came to a T-junction; the canyon before me was deeply set in the mountain but at least it wasn't dropping precipitously. Ironically, its floor was so level, it was hard to tell which way was down. To the left or to the right? My eyes started to play tricks. I walked a hundred yards to the right then swore I was going up. I retreated and went a hundred yards the other way before becoming convinced that too was up. I had to go some way. I chose to the right, at least that was south, the direction I wanted to travel.

Sometimes I was sure I was going down, and then I was sure I wasn't! There was no way of climbing out of the canyon. It was like being trapped in some frightening Victorian alley or backstreet. In places I was sandwiched between two vertical walls of rock 150 feet high and just 30 feet wide. A lone wild fig tree clung tight and flat against one of the walls as if breathing-in to let me pass.

Forcing myself to use every last moment of light, I came to another, much wider, cross canyon. There at the "T" where the "backstreet" spilled on to a major thoroughfare, I thought

I was seeing things. In the middle of an arid, rocky, wasteland that probably hadn't known rain for months, there was a pool of water deep enough to dive in and swim around. The water was stagnant and green but pure gold to me. After filtering and boiling, I sat drinking endless cups of coffee beneath a heaven slowly filling with bats and stars.

The immediate crisis was over, but the pool was just a life-raft; I was aboard, but still lost at sea in an ocean of rock. A more terrible struggle was about to begin.

The confluence of the canyons was sufficiently open-skied to allow me to pick up a distant, crackly radio station. A southern preacher was passionately pouring forth on the word of God, the coming tribulation, the certainty of judgment, the need to be saved, and the importance of sending contributions to keep the programme on the air.

For over a year I had listened to the ayatollahs of America pumping out their incredible interpretations of Christianity. Although possibly facing eternity sooner than most, I had no qualms about expressing my own increasingly strong opinions on the subject. I wrote:

> Why do so many Christians use their religion to look down on and condemn others? Where is the humility and compassion? Why are so many Christians paranoia-cally concerned about their own salvation? What would Christ have to say about such arrogance and selfishness?
>
> How can men be so blind as to miss the whole point of Christianity; to use the doctrine that bears Christ's name to further their own prejudices, insecurities and hatreds? Much of scripture is contradictory and confusing. Coherence and clarity must come from our hearts and our sense of what's right and wrong, from our sense of what's sound in Christ's teaching.

Christ's teaching is a guide for life. The Sermon on the Mount, the parable of the good Samaritan, the injunction to turn the other cheek, forgive and forget, rather than go in all guns blazing, blindly seeking revenge—isn't that the core of the message? Wasn't Christ's mission to teach us how to rise above the worst aspects of our potentially evil human nature; and to sow love, trust and mutual understanding rather than hate? To do unto others as we would have them do unto us.

Maybe God gives us such an unclear, contradictory message—an eye for an eye and turn the other cheek—so that we reveal what is really in our hearts by the doctrines we adhere to and cherish. That would be a good example of God's wisdom and justice; come the day of judgment the false and unworthy would have revealed themselves by their reading of His word. They would have spent their lives wasting time with the ego-massaging desire to judge, and their fundamentally selfish concern about their own salvation. Maybe the saved are those that say to the God which is being erroneously presented to us, "You are wrong. I will not serve you. My God should be and is a God of love and compassion." When Christians are willing to risk their eternal souls for what they believe in, then there is true faith, courage, and hope for the world.

I am a Christian. I made sense of much that I saw and experienced in terms of Christianity. My faith has been deepened, but I would rather be a Christ-like Moslem than an un-Christ-like Christian.

Next morning, I realized my problems were just beginning. Ahead there was an impossible drop, no way down or around.

I returned to the water hole to have a cup of tea and think about what to do. The rest of the day was spent exploring one canyon after another, vainly looking for a way out. A grove of prickly pear cactus satisfied my hunger. The slimy pads were better than nothing.

By late afternoon, I found an over-the-top animal trail that seemed to head towards the coast. Loading up with water, I reluctantly left the security of the pool and followed the trail through a maze of ridges and valleys. Eventually it led into a broad U-shaped valley which drained inland! Dilemma! Do I follow it down and away from the coast or up and towards the coast? I headed east directly to the Gulf. The climb up was gentle enough.

I began to look for a place to spend my second night in the mountains. Exhaustion was overtaking me. For two days I had been pushing myself to the limit, and beyond. Something was wrong.

The sun was sinking and I still felt hot, painfully, uncomfortably hot. The inexplicable aches returned. Columns of cacti started spinning faster and faster. My legs buckled as I struggled to put up the tent. Inside it I alternately shivered and sweated. All through the night a thousand images and ghosts raced through my mind—a white horse, the crack of a rifle, and a donkey calling in pain. Then I was alone, at night, by my fire, and a voice said, "You want to know if you can stand the pain of a rattlesnake bite?" The glowing embers of the burned-down fire suddenly coalesced into a hissing snake and shot into my leg. I woke sweating and groaning and frightened before drifting again into delirious oblivion.

The sergeant was back. "I'm here. It'll be all right. We'll go through this together. You're not alone." There he was, in that scarlet tunic as large as life. This time I knew him. Of course! I'd conjured up an image of something I hadn't seen for years, the portrait that used to fascinate me as a kid, the grandfather I'd never known except looking proudly down from the wall with his ribbons and medals—my grandfather with the red hair and the red moustache, Colour-Sergeant-Major Mackintosh of the Seaforth Highlanders. He died before I was born. But I knew him through that golden framed painting, through his medals and the stories my father told me of his deeds "holding together a tottering empire" from his first action at Omdurman in the Sudan to his last on some bloody First World War battlefield.

His service to King and Country was cut short by a piece of red-hot shrapnel ripping into his back. All day the kilted warrior lay groaning and delirious beneath the summer sun, while the battle raged around.

I found myself floating away from my body. I could see the tent below. I was rising out of the valley and into the starry, peaceful sky. It was a beautiful feeling but I didn't trust it. I didn't want to let go. I was fighting desperately to resist, and clung on as if clinging to life itself. A calming voice urged me not to struggle. It was his voice. I floated away then looked down, I was high above the ground, but instead of my tent below, there was a figure in a shell hole. A Sergeant! I woke up shouting: "You're not alone. You're not alone."

In between periods of feverish babble, I pondered my predicament. My life depended on being able to walk and I couldn't even stand. Suspecting that I hovered on the brink of heat stroke, I drank freely and licked salt from boots white-ringed from wading in the sea. Not able to face another slimy bit of cactus, I swallowed a multivitamin instead.

No matter what, I had to pack and get away before sunrise, to take my chances with the rattlesnakes rather than the heat of the day.

An hour before dawn, I eased on my backpack and struggled weakly along, fighting the desire to sink to my knees and lie down. I kept thinking of that poor burro. How valiantly he tried to keep his feet. He knew that if he went down it would be forever.

Wherever possible I used my machete to cut through the thorn and brush. Otherwise I would simply crash through. Nothing mattered except climbing to the head of the valley. I had convinced myself that the ocean and a fishcamp were down on the other side.

The stars disappeared. The sky went through its rainbow range of colours before settling to its brilliant blue. At last, I was coming to the end of the valley. Fresh air and sea birds ahead. Summoning all my strength and will-power, I made it to the top and looked beyond my boots to see a 500-foot sheer drop. There was no way down to the sea except by jumping. The disappointment was such, I had to laugh.

With the enormous morning sun staring me in the face, I backed away and collapsed onto a pile of loose red stones. A hummingbird darted in for a quick look at the strange creature crumpled, chuckling on the ground. A frigate bird swooped down. A vulture circled.

I began psyching myself up to use the Radio Distress Beacon. Would anyone pick it up? Could they get up to me in time? Nothing was certain. I had to try to save myself first.

Both sides of the valley were steep and rocky. Should I go north or south? I started up the marginally easier-looking north wall, and then changed my mind and headed south. I was nearing the top when I thought I heard someone calling me. It was beyond belief that anyone else was up there. I was obviously hearing things. But the sound continued, the only real thing in my whirling mind.

I called back and thus made the acquaintance of Francisco, a young Mexican boy up in the mountains looking for his goats. Seeing my condition, he took my pack and escorted me down those impossible-looking cliffs into his fishcamp where his family looked after me for a couple of days, till I had recovered sufficiently to be able to carry on.

Graham Mackintosh is the author of Into a Desert Place: A 3000 Mile Walk Around the Coast of Baja California, *from which this story was excerpted.*

BURIED

Nature teaches hard lessons.

THERE I WAS, UP TO MY NECK IN SNOW AND STUCK IN A tree. I was able to lift my head enough to watch the avalanche rumble on down the slope another seven or eight hundred feet and hit the group of clients who were in what they thought was an "island of safety." Oddly enough, the first thing I hear is Chuck, our helicopter pilot, coming through on my radio, which has miraculously remained attached to me.

"I can see him," Chuck is shouting. "He's stuck behind a tree."

Stuck is right. Not more than a couple of minutes ago, I had agreed to check out a slope for avalanche danger. As the tailgunner, or rear guide, of a helicopter ski outfit, I had waited up top while Darwin, the head guide, took our party of eight skiers down a steep powder slope. We knew there was a hazard out there, what heli ski guides would call a "moderate hazard," but we were managing it. Or so it appeared. Darwin and the rest of the party had skied down without mishap.

Darwin had radioed back up to me: "Hey, Pete, take a look at that other aspect, as an option for the next run."

So many things can change when you're on a mountain of snow. You might have a really solid layer of white powder, but the sun and the orientation of the slope can make the difference between one that is secure and one that's about to break off.

That's exactly what happened. I skied over to check out this slope, turned my skis downhill, got two turns into it and suddenly this thing pulled out and totally surprised me. It pulled out about a hundred feet behind me as I was skiing. My first indication that something was wrong was when the whole slope began sliding, moving to the left. As I'm turning, all of a sudden I find myself on my right hip, but I haven't fallen!"

I'm thinking, "This is weird," and then I look around and realize, Holy Shit, I'm in an avalanche.

I knew I was in deep shit and I was going down fast. I'm on my hip and the thing starts to break up. First, it's one big piece, but as it picks up speed it's starting to fracture and froth. I'm sinking down deeper into it. Accumulating speed.

I try to get up with my head, to look, because I can feel that I'm picking up speed. All this is happening in the first few seconds. I'm getting up on my hands and having trouble breathing, from all the powder froth. I'm not that deep in the avalanche but there's so much frothing and out-of-control washing machine action going on that it's all I can do to just keep my head above it to watch where I'm going. I know there are trees ahead.

I lose it. I'm in it, out of control. I get swept another couple hundred feet, then slammed into a stand of trees. I'm wrapped around one, my head going downhill on one side, my legs on the other, with the full force of the avalanche pressing against me. I feel tremendous pressure, as though my life is being squeezed out of me, but it lets up just before I feel I might black out.

Now, I'm stuck in a tree with the ski party in danger below me. I've had major wind knocked out of me and can hardly talk. Darwin has located most of the party. The next thing I hear on the radio is that one of the skiers, a seventeen-year-old girl, is missing, buried somewhere. I think, "Shit, Whittaker, good job, you kicked off this avalanche and not only messed yourself up, but now there's a girl buried in it."

I finally caught my breath and was able to reach my radio. The first thing I said, being at the time the macho-guide-stud-bolt, was, "Bring my skis back up to me. I'll ski out of here." My skis, gloves and poles had been ripped off by the force of the avalanche. My gloves were found later, down below, completely inside out.

The year before, I had just come back from the 1984 Everest expedition led by my father, Lou Whittaker. I had been able to spend a bunch of nights above 25,000 feet. I was twenty-five years old, strong and healthy. I'd just quit ski patrol at Snowbird and Greg Smith, the helicopter ski service owner, heard about it and offered me a job as a heli ski guide. I said, "Sure." I knew it was a really great job. And, a perfect off-season job for me. During summers, I worked as a guide on Mt. Rainier in Washington, with my father's guide service, Rainier Mountaineering, Inc.

So, I'm back from the Himalayas and feeling pretty cocky. Feeling like I've been around, been on the big mountains and all. I had been working as a rookie heli ski guide for a month when the avalanche happened.

Your first year, you learn an awful lot. You listen a lot. I'd had a lot of experience skiing because I'd grown up skiing and climbing. But heli guiding was a new thing and I spent most of my time at the rear of the ski party, where, in the hierarchy of heli skiing, rookies belong.

I knew a lot about avalanches, having grown up with Mt. Rainier as my backyard playground. I had even survived an avalanche that my dad had kicked off accidentally while we were climbing together, and, a few years later, watched in horror as a major ice fall buried eleven climbers. You learn quickly to pay attention to what a mountain is trying to tell you.

Even so, even with an understanding of the risk involved and the objective hazards present, things can get out of control in an instant. Before you can even think to react.

In helicopter ski guiding, we do what they call "slope evaluation." In addition to the many tests used to determine what the potential for avalanche is, we also conduct tests by throwing bombs out of the helicopter onto the slopes.

The year I started at Snowbird, we had a great heli pilot named Chuck. He had been shot down twice in Vietnam and had more mountain hours than any other pilot in the U.S. An unbelievable pilot.

We carried thirty bombs in the back of this Bell Jet Ranger. You sit with a case of bombs between your legs, all set with 90-second fuses. The first time I was bombardier, the head guide sat up front with the pilot and another guide sat to my right to hand me bombs. Each bomb is a two-pound hand charge. A mix used at most ski areas. Packs a pretty good punch.

The head guide figures out beforehand where we're going to fly to test slopes. Not only the slopes we'll be skiing on, but also the ones above us. The Wasatch Mountains are 11,000 feet or so, and Chuck flies us in and out and around the peaks, so we can get a look at different couloirs and slopes that we might want to ski.

I swear to God, Chuck's reaction to the first pull of the spitter on the bomb—the initial smell of sulfur in the cockpit—was predatory. He starts flying like we're in battle, diving and buzzing the slopes.

We pick a slope to test. Chuck gets the helicopter in position. Darwin yells, "Ready?" I yell back, "Ready!" He yells, "Go!" I pull the spitter on the bomb and suddenly realize that I'm holding a live bomb in my hands. It's a strange feeling.

There's a little window in the helicopter. I stick my arm out of it and wait for Darwin's commands. You don't throw the bombs, just drop them. Darwin is real good. When he yells "Now!" I drop a bomb. We do several in quick succession. Your adrenaline starts pumping. You've got to synchronize, not pull the spitter and drop the bomb on the floor of the cockpit in your hurry to get it out the window.

This is the safe way to check for avalanche danger. After we drop the charges, we hover over the area and listen to the bombs go off—sounds like "poof!" from the distance. Poof! A big crater appears in the side of the mountain. Poof! Black powder marks. Poof!—and the head guide yells, "It's going!" We've got an avalanche.

It's a classic slab avalanche. When it releases, you know that the underlayer has failed and you've got hundreds of yards of snow, a huge area, collapsing at the same time. It actually begins pulling away and moving as one piece. There's a fracture on top and one on the bottom. The whole piece kicks out and starts moving.

Some of these releases are between eight and twelve feet deep. That's a big avalanche. You watch these things start to come down first as one piece, then, as they pick up speed, they begin to break apart. The front turns into a wave.

Chuck likes to turn the ship around and fly right above the powder cloud. This avalanche we kicked off is going a hundred-forty miles an hour and that's just about as fast as the helicopter will go.

You realize that it's not the snow that's knocking over trees, it's the air blast that precedes the wave. Just shatters some of the trees. We ride above the avalanche, screaming down through a canyon.

Sometimes, a smaller avalanche will check itself when it first starts, and, if you're in it, you have time to point your skis downhill and actually get going faster than the slide. Get your speed up and try to do a big sweep turn and get out of the way. I've been able to do that a few times, ski out of the way. Sometimes, it works, and the danger passes you by. You feel like you're on a magic carpet ride. It's a tough call, though.

Another time, I was up near the starting zone and the fracture was only two or three feet uphill from my skis and I felt it start to go. I didn't have any room to sweep to the side, so I hammered my skis into the snow, trying to break down the slab beneath me. It worked. Everything else below me broke off and went sliding and I was left, just standing there. That technique came to me at that instant, out of a sense of self-preservation, I think. You know, when seconds count...

I've heard people give advice about what to do if you see an avalanche heading towards you. Like, "The first thing you do is take your skis off, then take off your poles...." and I picture some guy taking time to do this and waiting for the avalanche to hit him. On skis, you're pretty mobile. If you have a few seconds, you can usually move into a good position, such as behind a tree or just get out of the way.

If you get hit, though, staying on the surface is what you want to try to do. If it's a big avalanche and it really gets going, you're at the mercy of the slide. You're going to feel like you're in a washing machine, out of control. You just hope you don't hit anything.

The idea is to have your hands up around your face when you finally stop, to create a little air pocket. Maybe you can dig, too. Get out of your skis and poles, if they haven't been torn off you. Often, you'll be near enough to the surface and can pop out.

When I got wrapped around that tree, I was lucky that my head was above the snow. A lot of people aren't so lucky and they suffocate.

I didn't realize until later how broken up I was. After about ten minutes, while I was waiting to be rescued, I realized that I was bleeding internally. I could feel swelling in the left side of my abdomen. I was beginning to feel incredible pain, but I told the guides that I could maintain while they rescued the girl.

They found her in just a few minutes, thanks to the avalanche beepers we all were wearing, which emit a signal you can pick up through the snow on a receiver. She had been caught but not carried at the toe of the avalanche. She was down almost three feet. Face down, her skis had been ripped off and her legs were bent all the way up, almost touching the back of her head. At first, they thought she was really messed up. She wasn't breathing. But, they ventilated her, got her breathing.

Nice thing about this situation is, you've got the ambulance right there—the helicopter noses in and they carefully load the girl in the ship and Chuck flies her to the hospital in Salt Lake City in about six minutes.

In the meantime, the guides begin their rescue effort on me. By the time they get me dug out, the helicopter is back and takes me in. I spend a few days in intensive care, waiting to find out if my spleen will be removed. It's ruptured. My ribs are broken, my knee is blown out, but I'm mostly concerned about not having a scar from my sternum down to my abdomen.

The doctors put me on morphine and go through my back with a big needle to drain five hundred cc's of blood and fluid out of my abdomen. I start to improve. They operate on my knee, put a pin in it. I still don't have a hundred percent movement in it today. But, my spleen healed. If the helicopter hadn't been there, I'd have died in the backcountry.

I didn't ski or climb for a year afterwards. The doctors said I'd never be able to ski or climb on a professional level again. I decided to take an accounting class and a computer class, to prepare for another career. That didn't last long. I got real motivated about rehabilitation, and proved those doctors wrong. I couldn't see myself ending up as an accountant or computer jock.

What did I learn from this? I learned more respect and more humility, which is a good thing, because here I was, this hot shit helicopter guide.

I learned also not to be so concerned about making nice tracks and getting face shots when I'm skiing. I learned to be a little more conservative, a little more aware of that slope.

I also learned that there really is no such thing as an "island of safety." Safety is all relative. Now, I'm always prepared for the worst. Sometimes, I'm lucky.

Peter Whittaker carries on his family's mountaineering tradition. His Uncle Jim became the first American, in 1963, to summit Mt. Everest. His father, Lou, has led successful expeditions to Everest and Kangchenjunga. Peter makes his home at the base of Mt. Rainier with his wife Erika, a former member of the Austrian national ski team.

JOANNA GREENFIELD

HYENA

She just wanted to work with animals.

SPOTTED HYENAS ARE THE SHARKS OF THE SAVANNA, SUPER-predators and astounding recyclers of garbage. They hunt in large, giggling groups, running alongside their prey and eating chunks of its flesh until it slows down through loss of blood, or shock, or sheer hopelessness, and then the hyenas grab for the stomach and pull the animal to a halt with its own entrails or let it stumble into the loops and whorls of its own body. They eat the prey whole and cough back, like owls, the indigestible parts, such as hair and hooves....

I once saw a family of hyenas playing on an elephant skull. They rolled on their backs, biting gently at each other's legs. Two cubs squeezed under and then out of the elephant's mandible. A female turned on her side, paws in the air, and broke off a piece of the skull as if eating a biscuit in bed. Hyenas almost never kill humans—only now and then taking a piece from the cheek of a sleeping man, and that probably because some villagers used to put out their dead for hyenas, flies, and any vultures in the area. As the man jumps up—

perhaps he is a messenger between villages or someone searching for a bride—the hyena instantly, peaceably, retreats.

Africa is like no other place on earth, and there is no better place to watch animals. They roam sun-dazed on the savanna by the million, sniffing up the scent of dried grass, swishing their tails, eyes often half closed. Sometimes they ignore human beings, sometimes they stare, but always there is something to look at: impalas dancing together in a mock fight, giraffes slow—swinging across the horizon. In the distance, vervet monkeys hop through branches. An ostrich runs with tail rampant, all the while flapping its wings in agitation, like a maiden aunt caught in a shower. A baboon nurses its toe. A lion quietly chuffs to itself.

I had wanted to go to Africa since my childhood, in Connecticut. Before I was born, my eyes lost their attachment to each other, the instinctive knowledge of how to swivel together, how to analyze data in tandem. The vision of one eye is only slightly cloudy, but it withdraws from cooperation with the other. My eyes do not work like two halves of a whole, and I have no perception of depth, so human faces blend into their background and are unreadable. The unreadable is frightening. When I was a child, friendly voices could dig deep and sharp without warning: without depth perception, there is no warning. I had to learn about emotions, which are subtle and often masked, from animals, who signal theirs so much more clearly, with mane and tail and the position of the body. Human beings were a hazard.

There was only one thing that my eyes took in with ease. As the school bus crossed the marshes on a small cement bridge, we could see down the river to the horizon, and up the river toward a bend of trees. In the swamp that ran alongside it grew cattails and rushes, as naturally gold as they were tall. They were semi-translucent. Each blade glowed separately in the morning sun as if lit within. Together in their bending, high-feathered swamp, they bowed under the weightlessness of light. Sometimes there was mist rising from the water, and altogether it was the only masterpiece I ever saw in my suburban town. I don't know why I needed to see those rushes so badly, or how I knew Africa would be the same, but it was.

I had never wanted to work anywhere except in Africa, but after I graduated from college a wildlife-reserve director from Israel told me that he needed someone to set up a breeding site for endangered animals and I decided to go. When I got there, I was told that the project had been postponed and was asked if I'd mind taking a job as a volunteer at another reserve, cleaning enclosures. The reserve was dedicated to Biblical animals, many of them predators from the Israeli wild—hyenas, wolves, foxes, and one unmated leopard—attackers of kibbutz livestock. It was something to do, with animals, so I trudged off every day in the hundred-and-fourteen-degree heat with half a sandwich and a water canteen. I was being groomed for the job I'd initially been offered, but for the moment I sifted maggots for the lizards and snakes, and cleaned the fox, cat, hyena, wolf, and leopard corrals.

As the days got hotter, my fellow-workers and I carried gallon jugs of water in our wheelbarrows, poured it over our heads, and drank the rest until our stomachs were too full for food. It became a steady rhythm: sift dung, pour, drink, sift. We worked in pairs among the larger animals for safety, but toward the end of the month I was allowed to feed a young hyena and clean his cage. Efa had been taken from his parents as a cub because his mother rejected him. Also, he was a cross between a North African and an Israeli striped hyena, and nobody wanted him to confuse the gene pool further by mating. He was a beautiful animal. A mane trickled down sloped shoulders like a froth of leftover baby hair; he looked strangely helpless, as if weighed down by the tangled strands, and his back rounded to a dispirited slump. Even though he had a hyena's posture, he was like a German shepherd, a little dirty, but graceful, and so strong he didn't seem to have any muscles. His stripes twisted a bit at the ends and shimmered over the coat like feathers at rest. With his bat face and massed shoulders, he would have been at home in the sky, poised in a great leap, or swooping for prey. But here he was given aged meat, and he often left even that to rot before he ate it.

He had been, they said, an adorable cub, crying *"Maaaaa!"* to Shlomi, the gentlest of the workers and the one who reared him, and he followed Shlomi everywhere. Then he grew too big to run loose, and he started biting at people, so they put him in a corral—a square of desert surrounded by an electrified fence with a large water basin perched in the center.

Efa was bored and lonely. He flipped the basin over every day, attacking it as if it were prey. When we fed him in the morning, there was nowhere to put his water. He knocked over everything, so we had no choice: we had to put him in a holding cage outside his corral while we built a concrete pool that he couldn't move. This was worse. Locked in a cage, he rebelled. He refused to eat, and every box we gave him for shade was torn to pieces. After a few days, I walked by and saw him standing defiant in the cage, his shade box in splinters and his water overturned again. *"Maaaaaaa! Mmaaaa!"* he croaked at me. I made a note to return and water him when I'd finished with the others....

Efa was in a frenzy of *"Mmmaaaaaaaa"*s when I returned to his cage. He crouched like a baby, begging for something. I filled a water tray and unlatched the door that opened into a corridor running between the cage and the corral, then I closed it. If only I'd just squirted the hose into the cage, but instead I unlatched the cage door and bent over to put the dish down, talking to him. The mind, I found, is strange. It shut off during the attack, while my body continued to act, without thought or even sight. I don't remember him sinking his teeth into my arm, though I heard a little grating noise as his teeth chewed into the bone.

Everything was black and slow and exploding in my stomach. Vision returned gradually, like an ancient black-and-white television pulling dots and flashes to the center for a picture. I saw at a remove the hyena inside my right arm, and my other arm banging him on the head. My body, in the absence of a mind, had decided that this was the best thing to do. And scream. Scream in a thin angry hysteria that didn't sound like me. Where was everyone? My mind was so calm and remote that I frightened myself, but my stomach twisted. I hit harder, remembering the others he'd nipped. He'd always let go.

Efa blinked and surged back, jerking me forward. I stumbled out of my sandals into the sand, thinking, with fresh anxiety, I'll burn my feet. I tried to kick him between the legs, but it was awkward, and he was pulling me down by the arm, down and back into the cage. When I came back from Africa the first time, I took a class in self-defense so I'd feel safer with all the soldiers, guerrilla warriors, and policemen when I returned. I remembered the move I'd vowed to use on any attacker: a stab and grab at the jugular, to snap it inside the skin. But the hyena has callused skin on its throat, thick and rough, like eczema. I lost hope and felt the slowness of this death to be the worst insult. Hyenas don't kill fast, and I could end up in the sand watching my entrails get pulled through a cut in my stomach and eaten like spaghetti, with tugs and jerks. I started to get mad, an unfamiliar feeling creeping in to add an acid burn to the chill of my stomach. Another removal from myself. I never let myself get mad. I want peace. I tried to pinch his nostrils so he'd let go of my arm to breathe, but he shook his head, pulling me deeper into the cage.

I think it was then that he took out the first piece from my arm and swallowed it without breathing, because a terror of movement settled in me at that moment and lasted for months. He moved up the arm, and all the time those black, blank eyes evaluated me, like a shark's, calm and almost friendly. By this time, my right arm was a mangled mess of flesh, pushed-out globs of fat, and flashes of bone two inches long, but my slow TV mind, watching, saw it as whole, just trapped in the hyena's mouth, in a tug-of-war like the one I used to play with my dogs—only it was my arm now instead of a sock. It didn't hurt. It never did.

The hyena looked up at me with those indescribable eyes and surged back again, nearly pulling me into his face. I remembered self-defense class and the first lesson: "Poke the cockroach in the eyes." All the women had squealed, except me. "Ooooh, I could *never* do that." Ha, I'd thought. Anyone who wants to kill me has no right to live. I'd poke him in the eyes.

I looked at those eyes with my fingers poised to jab. It was for my family and my friends that I stuck my fingers in his eyes. I just wanted to stop watching myself get eaten, either be dead and at peace or be gone, but other lives were connected to mine. I'm not sure if I did more than touch them gently before he let go and whipped past me to cower against the door to the outside, the Negev desert.

Events like this teach you yourself. We all think we know what we would do, hero or coward, strong or weak. I expected strength, and the memory of my tin-whistle scream curdles my blood, but I am proud of the stupid thing I did next. He cowered and whimpered and essentially apologized, still with those blank unmoving eyes, and I stood still for a second. My arm felt light and shrunken, as if half of it were gone, but I didn't look. From the corridor, I had a choice of two doors: The one through which I'd entered, leading back to the desert, and the one opening onto the corral. I didn't think I could bend over him and unlatch the door to the desert. He'd just reach up and clamp onto my stomach. And I didn't want to open the door to the corral, or he'd drag me in and be able to attack the men if they ever came to help me. My body, still in control, made the good hand grab the bad elbow, and I beat him with my own arm, as if I had ripped it free to use as a club. "No!" I shouted. "No, no!" *Lo lo lo*, in Hebrew. I might even have said "Bad boy," but I hope not. It was the beating that damaged my hand permanently. I must have hit him hard enough to crush a ligament, because there is a lump on my hand to this day, five years later, but he didn't even blink. He came around behind me and grabbed my right leg, and again there was no pain—just the feeling that he and I were playing tug-of-war with my body—but I was afraid to pull too hard on the leg. He pulled the leg up, stretching me out in a line from the door, where I clung with the good hand to the mesh, like a dancer at the barre. It felt almost good, as if the whole thing were nearer to being over. In three moves I didn't feel, he took out most of the calf.

I opened the door to the desert and he ran out, with a quick shove that staggered me. I couldn't move the right leg, just crutched myself along on it into the Negev. He waited for me. The cold in my stomach was stabbing my breath away. The hyena and I were bonded now. Even if someone did come to help, there was still something left to finish between us. I was marked—his. I saw, in color, that he was going to knock me over, and I thought, in black-and-white, No, don't, you'll hurt my leg, I should keep it still.

A workman stood by a shed up-hill, leaning on a tool in the

sand. He watched me walk toward the office, with the hyena ahead and looking back at me. He was the only spectator I noticed, though I was told later, in the hospital, that some tourists, there to see the animals, were screaming for help, and three—or was it five?—soldiers had had their machine guns aimed at us throughout the whole thing. Israeli soldiers carry their arms everywhere when they're in uniform; but they must have been afraid to shoot. I don't know. Stories get told afterward. I didn't see anyone except the workman, looking on impassively, and the leopard, pacing inside her fence, roaring a little....

As I walked, the black-and-white faded, and color washed back in. I saw the blood for the first time. It was in my hair, had soaked into my clothes all the way to the skin, and was drying in a trickle from arm and legs. Each step left a cold puddle of blood around the right foot. I held up the arm and fumbled for the pressure point. The hyena trotted ahead of me as if he were afraid to be alone in the desert but was all right with me. Every now and then, he looked back, as if thinking about finishing me off—once again a predator, calm and competent, silver, and splashed with blood. But then men ran up shouting, and I stopped, and snapped, sorry even then for sounding like a bitch, "Get Efa and bring around the van."

Shlomi ran up and grabbed my good left arm, hustling me forward. Not so fast, I wanted to say, but I didn't. Every step felt more wrong, and I dragged back against moving until he almost shoved me forward.

In the van, blood sloshed around my feet and I tried to find the pressure point of the groin but gave up. I held up the arm instead, and pretended I knew what I was doing. Shlomi stopped to open the reserve gate, and then again to close it: As he got back in, I lost feeling in my right leg.

We drove for what seemed like a long time, then turned

into a kibbutz and roared past lines of women planting pineapples, past a cement yard, and then he was running me into a clinic past gasping women. And I wanted to apologize. I never cut in line. Shlomi pulled me forward while I stiffened up. Damn it. I wanted to be carried, I've done enough by myself, I remember thinking. But I made it to the examining table and Shlomi yelled for a doctor in Hebrew. A woman came in and told him there was no doctor—only nurses. They stopped telling me what was happening. Hands shaking, she yanked me forward and stuck my arm under a faucet. Hey. She turned on the water and it fell onto the bone and a minor nerve, full force. That was a sensation I wish I couldn't remember. No pain, but a tremendous feeling of wrongness. My insides were out.

She tried to get my leg into the sink, pulling at the ankle, and the shrivelled arm twitched in the air for balance. I tensed, so she couldn't; I wished later that I'd let her, because it was weeks before the dried blood and dirt peeled off. She told me to get on a stretcher, and then she poured hydrogen peroxide into the trenches in my leg. It foamed with a roar that spat froth in the air. That felt wrong, too. Shlomi grabbed the sink for support. I told him it didn't hurt. He wasn't listening. I was starting to feel better. Someone was making the decisions.

"Don't worry, Shlomi. I never wanted to dance ballet."

"No, I don't know, the leg is very bad."

Like all Israelis, he could make a statement of fact sound like an accusation. I knew it was bad, I just didn't see the need to dwell on it when I was so very surprised to be alive. The nurse picked up a towel and started wiping off the blood and dirt with brisk, scratchy strokes, and I cramped in the stomach again, worrying about infection. And what were we waiting for? We waited awhile, and then she gave me anti-shock injections.

"I'm not in shock," I said, and meant it. I thought I was thinking more clearly than she was. Shlomi told me that we were waiting for an ambulance. He was gray, with sick, in-turned eyes, the way I must have looked while the attack was happening. But I was over it, and he was just beginning. He and the nurse did not share my pleasure. In fact, they seemed taken aback at my jokes, so I stopped talking.

I had a new terror, but it was peaceful compared with the other, so I lay back. Fly home, microsurgery, I can spare the leg if something has to go, but I have to have the hand for grad-uate school. Helicopters, international flights, nerve damage.

The ambulance came. The nurse and Shlomi looked as bloodless as I felt. They pushed me around, telling me to get onto the gurney, and I tried to make them go so I could just roll onto it instead of jumping down from the table. They did, and wheeled me out in state through a crowd of horrified kibbutzniks. They showed no excitement over it; pain is too real to Israelis.

I am sure Efa crawled out to greet me with no intention to kill. He had cried to me like an infant in distress, hunched over and rounded. His ruff lay flat and soft and his tail hung down. He attacked me, I think, in a moment of thirst-induced delir-ium and loneliness. If he had wanted to eat or to attack, he could have taken my arm in a snap: one sharp jab and jerk, and the wrist would have been gone before I even noticed. If he had wanted to kill me, he could have leaped for my stomach as soon as he had pulled me down by the arm.

Cheetahs often catch hold of their prey's nose and run alongside it. As the victim stumbles and falls, or staggers, or tries to run, the cheetah holds tight, closing mouth and nos-trils in one stapled hold, or—with larger prey—biting into the throat to cut off air. Leopards like to leap down from trees for a quick crack of the back. Lions improvise. Each has its own specialty. Some leap up from behind, like a terrestrial leopard; some try a daring front leap, risking hooves and horns to bite into neck or face.

Hyenas are far more efficient. They catch hold of flesh, not with small nips and throwing of weight but by smoothly and quickly transferring chunks of it from toothold to stomach. Like human infants nursing, they seem to swallow without pausing for breath, as if food and air travelled in separate channels. They are the only predators adapted to eating bone. Their dung is white with it.

I heard a story of a young boy in Nairobi who was watching over a herd of goats and fell asleep leaning on his stick. A hyena appeared and opened the boy's stomach with one quick rip. For the hyena it might have been play, this trying on of assault. But he won, as he was bound to do. I was told that someone took the boy to a doctor and he died a while later. He could have lived; we don't need all our intestines, and the hyena had probably left enough behind. But maybe they didn't have the right antibiotics or sterile dressings. I would have liked to ask him what he saw in the hyena's eyes.

In the ambulance, the driver chatted for a bit, then said, "Don't close your eyes. If you feel faint, tell me and I'll stop right away."

To do what, watch me? I didn't tell him that I'd been exhausted for months—I'd got parasites in Africa—and always shut my eyes when I had the chance. I closed them now, and he asked me questions with an anxiety that warmed my heart. I love to be taken care of. It was good to be strapped down and bandaged, all decisions out of my hands after the hard ones, the life-and-death ones. It was also, I learned, a good thing to have the wounds hidden. Once they were open to the air, my stomach clenched with pain that made life temporarily not worth living. The arm, I finally noticed, was curled up on itself, like paper shrivelling inward in a fire, but heavy instead of too light.

We arrived at the hospital with a screech and a yank and a curse. The doors were stuck, but the driver pushed, and ran me in. Then he left with a wave of farewell. I waited and waited. A doctor came in and plowed my arm in search of a vein with blood, going deep under the muscle, to attach a saline drip. My nails were white, like things soaked in formaldehyde, and I was freezing. Bled white, I was, Nothing left to fill a test tube.

I asked the doctor to talk with the reserve's veterinarian before he did anything. Hyena bites are violently infectious. The animals' mouths are full of bacteria from rotten meat. He shrugged. But when Shlomi told him to wait for the vet he did. The vet told him to clean the holes out and leave them open for now, because the infection could kill me.

"The infection will probably take the leg anyway," the doctor told me. "The chances are fifty-fifty that we'll have to amputate."

I looked down once at the leg before they began cutting out the dirtier shreds of flesh and paring the whole surface of the wound. The holes were impossibly wide, more than twice the size of the hyena's face. I know now that skin and muscle are stretched over bone like canvas over a canoe. One thinks of skin as irrevocably bonded to flesh, and all as one entity. But skin is attached to flesh only with the lightest of bonds, and, once it has been ripped, the body gives way naturally, pulling the flesh back to its scaffolding of bone. The invisible woman, I thought, as the chill took me; I can see right through my leg.

I couldn't see all of it because of my bad eyesight, and the leg was still covered with blood-stuck sand, but it was strange the way the leg went down normally, then cut in to the bone, along the bone, and then out again to a normal ankle, except for a small gash on the side with fat poking out. I couldn't yet see the other hole. It was lower down, starting halfway past the one I could see, and continuing around the back of the leg to the other side, so almost the whole leg was girdled around. I still don't know how blood got to that stranded wall of flesh.

The doctor worked on the leg for an hour, clipping pieces of flesh out of the wounds with little scissor snips, as if my leg were a piece of cloth that he was carefully tailoring with dull tools. I asked for a larger dose of anesthetic, not because I felt any pain—I never felt any, really—but because I could feel the scissors scissoring away the flesh and I couldn't breathe. Between bouts of cutting, I kept joking, happy it was over, or might be over, and people crowded into the room to watch. No sterilization? Who cares? I was alive. They pumped saline into me so fast that my arm swelled and I had to go to the bathroom. For the first time, I realized how my life had changed. There is, after all, no simple dichotomy: intact and alive versus torn and dead.

They sent some of the people out and stuck a bedpan under the sheet. With one wrist locked to the I.V. and the other paralyzed, I couldn't wipe. Warrior to newborn babe in an hour. Someone brought me my sandals. They were dirty and covered with dried blood, like small dead animals.

I had expected the hyena bite in Africa, not in Israel. I had expected the price I paid for Africa to be high. The need that had driven me since I was eight years old had made me willing to risk anything, even death, to be in Africa watching animals. Anyone who works with animals expects to get hurt. You are a guest in their life—any intrusion is a threat to them. It is their separateness that makes them worthy of respect.

After the hospital, I went back to America for physical therapy and treatment of the parasites, which burned a path in my stomach for the next six months. Before I left, people from the reserve asked me to stand near Efa's cage. They wanted to know if his animosity was specific to me. He looked at me, again with those friendly blank eyes, and then rose up against the wire with a crash so loud that I thought he was breaking through. For one second, I saw his face coming toward me, mouth open, and I hopped back. They told me they were going to send him to a zoo where the keepers wouldn't have to go into the cage, but I heard later that a veterinarian came and put Efa to sleep. ("Forever asleep," the workers said.) Shlomi was there.

Back in America, too ill for school, I read about animals on my own. Then I went to graduate school, but I found the statistical and analytical approach to animals too reductive. So I gave it up. But I couldn't not return to Africa. Five years after the hyena bite, I went back. Without a joy, or any scientific purpose, I backpacked between Tanzania and Kenya, seeing the savanna in short bursts of safaris and hired cars and *matatu* buses.

Africa smells of nothing but dust, and that dust lingers with sweetness in the nose and like powder on the skin. It comes from everywhere, even the greenest grass, and it fingers into clothing like minuscule parasites. Shirts blossom red or brown, sometimes yellow, with dust; when clapped they puff into a cloud of color, like a dandelion blown adrift. With the wind in my face and the dust drifting over me, I have never felt so clean.

In spite of its color, the dust is translucent. African sunsets are famous. People say the dust rises into the atmosphere and reflects the sun's light. I think the particles rise, with their own separate colors, and the sun shines through them, heat through translucent splendor.

I believe that, even if you pass through quickly, there are landscapes that are particularly yours. Thousands of explorers returned home with shards of Africa embedded in their lungs. Breathe deeply enough, and you become part of that world, filled to the brim and clogged with its clays and dust.

In the Kenyan highlands, the nights are always cool, and there are so many stars that a book can be read by their light if there's no moon. Eyes sparkle in the light. At night, they reflect it back in small round circles. Snakes are tiny pinpricks in the grass, hares in a field sparkle like fireflies as they turn their heads to look at the car. Mice eyes are like snakes', but closer together. As we drive by, antelope flash one eye and then the other at us, white orbs of light in gray shadows. If you sit in the open mouth of your tent before the fire, the eyes of the hyenas shine green and gold, low down to the ground, and they look at you. People in Africa usually put their garbage pits too close to their camps, so we ate our dinner next to baboons screaming over a cabbage leaf, or hyenas snarling over bones. I hadn't told anyone here about the hyena bite. I liked to watch the hyenas rushing in and out of the pit, squabbling and rolling over each other, but still very friendly, trotting away flank to flank and stopping to look at me. An animal trainer told me that once you've been bitten badly enough to limp, even if the limp is almost imperceptible the animals will know, and from then on you are prey, not master.

Driving away from my tent camp in Africa, I came upon a den of hyenas. The first one stood like a statue on the great pan of rock, the kind I loved to play on as a child, full of towers and caves and little ledges, with the rock smooth underfoot. It was a silvery animal, very serious, like a young sentinel, and it wasn't until we saw the mother that we realized it was a hyena. Three generations lived in the den. Babies rolled in balls under the mother's feet and she pricked her ears at us and stepped clear, to watch with the sentinel. Water pooled in a curve before her, rocking with flashes of light in the wind, decadent somehow against the dried grasses. We moved and she made a noise and they disappeared—the babies first, then the mother, then another adult, who had been sleeping in the grass. The sentinel walked to the shaded side of the rock and stared at us from there.

I had almost died, eaten alive, and I was glad to be alive. The scars had healed. Three long dents ran around the arm and the leg, blurred with spider tracks of canine punctures. The one war wound, the bump that grew where I hit the hyena, still hurt, but I was back in Africa.

Joanna Greenfield is a graduate of the Columbia Creative Writing Program. This story is excerpted from her forthcoming book, In the Lion's Eye.

SEBASTIAN JUNGER

ESCAPE FROM KASHMIR

There are two ways out—escape or death.

THE GUERRILLAS APPEARED ON THE RIDGELINE SHORTLY
before dusk and walked down the bare hillside into the
Americans' camp without bothering to unsling their guns.
They were lean and dark and had everything they needed on
their persons: horse blankets over their shoulders, ammunition
belts across their chests, old tennis shoes on their feet. Most of
them were very young, but one was at least 30 and hard-
looking around the eyes—"a killer," as one witness said. Jane
Schelly, a schoolteacher from Spokane, Washington, watched
them come. "There were ten or twelve of them," she says, "and
they were dressed to move. They didn't point their guns or
anything, they just told us to sit down. Our guides told us they
were looking for Israelis." Schelly and her husband, Donald
Hutchings, were experienced trekkers in their early forties
who took a month every summer to travel somewhere in the
world—the Tatra mountains in Slovakia, the Annapurna
Massif, Bolivia. Hutchings, a neuropsychologist, was a skilled
technical climber who had led expeditions in Alaska and the

188

Cascade range. He knew about altitude sickness, he knew about ropes, and he was completely at ease on rock and in snow. The couple had considered climbing farther east, in Nepal, but had set their sights instead on the Zanskar Mountains in the Indian states of Jammu and Kashmir. For centuries, British colonists and Indian royalty had traveled to the region to escape the summer heat, and over the past twenty years it had become a mecca for Western trekkers who didn't want to test themselves in the higher areas of the Himalayas. It is a staggeringly beautiful land of pine forests and glaciers and—since an Indian-government massacre of 30 or 40 protesters in its capital, Srinagar, in 1990—simmering civil war.

The conflict had decimated tourism, but by 1995 Indian officials in Delhi had begun reassuring Westerners that the high country and parts of Srinagar were safe, so in June of that year, Schelly and Hutchings headed up there with only the vaguest misgivings. Even the State Department, which issues warnings about dangerous places (and had Kashmir on the list at the time), will admit that Americans visiting such places are far more likely to die in a car accident than as a result of a terrorist attack. Moreover, a few years earlier, Schelly and Hutchings had decided against going to Machu Picchu, in Peru, because of terrorist activity—but they later met dozens of travelers who had gone there without any trouble. There was no reason to think Kashmir would be any different. The couple hired two native guides and two ponymen (and their horses) and trekked up into the Zanskar Mountains. After ten days, on July 4, they were camped in the Lidder Valley, at 8,000 feet.

The militants, heads wrapped in scarves, secured Schelly and Hutchings's camp, rounded up a Japanese man and a pair of Swiss women who were camped nearby, and then left all of them under guard while the rest of the band hiked farther up the Lidder. Two kilometers away was a large meadow— the "Yellowstone" of Kashmir, as Schelly put it—that was guaranteed to yield a bonanza of Western trekkers. Sure enough the militants returned to the lower camp two hours later with a 42-year-old American named John Childs, his native guide, and two Englishmen, Keith Mangan and Paul Wells. Childs, separated with two daughters, was traveling without his family.

The leader of the militant group, Schelly would learn later, was Abdul Hamid Turki, a seasoned guerrilla who had fought the Russians in Afghanistan and was now a field commander for a Pakistan-based separatist group called Harkat-ul Ansar. He ordered all the hostages to sit down at the entrance to one tent. Childs, nervous, looked down at the ground, trying to avoid eye contact with anyone. He was already convinced that the guerrillas were going to kill him, and he was look-ing for a chance to escape. A cold rain started to fall, and Turki asked for all their passports. The documents were col-lected, the militants attempted to read the papers upside down, and then they declared that all the Western men would have to come with them to talk to their senior commander. That was a three-hour walk away, in the village of Aru; they would be detained overnight and released in the morning, said the militants. Schelly was to walk to the upper camp with one of her guides.

"After I left, the men (were told) to lie down and pull their jackets over their heads, and that if they looked up, they'd be shot," says Schelly, who learned these details later from Childs's guide. "The (kidnappers) went through the tents, stealing stuff. And then they took the guys off. By ten o'clock I'd gone to the upper camp and come back down (with the wife and the girlfriend of the Englishmen), and we all piled into one tent because we were still scared. I was awake at four the next morning, and I just kept looking down the trail thinking they'd be coming anytime now. It was six-thirty, and then seven, and then nine—that's when the knot in my stomach started."

Finally, Childs's guide returned. He had a note with him that he had been instructed to give to "the American woman." It said "For the American Government only," and it was a list of 21 people the militants wanted released from Indian prisons. The top three were Harkat-ul Ansar.

The kidnapped men walked most of the night. They weren't being taken to the "senior commander"—he didn't exist—they were just being led deep into the mountains. The deception reminded John Childs of the tactics the Nazis used to cajole people into the gas chambers, and made him all the more determined to escape. The men walked single file through dark forests of pines and then up past the tree line into the great alpine expanses of the Zanskar Range. It was wild, ungovernable country the Indian Army didn't even attempt to control, and Childs believed that there was no way anyone was going to save, or even find them. They were on their own.

"I was convinced they were going to shoot us, and so as soon as I heard someone chamber a round into one of those weapons, I was going to take off into the woods," says Childs. "At one point we crossed a stream—it was snow-melt season and the mountain streams were absolutely raging torrents—and I considered jumping in and flushing down to the bottom, but it would have been instant death."

Childs kept his eyes and ears open and waited. A chemical engineer for an explosives company, he was used to solving problems. This was just another one: how to escape from sixteen men with machine guns. There were personalities, quirks, rifts among his captors he was sure he could exploit. He started lagging while he walked, seeing if he could stretch the line out a little bit; he started taking mental notes of the terrain; he started probing for weaknesses in the group. "Escape is a mental thing," he says. "Ninety percent is getting yourself prepared to take advantage of an opportunity or create an opportunity. I knew that, given enough time, I'd get away."

Late that night they came upon a family of nomads at a cluster of three log huts. The head of the family stepped out into the darkness to give Turki a hug, then the militants and hostages all squeezed into the huts and fell into an exhausted sleep. A few hours later, as soon as it was light, Childs sat up and peered through a chink in the wall—alpine barrens and rock, nothing more. Escaping through the forest would have been at least a possibility, but crossing a mile of open meadow would be suicide. He'd be cut down by gunfire in the first twenty steps.

After the hostages were given a quick meal of *chapatis*, rice, and a local yogurt dish called *lassi*, they lined up on the trail and started walking again. This would become their routine in the next several days: up at dawn, hike all day, sleep in nomads' huts at night. The militants bought—or took—whatever food they wanted from the nomads and never had to carry more than a blanket and their guns. They told the hostages that they had been trained in Pakistan, near the town of Gilgit, and had come across the border on foot. They'd been in the mountains for months together and were prepared to die for their cause. When Donald Hutchings tried to engage them in talk about their families, one of the militants just patted his gun and said, "This is my family."

India and Pakistan have fought three wars over Kashmir, and Turki's band was the latest permutation in the 50-year conflict. Harkat-ul Ansar (HUA) is committed to overthrowing Indian (thus, Hindu) rule in Kashmir and absorbing the state into the Islamic Republic of Pakistan. Since 1990, the "militancy," as the rebel movement is known, has been waging a sporadic guerrilla campaign against Indian authority with automatic rifles, hand grenades, and other small arms acquired from Pakistan. Turki called the group he commanded Al Faran, a reference to a mountain in Saudi Arabia near where the Islamic prophet, Mohammed, was born. The first time anyone had ever heard of Al Faran was on July 4, 1995, when they came walking down out of the mountains into Schelly and Hutchings's camp.

The militants led the hostages by day through snowfields and high passes, traveling north. Childs's impression was that they were simply marking time in the high country, avoiding the pony trails in the valleys where they might run into Indian soldiers. As the day wore on, the militants became less worried about being caught, and their vigilance slackened a bit. Turki remained dour and implacable, but the younger ones warmed up to the hostages. They called Don Hutchings *"cha-cha,"* meaning "uncle," and practiced their high-school English whenever they could. Far from being threatening or abusive, they did anything they could to keep the hostages healthy— bandaging their blisters, giving them the best food, making sure they were warm enough at night. Not only did the hostages represent possible freedom for 21 separatists rotting in Indian jails, but they were also the only protection Al Faran had from the Indian Military. They were a commodity, and they were treated as such.

"It was like a Boy Scout troop with AK-47s," says Childs. "The youngest militant was sixteen or so, a Kashmiri kid who'd been recruited to the cause. He hadn't been issued a weapon yet because he hadn't been through training; he was educated and bright, and his English was good. Turki was dead serious, though, and I didn't let any kind of camaraderie fool me. If he told them to kill someone, these guys wouldn't hesitate for a second, they were too well trained."

By the second day, Childs had noticed an interesting—and horrifying—dynamic. The hostages, all desperately scared, turned to one another for comfort and support. They talked about their families, their homes, and their fears. But they had also been thrown into a ruthless kind of competition. They knew that if the militants were forced to prove their intent, they would shoot one of the hostages. That much was clear—but who would it be? An American? A Brit? A weak hiker? A brave man? A coward?

Since the hostages didn't know the answer, they did the next best thing: they tried to make as little an impression on their captors as possible. They didn't complain, they didn't cry, they didn't do *anything* that might cause them to be noticed. They blended in as completely as possible and hoped that, if the time came to kill people, they'd be invisible to the man with the gun.

Childs quickly realized that he was losing the competition to not stand out.

"I was in really rough shape—my boots weren't broken in, and I'd gotten blisters on my heels before I was captured," he says. "The days went on and the skin was rubbed literally to the bone. By the fourth day I was having trouble keeping up." Childs believed that he and Hutchings, the U.S. citizens, were the most valuable hostages, "but you could burn one American and still have one left over."

From time to time the hostages discussed the possibility of trying to escape en masse, but the consensus was that they would be putting themselves at terrible risk. Keith Mangan, in particular, was convinced that the situation would resolve itself peacefully—"Look, these things usually end without any tragedies," he told the others at one point. Childs wasn't so sure. Not only did he believe that Turki would kill them without a second thought, he felt singled out for the execution. Adding to his misery, he had come down with a devastating case of dysentery. By the end of the first day he was stepping off the trail every hour or so to drop his pants. A militant always gave him a Lomotil pill and followed him, so after a while Childs started relieving himself in the middle of the trail, in front of everyone. Soon they were waving him away in disgust, and he thought, *This is going to be useful. I don't know how, but it will.*

The next time a militant put a pill in his mouth, Childs didn't swallow. He waited until the man looked the other way, then he spit the medicine out onto the ground.

It took six hours for Jane Schelly to hike out to Pahalgam, a jumping-off point for people heading into Kashmir's high country. The entire trekking population of the valley—some 60 or 70 people—was by the end walking out with her, and when they arrived at the Pahalgam police station, utter pandemonium broke out. Schelly informed an officer that her husband had been abducted, and she was taken into a back room and interrogated. "I had to decide whether to give them the note or not," she says, "because it said 'For the American Government only.' I looked over at my guide, and he nodded and I thought, If they're going to help, let's get this show on the road. So I gave it to them, they copied down the names, and then I went to the U.N. post. That was at 8 p.m.; they called the (American) embassy, and things were kicked into motion."

The United Nations has had a presence in Kashmir since 1949, after Britain formally relinquished control of its Indian colony and the subcontinent sank into ethnic chaos. The

British government's last administrative act was to draw a border between the Muslim majority in Pakistan and the Hindu majority in India, and that sent six million people fleeing in one direction or the other. Hindu mobs attacked trains packed with Muslims trying to cross into Pakistan, and Muslims did the same thing to Hindus going in the other direction. Trains plowed across the border between Amritsar and Lahore with blood literally dripping from their doors.

While half a million people were being slaughtered, the semi-independent state of Kashmir was trying to decide whether to incorporate itself into India or into Pakistan. Kashmir was primarily Muslim, but it was ruled by a Hindu maharajah, and that inspired an army of Pakistani bandits to cross the border and try to take Srinagar in a lightning raid. They were slowed by their taste for pillage, however, which allowed Indian troops to rush into the area and defend the city. War broke out between India and Pakistan, and the nascent U.N. was finally forced to divide Kashmir and demilitarize the border. Fighting continued to flare up for the next 40 years, and a surge in Pakistani-backed guerrilla activity again brought the two nations to the brink of war in 1990. This time the stakes were higher, though: India had hundreds of thousands of troops in Kashmir, and both nations reportedly had the capacity to deliver nuclear weapons. Diplomats defused that crisis, but American envoys in Delhi still considered Kashmir to be the world's most likely flash point for a nuclear war.

By the time Jane Schelly and Donald Hutchings showed up in Srinagar, as many as 30,000 locals had been killed since '92, and Kashmir had been turned into a virtual police state. The brutal tactics employed by the Indian Army had brought a certain amount of stability to the area—it was alleged, for example, that security forces machine-gunned every member

of a household that had any association with the militants—
but the war continued to rumble on in the hills. In 1994, two
Brits had been kidnapped by militants and held in exchange
for twenty or so HUA guerrillas serving time in Indian jails.
The Indian government had refused to bargain, and after seventeen days the militants relented and let the hostages go.
They even gave their prisoners locally made wall clocks as
souvenirs of the adventure.

Schelly spent her first night out of the mountains at the
U.N. post, and the next day she moved to a secure Indian-
government compound. High-level British, German, and
American embassy officials flew up on the afternoon flight
from Delhi, and by July 7 a formidable diplomatic machine
was in gear. Terrorism experts—unnamed in the press—were
flown in from London, Bonn, and Washington, D.C.
Negotiation and hostage-release specialists were made available to the Indian authorities. Surveillance satellites reportedly tried to locate the militants on the ground, and the
Delta Force, a branch of the U.S. Special Forces, was in the
area being readied for possible deployment. Indian security
forces began working their informants in the separatist
movement, and Urdu-speaking agents started trying to maneuver between brutally simple parameters for negotiation:
no ransom and no prisoner exchanges. Any concession to the
guerrillas' demands, it was feared, would only encourage
more kidnappings.

Still, there was some hope that Al Faran could be eased toward compromise. Communication was carried out by notes
sent along an impenetrable network of local journalists, militants, and nomadic hill people. Hamstrung, on the one hand,
by an Indian government that was not entirely displeased
with a situation that made Pakistan look bad and, on the
other, by a U.S. policy that forbade concessions to terrorists,

negotiators found themselves with almost no "wiggle-room," as they say. The best they could do was relay messages to Al Faran that pointed out the immeasurable harm the kidnappings had done to the Kashmiri cause; the only way to regain credibility, said the negotiators, was to let the hostages go. To encourage this line of thought, the U.S. government left the negotiating to the Indians—whose country it was, after all—and started pulling strings elsewhere in the Islamic world. They persuaded a Saudi cleric to condemn the kidnappings as un-Islamic, and they tried to massage some of their contacts in Pakistan.

"Al Faran was clearly an HUA-affiliated group, and what we know about HUA is that it's not very hierarchical," says a U.S. government source who closely followed the incident. "It's not at all clear that Al Faran was even interested in communicating with (HUA) headquarters. If we'd had anything suggesting a tightly hierarchical organization, it would have been much easier to negotiate. And they had very poor, unsophisticated decision making. These were *not* people with a Plan B."

By the end of the third day, John Childs could barely walk, and the militants seemed to be heading deeper and deeper into the mountains. They were, in fact, just walking in circles, dodging Indian military. To keep himself from sinking into despair. Childs devoted every waking moment to planning his escape. He knew the militants' sole advantage was their incredible mobility; without that, it would be only a matter of time before they were discovered by an army patrol. Which meant that if any of the hostages escaped, the militants wouldn't be able to waste too much time searching; they'd have to look quickly and then get moving again.

"My first objective was to get fifty meters away from them," Childs says. "And then five hundred meters, and then five kilometers. I knew that every bit increased the area they had to search by the square of the distance. And I knew there was no way this guy Turki was going to scatter his crew all over creation looking for me. He couldn't afford to look for me for more than six hours, so if I could stay away from them for that long, my only problem would be not being seen by the nomads."

That meant hiding during the day and traveling at night, which strongly favored an escape after dark. And that was fortunate, because Childs had one ironclad reason for getting up over and over again during the night: dysentery was still raging through his insides. The militants always posted a sentry after dark, but the hostages weren't tied up when they slept, so the sight of Childs getting up to relieve himself was by now routine.

In contrast to Childs, the other hostages seemed to be doing fairly well. The two Brits, Wells, 24, and Mangan, 34, were depressed but physically strong, and Hutchings was fully in his element. When Mangan came down with altitude sickness, Hutchings had him pressure-breathing and rest-stepping as he walked; when the group got lost in a whiteout, he took charge and told them which way to go. At one point Wells muttered how he would like to grab one of the hand grenades and blow all the militants away, but Hutchings always personable and helpful—"it's a lot tougher to kill a smiling face," he said. Hutchings had years of psychological training; if anyone could manipulate the situation, he could.

It wasn't until the fourth day, as they were crossing yet another valley, that the militants made their first mistake: they visited a familiar place. It wasn't much, but it was all Childs had.

"We were in the valley that the pilgrims take to Amarnath Cave," Childs says. "And Don knew where we were; he'd been there before. He said, 'Okay, down the valley is Pahalgam and up the valley is the cave.'"

Childs thought about that for the rest of the day. He wasn't going to be able to keep up with the group for long, and Turki wouldn't hesitate to have him shot. Not only would that free up the group; it would also send a message to the authorities, who obviously hadn't given in to the militants yet. If he was going to escape, he'd have to do it soon.

"So, are we going to spend the night here?" Childs asked Turki that afternoon, as they were taking a break. He knew the answer, but he wanted to hear what Turki had to say. "No, too much danger," Turki replied, waving his arm down the valley—Indian military. *They wouldn't dare spend much time searching for someone*, in other words.

That night, the militants made camp along the east branch of the Lidder river, sleeping in a cluster of stone huts generally used by pilgrims on their way to Amarnath Cave. Childs, rolled up in a horse blanket, lay on the dirt floor of a hut and considered his possible avenue of escape. The camp was at the mouth of two huge valleys that fed into the valley leading to Pahalgam, and Childs's plan was to escape by climbing *up*, in the opposite direction of what the militants would expect. He'd hide in the snowfields before dawn, stay until dark, and then start down toward Pahalgam. It was a three-day walk, he figured; he had no food, no bedding, and the valley was filled with nomads who might report his location to the militants. It was, at best, a long shot, but it was better than the odds he had now.

And then, exhausted by four days of forced marches, Childs fell asleep.

"There had been other opportunities to escape, but of course you never know if it's the right time," says Childs "It's not a movie, where you know when it's going to end. You keep asking yourself, 'Is this the best time, or will there be a better time with less risk?' It took a huge effort to focus my thoughts and say, *'Okay, you've got to do this now. You've got to do it when you're tired and not feeling well.'"*

Childs woke up in the middle of the night. It was quiet except for the sound of people snoring and the crash of the river. The dysentery was roiling through his system, so he fumbled in the dark and grabbed his hiking boots—knocking over a metal grate in the process—and crept out of the hut. Ordinarily the sentry would greet him and escort him out of camp. But this time no one stirred—the sentry seemed to be asleep. Childs walked out of camp, relieved himself, and then stole back into bed, wondering what to do.

"You can be passive and not make a decision that may save your life," he says, "or you can accept death as a possibility. That was the crux of the whole thing."

Childs lay in bed for an hour, preparing himself, and then he got up again. He decided that if anyone stopped him, he'd just claim he was having another bout of dysentery. He thought about waking up the other hostages, but there didn't seem to be any way to do that quietly, the others also lacked his pretext for getting up. Childs stepped out of the hut and waited for someone to say something; silence. He edged out of the firelight into the darkness beyond the huts; more silence. There was always the possibility that someone was watching him surreptitiously—or even had a gun trained on him—but that was a chance he had to take. He stood motionless for a moment, frozen at the point of no return, and then he started to run.

"I thought I was in their cross hairs the whole time," he says. "It was like a dream where you run and run and you're not getting anywhere because your feet are bogging down. I kept expecting to hear a ruckus behind me, but I never saw any of them again."

Childs took off straight up a ridge between the two valleys. He was in his stocking feet, and all he had on was long underwear, Gore-Tex pants, a wool shirt, and a pair of pile pants wrapped around his head. He walked and ran as hard as he could until the ridge got too steep to climb without boots, and then he put them on and kept going. He knew the militants would wake up early for morning prayers, and he had to get as far away as possible before then. He hammered upward for the next three hours, and when dawn came he crept into a cleft in a rock, drew in a few stones to conceal himself, and settled down to wait. As it got lighter he noticed that anyone walking along the ridge would stumble right into him, so he violated his rule against traveling during the day and continued higher up. He was in the snow zone now, really rugged country; the next hiding spot he found seemed perfect, until it became apparent that he was resting on solid ice. He wound up moving to a small patch of moss on a hillside. There were glaciers and peaks all around him, and he was sure no one would follow him up that high; he was at least at 12,000 feet.

By midmorning a drizzling sleet had started to fall, and Childs endured that for a few hours—resting on the moss, dozing from time to time—before starting out for Pahalgam. He was almost down at the bottom of one of the side canyons when he heard a helicopter. The sound of the rotors faded in and out, then seemed to head straight toward him. Since he hadn't heard any aircraft in five days, his first thought was that there must have been a negotiated release of the hostages and now he was stranded in the high mountains with no food and no way to call for help.

"I stood there kind of dumbfounded," he says, "and I started waving my pants around over my head. The pilot circled and I could see there was a soldier in there; he had his gun pointed at me. I was a mess by that point—I hadn't bathed in five days and had mud smeared all over me and looked like a wild man of the mountains. The pilot landed on one skid, I ran up, and (a soldier) said, 'Are you German?' I said, 'No, I'm American. I just escaped from the militants.' He said, 'It's a miracle from God,' and hauled me on-board."

The militants, as Childs had thought, had searched down-valley when they realized he was gone. They didn't find him, but they stumbled across two other trekkers, Dirk Hasert of Germany and Hans Christian Ostro of Norway—they were subsequently reported missing and were, in fact, the people the helicopter crew had been searching for. Rebel sources in Srinagar say that Ostro was belligerent toward the militants from the start, telling them that what they were doing was cowardly and un-Islamic; they also claim he was armed with a knife and had tried to use it. That is impossible to verify, but suffice it to say that Ostro succeeded in sticking out in the group.

Childs was brought back to Srinagar in triumph and im-mediately debriefed in the presence of British and American embassy officials. It was the first of endless debriefings over the next several days—"I spent more time in captivity by the State Department than by the militants," he said later. Childs was then taken to a secure guest house, where he was intro-duced to Jane Schelly. For Schelly, the chance to talk to some-one who'd seen her husband only hours earlier was a relief beyond words.

"Do they have enough food and drinking water?" she wanted to know. "Do they have enough clothing? Do they know that the women are okay?"

Everything Childs had to say about the hostages was posi-tive—they'd suffered no abuse, and the situation seemed sim-ilar to the peacefully resolved kidnappings of a year earlier. The current hostage team—referred to as "G-4" because the governments of four Western countries were involved—had no reason to believe that this case would be different. While Indian security kept up a steady dialogue with Al Faran, the G-4 team continued to pressure Pakistan to intervene with HUA. (Pakistani officials were stubbornly claiming that the incident had been staged by India to make them look bad.) A rescue was deemed to be too risky; even Indian Army patrols were warned away from areas where the militants might be. Everyone, including the hostages, was worried that a surprise encounter could erupt into a firefight.

Childs flew back to Delhi two days after his escape, speaking to reporters at the airport despite the efforts of officials to bundle him into an embassy car. A few days later, he stepped off an airplane at Connecticut's Bradley Field, and news crews taped him sweeping his two young daughters up into his arms. He'd gone from the mountains of Kashmir to Hartford in the space of a week, and it rattled him. "Had circumstances been a little different, I'd be dead," he says. "You expect to live out your normal life span, but it could be over in a second. At the time, I thought I'd never see my kids again. Now every breath I take is something I didn't expect."

While Childs was facing the news cameras back home, Jane Schelly was still in Srinagar, working frantically for the release of her husband. "Please let Donald go," she sobbed at a press conference, holding on to Keith Mangan's wife, Julie. "In the name of God, please let our loved ones go." Al Faran responded by passing along a statement that said they had let Childs escape on purpose, but that they would resort to an "extreme step" if India didn't release the HUA rebels. They also sent a photograph of the five hostages sitting on pine boughs in a stone hut, their hands tied behind their backs, their eyes downcast. On an accompanying tape, Don Hutchings said, "Jane, I want you to know that I am okay. But

I do not know whether I will die today or tomorrow. I appeal to the American and Indian governments for help."

The G-4 team decided, for security's sake, to move Schelly, the German woman, and the two English women back to the British embassy's guest house in Delhi. Negotiations remained deadlocked, and one week later some very bad news came in: the militants had supposedly run into an Indian Army patrol near Pahalgam, and two hostages had been wounded in the ensuing gunfight. The Indian government denied that the encounter had taken place, so Al Faran released some photos showing Hutchings lying on the floor of a house with his abdomen wrapped in bloody bandages. There was no blood on his pants, though, and he seemed to be refusing to look into the camera—refusing, perhaps, to cooperate with the deception. The consensus at the U.S. embassy was that the photos had been staged, an opinion Schelly shared.

On an audiotape sent with the photos, Hans Christian Ostro asked the Indian government to give in to Al Faran's demands, pointing out that it was tourist officials in Delhi who had misled him into thinking Kashmir was safe. "I even went to the leader of the tourist office in Srinagar, and he gave me his card and said that if there was anything, I could call him," Ostro said at the end of the tape. "Well, Mr. Naseer, I'm calling you now."

Another week passed, and still there was no breakthrough in the negotiations. Britain's Special Air Squadron and Germany's elite counterterrorism force, the GS-9, had by now joined the U.S. Army's Delta Force in Kashmir, even though an Entebbe-type rescue operation was unlikely, the authorities had no idea where Al Faran was, and there were also delicate sovereignty issues to work out with India. The feeling among the G-4 negotiators was that, as with the previous kidnapping, Al Faran would eventually give in.

They didn't.

On August 14, 1995, "we were at the German ambassador's residence, having lunch with the other families," recalls Schelly. "And during the meal several embassy people were called out of the room, and then more people were called out, and I didn't think anything of it. The German ambassador was called out just prior to dessert. We were eating cherries jubilee, and the next time I looked over, his ice cream had melted all over the place. And then I began to wonder."

While the families retired to a sitting room for coffee, a group of embassy officials talked somberly in a corner. Eventually one of them came over and reported that the body of a Caucasian man had been found in the village of Seer, outside Srinagar, but they didn't know if he was one of the hostages.

In fact, they did know, but they weren't saying. Cars came to pick up the families, the Ostros' car arriving first. After they had pulled away, the German ambassador put his arm around Schelly and said, "It's not your husband." It was not until that moment that Jane Schelly finally accepted the possibility that she might never see her husband again.

The body was that of Hans Christian Ostro. The guerrillas had cut off his head, carved "Al Faran" in Urdu on his chest, and dumped his body by an irrigation ditch. His head was found 40 yards into the underbrush, and a note in his pocket warned that the other hostages would suffer the same fate if the HUA prisoners weren't released within 48 hours. The families of the remaining hostages were told that Ostro's chest had been carved after he was dead, that he had been "peaceful" when he died, and that he hadn't been killed in front of the other hostages—though how the officials could know that is unfathomable. However peaceful Ostro's death, though, he may have known it was coming. Medical examiners found a good-bye note hidden in his underwear.

The G-4 team—now down to G-3—responded by demanding proof that the other hostages still lived. The militants passed along a photograph of the four holding a dated newspaper and also arranged for a radio conversation between Donald Hutchings and the Indian authorities. At 10:45 on the morning of August 21, a negotiator raised the guerrillas on a military radio, and Hutchings was put on:

"Don Hutchings, this is 108. When you are ready please...tell me 'One, two, three, four, five.'"

"One, two, three, four, five."

"The first message is...from your families. Quote, 'We are all staying together in Delhi and we all send our love and prayers. We are helping each other. Be as strong as we are. Over.'"

"Okay, I have the message."

"Now, Don Hutchings, there (is) a set of questions for you. You'll have to provide me with the answers because I don't know them...Am I clear to you?"

"Yes."

"What are the names of your pets? I repeat, what are the names of your pets?"

"My pets' names are Bodie, B.O.D.I.E., and Homer."

Hutchings's existence was confirmed. The negotiator continued with personal questions for each of the other hostages and then signed off, telling Hutchings to "have faith in God and strength in yourself." Within days of the radio interview, Al Faran began renewing their threats to kill the hostages, and their tone was so antagonistic that members of G-3 privately admitted that they thought the odds of the hostages' surviving were only 50-50. September crawled by, and then October, and the winter snows started to come to Kashmir. Reports of frostbite and illness among the hostages began to drift in. And then, on December 4, the inevitable happened: Al Faran ran into the Indian Army.

The guerrillas were passing through the village of Mominabad early in the morning when a patrol of a dozen Indian soldiers spotted them from the marketplace and someone opened fire. According to Indian military officials, there were no hostages with them—they were presumably being held nearby—but that's impossible to confirm. The militants jumped a barbed-wire fence, splashed across a shallow stream, and then ran through a patch of scrub willow. They headed across a dry rice paddy, machine-gun fire hammering behind them, the villagers diving into their mud houses and slamming their doors shut. The militants made it across the paddy and took a stand farther upriver, near the small village of Dubrin, and the Indian patrol called for reinforcements. Soon dozens of troops were firing on the rebels, who held off the army for six hours until dark fell, when they left their dead and ran.

Turki was killed, along with four other Al Faranis. Three days after the gunfight, the British ambassador in Delhi received a phone call from a man claiming to be with Al Faran and offering new terms of release: $1.2 million in ransom and safe passage to Pakistan. "You know, you know, we have been treating (the hostages) as our guests for the last five months plus," he complained. "You can expect that we have spent lots of money." The ambassador demanded proof that the hostages were still alive, but the man never called again.

And that was it. From time to time, over the next few months, nomads would report seeing the hostages up in the mountains, but those reports came to be suspect when it was revealed that the nomads were making money both as paid police informants and as messengers and suppliers for the kidnappers. In April 1996, a captured HUA militant claimed that the hostages had been executed about a week after the fight at Dubrin, in retaliation for Turki's death, and that the bodies were buried in a village called Magam. The Indian Army scoured the woods and fields around Magam for weeks without finding anything.

"You want to be optimistic, your heart says be optimistic, but your mind says, 'Sucker, you've gotten your hopes up before,'" says Schelly. "We had a full moon right before Id-ul-Fitr (a feast day at the end of Ramadan), and a friend of Don's said, 'This is the last full moon that's going to pass before Don comes back.' I was so convinced they would release him for Id-ul-Fitr that I packed my bags and got my hair cut. At one point I had to pull the car over on the way home from work and throw up, I was so worked up."

Id-ul-Fitr came and went, as did the one-year anniversary of the kidnappings, without any word from Al Faran. Reports continued to trickle in from the nomads, but nothing could be confirmed. Schelly went back to Kashmir in the summer of 1996 to meet with HUA leaders, and she returned there a few months later to start up a reward program. Announcements in local newspapers, on local radio shows, and even on the backs of match-books offered money to anyone who would come forward with information. The U.S. government also offered a reward, and India followed suit.

"It's very difficult to say if the program will be successful," says Len Scensny of the State Department's South Asia bureau. "We haven't had verifiable contact with the hostages in over a year, and we have no current information of their well-being. It's been an ongoing subject of discussion with very senior officials in both India and Pakistan."

Meanwhile, John Childs has resumed his life in America—working, jogging, spending time with his daughters. People who know Childs have made joking references to Rambo, which bothers him, and some even ask why he didn't help the others escape. It's a question that still troubles him. "I rationalize it and say, 'I couldn't have done it any other way,' but without having done it another way I'll never know," he says. "I ask myself constantly, 'Should I have done anything different?' Sitting here in my office it's one thing, but when I actually made the decision to escape I was tired, I was injured, I was miserable, I was terrified. It revealed something about my character, and I'm not even sure if I'm proud of it or not."

And Jane's hopes are slowly waning. While promoting the reward program in the fall of 1996, she decided to visit the village of Seer, where Ostro's headless body had been found. She talked with the villagers through an interpreter and then walked along a dirt path by the irrigation ditch where, among the rice paddies, two women had spotted the body a year earlier. "It was so incongruous," says Schelly. "The village was on a little pass, and when I was there everyone was harvesting the rice. There (were) stacks of rice straw in the fields and mountain peaks in the distance. It was probably one of the most beautiful spots I've ever seen in my life."

If Don Hutchings is still alive, he's probably looking out at a scene very much like that one—iron-gray mountains, a scattering of mud huts, and a dozen villagers, cutting their way across the rice paddies at dusk. One of them, undoubtedly, knows Hutchings is there; one of them, undoubtedly, wonders if telling the army would put his family in jeopardy. He decides to say nothing. And Don Hutchings, peering out through a chink in the wall, watches night come sweeping up his valley one more time.

Sebastian Junger also contributed "Ditching at Sea" in Part One.

ROBERT K. WILCOX

FLYING BLIND

Sometimes only your training can save you.

SECOND LIEUTENANT KEITH BEAN, CALL SIGN "BEAMER,"
made the mistake of going to his radar too soon.

A twenty-three-year-old F-16 "Fighting Falcon" pilot at
Utah's Hill Air Force Base, he had just lifted off on a training
flight into a dark, moonless night of horrendous weather. His
instructor, "Moose" Mullard, was already in a climbing west-
erly turn two nautical miles ahead of him.

His first task was to follow.

He didn't want to mess up right at the start.

So, making his own climbing turn, only seconds into the
flight, he looked back inside the cockpit to check for Moose
on his radar screen, a glowing green rectangle between his
knees. Thus, he eliminated his main source of spatial orientation—sight of the outside.

"What I should be doing is looking at my instruments, flying the airplane by cross-checking all the gauges, and looking
back out," the future Air Force F-16 Fighter Weapons School
instructor recalled. "Radar trail," they called it.

But he was preoccupied with the radar.

Not that sight outside the cockpit that night would have made much difference.

It was winter at Hill, February 1983, and the storm they were banking into over the Great Salt Lake was a black, cloud-filled mountain of rain nearing snow. It billowed from an 800-foot floor to a 15,000-foot ceiling, and was probably 50 miles thick—an immense, rain-slashed rectangle with visibility of barely a few feet and no hint of the orienting horizon.

Beam's mistake in these first few seconds was about to chillingly introduce him to the most common cause of accidental flight death in the Air Force (and probably the Navy, too)—spatial disorientation, often called "vertigo"—and begin for him a night of contained terror and surrealism he'd never forget.

In fact, Hill had recently had two F-16 crashes from spatial disorientation, one resulting in the pilot's death. Both jets had gone into the Great Salt Lake, according to Scott Logan, a fellow student with Beam who also roomed with him. There had been so many such crashes, according to Logan, that a local newspaper cartoon showed F-16's clogging an effort to drain water from the lake with a pump.

But a new plane—as some of those in the lake were—was going to have its troubles, and so Beam, a confident pilot and former soccer star at the Air Force Academy, was not dwelling on other pilots' misfortunes.

His attention was focused solely on the green radar screen.

It wasn't more than twenty seconds into the flight that he found Moose. The instructor was also flying a Falcon—or Viper, as its pilots preferred to call the nimble little single-seater. Powered by a lone, potent Pratt and Whitney engine with afterburner, the Viper was the Air Force's newest fighter, although its relatively modest 25-mile-range radar was not one of its touted features.

In order to be nimble, the fighter had to give up some long-range capability.

Revolutionary, however, was its new "fly-by-wire" flight control system. Previous jets had used slower, harder-to-move hydraulics to transmit the pilot's will to the control surfaces. But the "Electric Jet," as the F-16 was sometimes called, used lightning fast electrical impulses, plus a computer, to quickly and precisely steer the plane.

If the pilot wasn't exactly correct in his movement of stick and rudder, the computer would compensate.

The light F-16, which also doubled as a bomber, was a maneuvering marvel. Just a slight amount of pressure or movement on the jet's small, side-mounted stick (another innovation) was all it took for the pilot to instantly send the plane into a nine-G turn, which was about the limit of any pilot's endurance. But precisely because of its smoothness, the jet gave no seat-of-the-pants indications of trouble.

Even the wind roaring by outside was barely audible.

Beam couldn't feel he was in danger.

"I was at about two thousand feet and supposed to be in a slight, thirty-degree turn to the right," he remembers. But having found Moose and glancing at his instruments, he was surprised to see that he was in a much harder turn, approximately sixty degrees. "I'm getting slow. My nose is pointed much higher than I wanted."

In fact, the bubble-canopied jet was rolling upward, and as a result slowing from 300 to 150 knots and in danger of departing from controlled flight, which, at 2,000 feet, left Beam little time or space in which to recover.

"We have a warning horn in the cockpit, so I think I would have heard it," he said, reacting to the possibility that he would have gone right on over and crashed into the ground or the lake (whichever was below him). "But you never know.

Things were happening pretty fast. I'd gone into the weather and gotten a little disoriented...My body (with no references from outside) was telling me we were still in the turn, but my eyes (on the instruments) were showing something else."

It took him a few seconds to react. "You're confused. You say, Hey. What's going on here?"

He checked a backup attitude direction indicator (ADI). It verified the main ADI, showing he was in a much steeper turn than he thought.

His slowing flight speed cinched it.

The jet was teetering on the brink of stall or worse. The delicate motion sensors in his ears were deceiving him. He knew he had to act fast.

He quickly added power, while at the same time dipping a wing lower, putting the plane in a suddenly steeper turn. This dropped the nose quickly, slicing it downward, enabling the wings to catch air and start the jet flying again, albeit in the wrong direction—toward the ground.

But the quick dive increased airspeed and he was able to pull the nose back up. In a matter of seconds he was back on course, following Moose.

It had been a close call.

"Once it's over it makes your heart pound a little," he says. "But it could have been worse. I'd rather have my nose pointed up and getting slow than all of a sudden popping out of the weather at eight hundred feet and seeing the ground rushing up."

He settled down.

He didn't know it, but that was only the beginning.

He was now three and half miles in trail and climbing, which was something the F-16 did very well. Its thrust-to-weight ratio, or ability to accelerate while going up against gravity, was as good as or better than the ratio of any other jet in the world at that time. He felt better with Moose on the radar and he was watching his instruments carefully.

Since starting flight training a year and a half before, Beam, a bachelor, sharing a condominium with Logan and Mike Loida, another Viper student, had been briefed adequately on the possibility of vertigo and disorientation. The solution, his instructors had always emphasized, was trust your instruments.

Still, many students, having just been through what he had, would have alerted their instructor. But Beam was very competitive, about to graduate from the RTU (Replacement Training Unit) and be assigned to his first operational squadron. He didn't want to jeopardize that—not that alerting would have hurt his standing. It was just the principle. He'd distinguished himself by even getting picked to train for the Falcon, which was few in number at that time and given to only the best basic flight students. He was now getting known as a "natural," which was ironic for a guy who'd "puked (his) guts out" on his first basic training flight and then taken half the course to begin to feel comfortable.

But he felt he was now in control of his disorientation. This was his first night flight alone in the F-16 cockpit. He'd gut it out.

At about 15,000 feet they broke out of the weather into a black, moonless void; first Moose, then Beam. "Darker than crap," he remembers. Only a few stars and the lights of Moose's jet were visible; blue on the right wing tip and fuselage, red on the left.

It was like flying in outer space—no way to tell where the ground or horizon was, just pinholes of light twinkling in the void.

Moose started a gentle turn, the lights of his plane moving eerily in Beam's vision.

They were going to get gas.

Perhaps 50 miles away, a four-engine KC-135 jet tanker streaked toward them unseen. It was above them at approximately 20,000 feet, on the downward leg of a huge, race-track-like orbit, which the two Vipers would enter for their rendezvous after the tanker had turned in front of them and started its return.

They'd approach the tanker from behind.

Tanking was one of two major tasks in the training flight: bombing, which they would do next, was the other. Moose was in contact with the tanker as he started his slow, climbing turn toward it, dipping his wings slightly, about thirty degrees.

As they'd briefed earlier, Beam now closed the distance between his and Moose's jet by cutting across Moose's soft arc to join him close abreast and a little below. The two jets then continued the turn in unison. Beam tucked under Moose, keeping good visual on his leader, concentrating on his colored lights in order to maintain their very slim separation; Moose giving all his attention to the coming rendezvous, which would be especially dangerous in the moonless night.

In the fleeting seconds as their duet continued, Beam felt the turn getting steeper. Soon he believed it was a full ninety degrees, which was exceptionally tight, perhaps putting their wings perpendicular to the horizon, had they been able to see the horizon. But he didn't dare take his eyes off Moose. The two jets were dangerously close and he didn't want a recurrence of what had happened when he'd looked inside his cockpit before.

"I wasn't sure what he was doing," he says about his leader. "All I could see was his wing. I was just hanging on for dear life." And since Beam hadn't mentioned his earlier vertigo, Moose wasn't radioing that they were, in fact—contrary to what Beam was now feeling—still in the gentle, thirty-degree turn. "I'm getting the 'leans' real bad, but I think that's just because we're in this severe turn."

As had happened earlier, the tiny chambers in Beam's inner ear, deprived of other input, such as vision, were deceived again—but this time in an opposite way. Where before he hadn't realized he was in a curling climb, now the fluids, which jostled hairlike nerve endings to give him a sense of balance and direction, were tricked by the smoothness of Moose's gentle turn and were sending Beam's brain signals falsely indicating he was in a hard right turn.

He reacted accordingly.

"If I'm in a ninety-degree turn," he says, "then I'm going to have to be rolled up under (Moose) pretty tight." In effect, he moved a little closer to Moose, who was still not watching him, increasing the danger of their proximity.

"I think I'm looking up at him over my left canopy rail," he remembers. "The closer I get to him, the harder it is to see him as the turn gets steeper."

At least that's the way it appeared to Beam.

In reality, he wasn't below Moose—he was above him. When he thought he was moving up to Moose, he was actually moving down.

In the near-mystical black void, he'd totally lost his sense of up and down, just as two objects revolving around each other might do in outer space. There was nothing with which to judge his relative position. His only visual reference was Moose's blue lighted wing tip, to which he had welded himself without cognizance of the horizon or anything else.

In addition, reaching the point in the turn that put them in a straight course to the tanker, Moose, aware of the disorientation dangers of such a night, had gently leveled his wings back to the horizon, thus ceasing the turn, which was why Beam was finding it harder to see him. By leveling, Moose had changed the positional relationship between the two jets. Beam was having to look harder over his cockpit to keep his instructor in view and in proper alignment. But he did it, unknowingly leveling his own jet in the process and maintaining the precarious slight hover, leans and all.

Luckily, they finally sighted the lights of the tanker, which alerted Beam that something was wrong. Because of the radio communication, Beam knew they were climbing to get gas. But the tiny lights coming toward him in the distance seemed below him—at least that was the way he was perceiving them.

"The tanker's saying he's at twenty thousand and we're to come in at eighteen," he remembers. "That's when I thought, Whoa, something's messed up. How can he be two thousand feet above us when I'm looking down towards the ground at him?"

The realization was startling. He looked at his instruments. In addition to showing that the ground was actually in the opposite direction, they indicated that he and Moose had straightened out into level flight, although he was slightly above Moose. "I thought, Oh man, I'm screwed up again."

It was a scary feeling. In effect, he'd been flying blind, unaware of where he really was, not in control of where he was going. Thinking he was below Moose and turning, he now realized he was above and flying straight and level. Worse, he had to maintain that level flight path despite the contrary turning feelings his inner ears were still giving him.

"It was so hard," he remembers. "You keep glancing at the gauges, saying, 'We're not in this turn (that he kept feeling he was in). We're straight and level. We're straight and level.' It's the hardest thing to make yourself do...You want to do one thing because of the seat-of-the-pants feeling...(but) you force yourself to do the correct thing because of the facts."

He still wanted to turn, curl up "under" Moose, which, in

reality, would have forced the two planes dangerously closer. But "you say to yourself, 'Get your ass down. Get your ass down....' You've got to fight it or it'll end up killing you."

Again, he didn't tell Moose. "I probably should have, because he'd mentioned in the brief that something like this could happen. You can fly on auto pilot, get away, and watch your gauges until you're all right. But I thought I'd just gut it out and (the disorientation) would go away."

He was partially right.

The tanker turned in front of them and he fought the urges, watching his gauges, staying straight and level. They made their way up behind the large, four-engine tanker, and Moose positioned his Viper beneath its giant tail.

An operator looking out a window extended a long boom to a small, lighted receptacle on the F–16's fuselage. Meanwhile, Beam, still struggling, moved up to a position a little above and perhaps ten yards off the tanker's dark right wing tip to await his turn.

"Once I got on his wing, the leans started going away. I'm feeling better. Up feels like up...But it was still really dark and the tanker had this light...A nacelle light, I believe, somewhere over the wings on its fuselage...It was really bright. It was blinding me."

He tried a few different positions, but the light was always in his face. "It was bugging me. I couldn't see anything."

He decided to maneuver the tanker's wing between him and the light, hoping that would give him some perspective. He flew forward and down a little bit and finally thought he was okay until the tanker's eight-foot-wide wing tip suddenly stabbed at him out of the dark.

"It was a big chunk of metal, not more than a foot from my canopy. I wasn't supposed to be that close. It kind of scared me and I obviously moved away."

His disorientation had eased, but now he was blind with or without the light. "I had no depth perception. I had to do something."

Moose had briefed him on a procedure: Ask the tanker to turn down the nacelle light and turn on its dimmer landing lights, located where the wing met the fuselage. When they complied, everything cleared up. He could finally see the wing and where he properly should have been positioned.

That's nice, he remembers feeling.

He waited his turn and then got his own gas.

It took five minutes to fill his tanks. They'd been in the air approximately half an hour.

But now, in order to take their practice bombing runs, they had to go back through the bad weather.

He was not looking forward to it.

They went into close "fingertip" formation—their wing tips barely three feet apart—Moose leading, and descended into the weather. The range, called "Eagle," was about thirty miles away. They were to drop to the storm's bottom, come out underneath it, and commence some low-level bombing passes.

Back in the soup, Beam started getting the leans again.

The weather was moving in a direction opposite to their course. They broke out of it at about 2,000 feet, 15 miles from the range.

"Once we got past the squall line," he remembers, "there were like a bizillion stars, but no moon and no horizon." The range had lights on it but they just blended in. "You couldn't tell where the ground was. It was like a black hole. I just had this sensation I was flying upside down."

They'd moved farther apart by this time, but he could plainly see Moose's jet, about one hundred feet away.

"I felt like I was looking up through my canopy at the

ground, but I kept looking over at Moose, and he was flying the same attitude that I was. If I was messed up, so was he."

He, of course, also checked his instruments. They showed he was straight and level.

"It was just the weirdest, strangest feeling," he remembers, "the worst I'd been all night."

He didn't like it, he said. He was scared. But that was to be expected. At least he understood what was happening this time.

"I know that the more I feel like this, the more I just have to concentrate on my instruments. They're what are going to keep me alive."

Unlike a few moments before, he was now back at 2,000 feet, a very short distance between him and a crash.

"You keep cross-checking your gauges," he says. "Nope, nope, nope. There are the stars and there is the ground. Am I climbing or diving? Is my altitude changing? No, altitude's staying the same. ADI says we're straight and level. His airplane is doing the same thing as mine so we've got to be straight and level."

He says he decided that if he didn't come out of it soon, he'd radio Moose and "go home."

But the focus on his instruments—perhaps the cross-checking with Moose's airplane—finally paid off. Half a minute before they arrived at the point where they were to split and begin separate runs, he began to feel more like he was rightside up.

"My body is starting to say it's getting better. It's getting better. We're not quite so upside down anymore. I'm just flying the instruments. I'm not looking outside."

By the time they were on their actual run he was back to normal.

But he knew how insidious the disorientation was.

As he had been briefed previously, he then took the lead on

the second run—a low-level route back through the bad weather with him showing Moose the way. Moose was characteristically silent.

The rest of the flight was uneventful.

When they got back, Beam finally told Moose about his disorientation. Moose wasn't happy. Beam should have told his instructor, he said. Vertigo is a dangerous affliction. Suppose it had occurred during combat? Then he told Beam something Beam wasn't expecting—he (Moose) had experienced disorientation when Beam had been the leader.

Robert K. Wilcox is the author of six books including Wings of Fury, *from which this story was excerpted. He writes for film and television and has worked as a stringer for* The New York Times. *He began his career as a police reporter for the* Miami News, *and during the Vietnam War served as an Air Force information officer. He lives in Los Angeles.*

BARBARA J. EUSER

DESCENT FROM MOUNT COMMUNISM

Some experiences are better forgotten.

FIVE CLIMBERS TRUDGED ACROSS THE 20,000 FOOT HIGH plateau dragging a long object wrapped in a nylon tent. With each step, they sank thigh-deep in the recent snow. Wrapped inside the tent was a sixth member of the climbing team. She had fallen into a coma two days earlier. The only way to get her off the mountain was to drag her along in a makeshift sled.

I remember the fall a couple of days earlier. In the morning, we had come across three members of a German climbing team that had been stranded on the side of Mt. Communism at about 22,000 feet. (At 24,500 feet, Mount Communism is the highest peak in the former Soviet Union.) The four members of our team who had made it as high as 23,800 feet were retreating. Three days before, an avalanche had swept away three members of another team camped above us. Our tent had collapsed in the accumulating snow, despite our repeated efforts to dig it out. The time allotted to us to reach the summit of Mt. Communism had run out. In the strictly controlled climbing environment, we had agreed to make our final summit attempt by a specific date. When the weather didn't cooperate, we were required to descend. Two members of an Austrian team had camped near us and turned back the same day we did. On the descent, we all spent one night at our previous campsite at 23,000 feet.

Descending in a white-out the next morning, we came across an abandoned-looking tent. The three Germans inside were in bad shape. We had heard them on our radio days earlier calling for assistance. But because of the storm, no one had been able to reach them. They were badly dehydrated and unable to walk steadily. As we helped them get ready to join us in the descent, we realized they had lost their fine motor skills. They were unable to put on their own crampons. They were letting their gloves blow away in the gusting wind. We buckled their crampons, dressed them in their hats and gloves, handed them their ice axes. Then we roped them together so they could descend in parallel with us. That was too much for them to accomplish. They couldn't walk together. One of them kept falling down and the other two were too weak to assist him. The two Austrians left our rope to climb down by themselves. We added the three unsteady Germans to our rope.

The blowing snow was so thick we could not see where we were heading. The climb up had not been extremely steep, just tediously uphill. However, as we headed down to the camp on the 20,000 foot plateau below us, we blindly veered off course, onto steeper and steeper terrain. I was the last person on the rope. My friend Jini was just ahead of me. All at once, the rope connecting us jerked tight and I was pulled off balance. Jini was already sliding down, flipping over into arrest position, jamming her ice axe into the snow. As soon as I started falling, I did the same. The full weight of my body and the heavy pack on my back were forcing my ice axe into the snow, willing it to hold us, willing us to stop sliding. Then I was plucked backwards off the snow, flying downward through the air, until I hit the snow, sliding down head first on my back, ice axe stilled clutched in my gloves.

The seven of us were in a snow slide—perhaps in falling we had fractured the fresh, unstable powder. I realized the snow and climbers were sliding down the mountain together, then all of a sudden I stopped moving. Like an anchor, the snow had caught me fast. All the others on the rope were arrested in sequence, like dolls on a long rubber band. It took a moment for me to realize I could still breathe. My face was up, covered with only a light layer of snow. I couldn't move, my arms pinned in the snow by the straps of my backpack. Gratefully, I sucked in air. After the initial relief, I began struggling to free my arms. Gradually, I worked my shoulders out of the pack straps and my arms followed to the surface. At that moment, the leader of our rope reached me. He told me all the others were safe, regrouping after our fall. One colleague had been suspended in the air over a small cliff when the rope jerked taut. With careful maneuvering the others had eased him down. Slowly, we assembled our gear and our selves. From where our fall ended, it was only an hour's hike down to our previous campsite on the 20,000 foot high plateau.

We reached the plateau, unroped and walked along together, chatting and joking in the aftermath of near disaster. Then I fell over. Momentarily, I had lost consciousness. Someone called "Hey, get up!" and dazedly, I did. When asked what had happened I couldn't say. I knew I hadn't tripped over my crampon or fallen for any obvious reason. Mystified, I walked on slowly. Putting up the tent that evening seemed like a terrible effort and I sat to the side, watching my climbing partners do the work. I had no excuse, I just couldn't make myself participate. After a dinner of freeze-dried stew, we crawled into our sleeping bags. It was days before someone pulled me out of mine.

Jini, my closest friend on the expedition, told me the next part of this story, about the days I can't remember.

The next morning after our fall, I didn't get out of bed in the morning, despite the exhortations of my partners. Finally, they realized I wasn't asleep, but unconscious. The four members of our team, plus two more who had descended from our 23,000 foot camp because one was experiencing symptoms of pulmonary edema, were at one end of a 20,000 foot high plateau, a prominent feature of Mt. Communism. It was six miles across the plateau to the other end, which was another day's climb along a rock ridge and down a steep slope to a camp at 16,000 feet. Then there was one more day's hike across a serrated glacier to a base camp at 13,000 feet.

My unconscious condition presented a serious problem to my partners. The day before we had been involved in a serious fall because we were trying to accommodate members of another climbing party who were not able to descend by themselves. With the descent to lower altitude and plenty of fluids, their condition had improved and they were able to continue on their own. However, now I was a serious liability to my partners. The doctor who was with us was only able to say that other than being unconscious, I was in apparently good condition. He couldn't conjecture about whether I was suffering brain damage in connection to being in a coma. However, the longer I stayed in a coma, the more likely brain damage would be.

During the series of storms that had buffeted the mountain while we were making our way toward the summit, several feet of snow had fallen on the plateau. It was beginning to consolidate, but breaking trail was an arduous task. Every footstep meant sinking to one's thighs. In planning for the expedition, we had carefully included backpackers' snowshoes in our gear, but when we initially arrived on the plateau, it was hard-packed glacier ice. There seemed no good reason to carry snowshoes on our backs all the way to the other end of the plateau just to carry them back again. It was a decision much regretted over the next couple of days.

My colleagues determined to drag me off the mountain. There is no alternative in a situation like that: a climbing team has to depend on its own ingenuity. They wrapped the tent around me like a colorful cocoon and took a photograph. Then they started dragging me through the hip-deep snow. It took two days to go six miles. No one was sure whether they were dragging a person or a vegetable. But they didn't consider abandoning their burden.

That night, I showed a sign of consciousness. Some event during the day had caused a disagreement and it continued in the tent after supper. I had been placed, still in my sleeping bag, between two of my partners in an attempt to keep me as warm as possible. The argument got more and more heated. My partners were yelling at each other. Suddenly, I sat up in my sleeping bag and shouted "Stop it now!" Then I slumped back down. I vaguely remember being irritated enough, even in my unconscious state, to want to make them stop.

Once they arrived with their package at the beginning of the plateau, they faced a bigger challenge. The rock ridge we had traversed to arrive at the plateau was narrow and exposed. There was no way to drag a body along it. They decided to put me in a backpack and carry me. They emptied my pack and cut holes in the bottom corners for my legs to stick out. Several days earlier, the strongest member of our team had gone all the way down to the base camp at 13,000 feet with another member who had shown signs of pulmonary edema. We were in touch with the base camp every day by radio.

Steve had been summoned back up to the plateau to help with my evacuation. Somehow my colleagues stuffed me into my backpack. My legs stuck out the holes of the backpack, but the painful position brought me to semi-consciousness. I have a vivid impression of Steve staggering under my essentially dead weight on his back. I was too heavy for him. He couldn't hope to negotiate the delicate ridge while barely able to maintain himself upright. I remember the view, looking over his shoulder down from the plateau onto blue and white plains below.

There was a team of Russian climbers about to begin their descent of the ridge. My team members appealed to them for help. Someone volunteered. Again I was hoisted onto a man's back. The backpack hurt my legs and I remember the impression of patterned mitten-backs. The design seemed to me like the totem pole designs of the Indians in the Pacific Northwest. Then as my savior carefully inched his way along the ridge, holding onto the rock pinnacles with his hands as we passed along the edge of the cliffs below, I had the impression that we were working our way around the perimeter of a stone cathedral. Those moments of semi-consciousness were brief and I'm not sure anyone remarked on them. But they are all I have of four days' time.

Jini told me that the next section of the descent also affected me, though I do not remember. The steep climb up the snow had been accomplished on fixed ropes traversing the slope. There was no way to drag me down, and there was no need for the person who had managed to carry me along the ridge to risk himself further. Wrapped in the tent once again, my colleagues lowered me on ropes to the base of the slope. As they belayed me down, I began to travel faster and faster. Finally, I sat up and screamed. Amazed, my belayers stopped me and resumed at a slower pace. On the fourth day, my climbing partners faced a glacier melted into icy points. There was no way to drag me across the uneven surface. A stretcher was brought from the base camp and my colleagues and other volunteers took turns negotiating the difficult terrain without dumping me.

That night I dreamt I had malaria. I thought I was sweating in my sleeping bag. It was wet and sticky. I was beginning to come to and I was peeing for the first time in days.

The next day, at the 13,000 foot base camp, I was examined by all the medical personnel at the camp. Discussions went on at length. People crowded around the cot where I was lying. I could see and hear them, but I couldn't move. Someone pinned a brass bear to the collar of my shirt. From the discussion in Russian, which I do not speak, I got the impression that there was some special connection between us. Perhaps he was the person who carried me across the rock ridge.

I was taken by helicopter directly to the city of Osh, bypassing the helicopter ride to the base camp at 11,000 feet and the day-long bus ride between there and Osh. I was put in the hospital. Still unable to move, I watched and listened to the nurses discussing me in sympathetic tones. They fingered my long hair and talked about whether it was so matted it should just be cut off. Instead, a nurse on night duty decided to try to untangle it. She sat patiently beside me for hours, combing the knots out of my hair. The doctor on our climbing team insisted that I not receive any medical treatment at the hospital in Osh. The hospital facilities made me think of something from a 1930s movie. The nursing care was excellent, however, and I regained a bit of muscular control. After a couple of days, I stood and took a few unsteady steps. My climbing partners called me "Lurch." It was a great relief to be able to joke about it.

Despite various tests I took over the ensuing months, no

one could say what caused me to lapse into a coma. Perhaps my brain swelled after hitting against my skull when I acted as an anchor during our fall down the mountain. Or perhaps I suffered from high-altitude cerebral edema. I will never know for certain. For some reason, I recovered completely from four days of unconsciousness at 20,000 feet. I ask myself why. I am filled with a sense that I have a debt to repay. I cannot pay it directly, but such debts are rarely paid to whomever or whatever they are owed. The debt for the years which were added to my life through no effort of my own is enormous. It will take the rest of my life and all my creative efforts to compensate for the dispensation.

Barbara J. Euser is a former U.S. Foreign Service Officer who has served in China and France, accompanied by her husband and two daughters. Since the events on Mt. Communism, she has not participated in any mountaineering expeditions. She is teaching her daughters to rock-climb and has developed a passion for sailing. In her family's 34-foot sloop, she made her first transatlantic crossing with one sailing partner.

KEVIN KERTSCHER

SHAKING IN THE CONGO

Sudden illness makes a difficult situation desperate.

JAN AND DAVE AND I HIKED OUT TO THE POLICE CHECKPOINT on the eastern edge of town where all trucks had to stop for inspection. Everyone in the campground had been worrying so much about rushing to beat the heavy rains that we were all almost frantic. We figured we were the last or the second-to-last boatload of travelers who would make it through before three months of rains would almost completely shut down the muddy roads, turning a four day journey into four weeks or longer. I had read stories about trucks getting stuck so badly in deep mud holes that other drivers finally had to just fill dirt in around them and drive right over. Because the rains had already started a little, we figured there would be a last minute rush by transport trucks to get across, but that wasn't the case. We sat there all day without one truck leaving town.

I read a bit and when music from a nearby bar made it difficult to concentrate, I just sat back and watched the movements of the little town. Late in the afternoon I started feeling strange, and by six I could tell that I had a fever. When I went into my second cycle of chills, both Jan and Dave said, "You've got malaria." Jan had just gotten over malaria a couple of weeks before, and Dave's original traveling partner had been sent home from Ghana with it. Worse yet, there had been two tourists on the boat who were suffering from it and the mosquitoes had been pretty bad in Kisangani. I tried to remember the times that I had missed taking my daily antimalarial pills and how many times I had been bitten. I had tried to be careful, but obviously I had not been careful enough. About eight o'clock, I decided to take Fansidar, a malarial prophylaxis that at the time had no resistant strains. As advised by the doctor in Paris, I had been saving it only in case I got sick, using older medications as my day-to-day precaution.

As I was taking a whole week's dosage as instructed, a truck pulled up heading our way. Though I had already set up my tent and was ready to crawl in for the night, I gathered my stuff together and climbed up top with the others. We set out into the jungle in the dark, and almost immediately the road was so bumpy that I felt like my fillings were going to drop out. I was feverish and dizzy and when I tried to sleep, my head would get jolted from side to side. By the time I realized that a megadose of Fansidar might be kind of hard on my stomach, it was already too late.

Not far into the trip, the truck got a flat tire, and while they were fixing it, I walked a little ways down the dark road behind the truck, worried that I was going to get sick. My stomach heaved and shook a few times, but I kept myself from throwing up because I didn't want to lose the medicine I had just taken. When the truck broke down again a little while later I was feeling even worse and when I walked down the road, I had an attack of diarrhea. I climbed back up, feeling a little better and hoping that I could just settle down for the night, but I got attacks again and again and again, sharp cramps stabbing at my insides. Each time when I was just about to bang on the roof and say, "Stop the truck!" one of the tires would go out and they would stop in the middle of the dirt road and take it off and bang on it a bit while I ran out of sight.

By the fifth or sixth time, I was feeling dizzy and shaky and horribly wrung out. When I told Jan and Dave that I was getting worse, they worried, but they were sure that when the medication kicked in I'd start to feel better. Though it was only about midnight, I felt an intense need to sleep. If I could just lie down for a bit in a stationary place, I'd be all right, I thought. Everyone else on top of the truck was sleeping as best they could while we bounced slowly along between the trees.

When we stopped the next time, the tire was in bad shape, and when I went down the road to squat down, I could see the big truck in silhouette and the men pounding on the tire with their wrenches. I woke up to the sound of the horn honking, probably twenty minutes later, and I could hear the driver revving the engine. I was lying in the middle of the road with my pants halfway down and barely had the strength to pull them back up. It was so dark that I could hardly even see where the black trees gave way to the sky, and all I wanted to do was to find a spot to go to sleep. "Go on," I yelled, eyeing the ditch by the side of the road, thinking that I could crawl over there and sleep for a while and catch another truck in the morning. I didn't care about bugs or animals. I just didn't want to get run over. But then I woke up again to more incessant honking and I was still in the middle of the road and the truck was still fifty yards ahead, waiting for me.

I pulled myself up and got over to the truck. The driver said something to me angrily in Lingala and motioned for me to get back up top. My head was just up to the top rung when I passed out and fell ten feet to the road, landing with a big thump. I couldn't see straight when I opened my eyes, but I remember thinking, Ha! Now they'll know I'm sick. As my vision cleared a bit, I could see panic and concern in the driver's face. He touched the back of my head to see if I was bleeding, and I could feel the bump already forming. Some of the other passengers woke up Jan and Dave and I emphatically told them to leave me.

"I can't go any further in this truck," I said, "I just need to sleep. I'll be fine."

"Just come to the next village," Jan said after speaking with the driver. "He says it's not far."

With their help I got back up on the truck and when I woke up again, we were in a small village. Jan and Dave got our packs down while I ran behind a tree. I got my sleeping bag out and curled up in it with a sense of enormous relief. I was half surprised that the others had stayed with me. I was glad that they had, but I was especially surprised when I realized that the truck was staying too. "I'll be fine in a couple of hours," I said to Jan, "then we can get moving."

"No worries," he said, "just take it easy for a bit." They insisted that I drink some water, but it just kicked my stomach into action again. Each time I went behind a tree, I felt better for a little while. When they woke me up in the morning, it was still dark, but I had slept for nearly two hours straight and I was feeling much better. I told everyone I was good to go, but by the time we were loaded up, I had already had two more bouts. When I got a third attack and had to climb down, I told them to go on without me. They didn't want to leave me, but they didn't want to be stuck waiting for me to get better either. When the driver said he couldn't wait any longer, Dave announced that he was going to go on and I convinced Jan to go on with him.

I went back to sleep for another couple of hours in the clearing where we had stopped and then woke up when I heard another truck coming. By the time I got on my feet it had already gone by. But the sun was up and I felt so much better that I crossed the road to be in a good spot when the next one came. My stomach felt more empty than it ever had and my clothes and sleeping bag were covered with the red dirt of the village. Although I was a little dizzy, I felt great compared to the night before.

Up and down the dirt road on both sides were little grass and bamboo huts. A few were stirring here and there, but most of the village was still asleep. There were tall trees and dense jungle all around, but all the yards were cleared of vegetation and swept clean of everything but dirt, in the traditional fashion. I felt a little awkward just sitting out in their quiet neighborhood, but I didn't have much choice but to wait for another ride to come along.

I was planning to clean myself up a bit, but the effort of moving across the street made me exhausted again. I sat down on the ground, leaned against my pack and before I knew it, I was curled up on the ground, sleeping again. Dozing in and out, I heard the village waking up, and I could feel the sun clear the trees and get hotter on my face. I could hear children coming and going and I was thinking that there must be a schoolyard nearby when I felt a little hand poking at my shoulder. I woke up like Gulliver, surrounded by a crowd of wide-eyed kids, one of them leaning close. They all took a few steps back when I sat up and tried to speak. And they stayed clear when I shuffled across the road to go behind a tree. I could not even get completely out of their view and a few of them moved around anyway to get a better idea of what I was doing.

When I came back a couple of them seemed very worried. They tried to speak to me but I couldn't understand them.

"Je suis malade," I said to them, holding my stomach, then lying down to go to sleep again. *"Je suis malade, c'est tout."* Some of them went off to school, but soon the crowd was back, and a tall, kind-faced man whom I took to be their teacher was shaking me awake. He could speak some French, and when I told him as best I could what had happened, he seemed very concerned. He told me that I should not travel and he and the kids helped me get my stuff to a shady spot in front of an abandoned hut a little ways down the road. It even had an outhouse in the back. We got my tent set up and he tried to get me to eat or drink something, but I wouldn't. I knew I was dehydrated, but I also knew I couldn't hold anything down and I figured getting my system active again would just make things worse.

They promised to come check on me and went back to school while I fell asleep, unable to keep my eyes open. I heard a couple of jeeps and trucks pass at different times, and at one point I heard one of them come back. It was Gerwin, and he was stunned when he saw me there.

"What happened?" he asked. I could see on his face that I looked pretty bad. When I explained it to him, he looked distraught. He started asking me about the foods I had with me and then he tried to insist that I drink some fluids. I wouldn't do it.

"You are dehydrated," he said. "You will have to replenish your salts soon or you will be in worse trouble." I was thinking that at least now I could get a ride with him and his friend Horst, a reticent German who owned the truck he was traveling in. But he wouldn't hear of it. He said he thought I should go back to Kisangani to the hospital, and that no matter what I shouldn't travel for a few days. I could tell that he felt awful about leaving, but Horst wouldn't wait for me to get better and if he hadn't wanted me in his truck healthy, he certainly didn't want me in there sick. Gerwin gave me a few packs of a powdered, Gatorade-like drink and told me to make some as soon as I felt able. Then he gave me a couple of rolls of toilet paper and left. Horst waved disdainfully as they pulled off. I never saw Gerwin again, but he may have saved my life.

By midafternoon I started having trouble thinking straight and I was having trouble moving my arms and legs. It was like they weren't entirely connected to my body. I'd had to go back to the outhouse behind the empty hut a few times, but my stomach was feeling a little better. With the encouragement of the teacher, I mixed some of the powder with my water and drank a bit. It instantly made me feel better and though I wasn't able to hold it very long, my head cleared up a little and my joints felt reconnected. I kept making myself drink the solution, and in the evening I ate a little papaya and manioc paste that the teacher brought me. For a while I started feeling better, but during the night, in the middle of an awful rainstorm, things got bad again. My stomach and intestines lurched as the rain poured and poured, and I had to limp back and forth to the outhouse in the mud. Inside, water started dripping in, but by about three in the morning I was so exhausted from the ordeal that I just collapsed on top of my bag, mud and all, and fell asleep for the rest of the night.

When I woke up in the morning, I felt better, but I could tell that my system was still out of balance. I mixed more of the powder, and changed my clothes, putting the disgustingly filthy socks and shorts and underwear outside my tent. Before school, the teacher woke me up again and gave me some pineapple for breakfast with coffee, which he said was a medicament. By midmorning I felt so good that I read for a while and was thinking that I might even be able to travel on. At lunchtime, the teacher brought me more coffee and some papaya and bananas and manioc paste. The manioc paste would stop the diarrhea, he said, and the papayas and bananas would help me get better. Only later did I figure out that my electrolyte system was probably out of balance and that both were rich in potassium and glucose, just like the powdered solution I had been drinking.

One by one, most of the other tourists from the boat came by. They would stop and talk and wish me luck, and then give me some toilet paper before leaving. One guy whom I had talked to occasionally on the boat didn't even stop. He looked petrified that I might ask him for something. I could tell that the kids thought it was very strange that no one gave me a ride, but they loved the point in the conversation when toilet paper was handed over. After the fifth or sixth time it happened, they were waiting for the exchange and laughed when the roll was produced. I laughed too, feeling embarrassed but appreciating the absurdity of it.

By midafternoon I was feeling good enough that I decided to just keep heading east in small increments. I had no symptoms of malaria and I could tell that my stomach was getting more stable. I was even feeling a little hungry. I slowly packed my things, moving the stuff that was still damp into the sun and then packing it up when it dried. To my surprise, my down sleeping bag hadn't suffered much at all, but my tent was pretty dirty. I wiped them both down and hung them from the tree branches, resting between each effort. I noticed that the dirty clothes I had left piled outside my tent were missing. I felt bad for anyone who was willing to steal them in that condition—I knew I was never going to be able to use them again. But then one of the students who had been particularly worried about me came walking up the hill from a nearby stream with the clothes thoroughly washed and neatly folded. They looked better than they had in a month. I was floored. I tried to give him money, but he wouldn't take it and when I asked the teacher about it, he said, "It is not a problem. He sees that you need help and he is happy to help you."

Kevin Kertscher is the author of Africa Solo: A Journey Across the Sahara, Sahel and Congo, *from which this story was excerpted. He is an independent filmmaker who lives in Boston.*

PETER NICHOLS

PUMPING

On a solo Atlantic crossing, a sailor is confronted
with a true survival test.

AT 0500, JUST BEFORE DAWN, THE ALARM WAKES ME. SWINGING
my feet off the bunk, I touch water before floor.

Real panic. Before I know it I'm up in the cockpit pumping for all I'm worth—so frenziedly that part of my mind is
wondering about the age and strength left in the sun-faded
rubber diaphragm C-clamped on the pump's exterior. I have
a spare, but it would rattle me further if this broke and I had
to repair it right now. Pump-pump-pump-pump-pump-
pump. After a while—I've forgotten to count or look at my
watch—I look down the companionway: water's no longer
visible over the wet floorboards. I slow down a bit, catch my
breath. Several deep breaths. What a way to wake up!

I start thinking: I was in the lee bunk—the lower side of the
boat now that it's well heeled with wind in the sails for the
first time in weeks. Water just under the floor when the boat
is becalmed and upright would overflow on the lee side when
moving and heeled. No need for panic. But water over the
floorboards is above the threshold of my peace of mind.

Five minutes later I know with certainty there's a shitload more water coming in now. Still no suck from the bilge and I've been at it for ten minutes at least. I stop and go below and pull up a floorboard. The bilge appears half full. Je-sus Christ.

Up in the cockpit I pump like a mad metronome. Of course, I think, the bilge is V-shaped so what looks half full is really probably only a quarter full. I normally see half a glass of water as half full, but I have just become a fervent half-empty man.

Another five minutes until I hear the sucking of air from bilge. I go below, up into the bow, and what I see is a waking nightmare that makes my gut feel suddenly full of ice: water is welling in, steadily, along half the seams in the hull below the waterline, on both sides. The inside of the planking up here looks as if a hose is being played across it. I pull sails, duffel bags, coils of rope wildly away from the hull to see how far aft this continues. Not far, thank God, not too far: it stops about six feet or so back from the stem. The planking is dry aft of this. The water's getting under the sheathing, of course, and coming in through the seams, which haven't been caulked for a decade at least. You can't caulk them if you can't get at them, but the water sure can. I stare for a few minutes, trying to think—of what, I don't know. Through the hatch light overhead I can see that it's dawn.

I go aft and start making coffee.

Okay. I can still pump it out, I can keep it below the floorboards. But no question about it now: the faster I sail, the more water comes in. However, we're doing about five knots now, we won't go much faster than this, so maybe it'll stabilize at this rate.

Not a hope. The leak got progressively worse over the last two weeks while we were practically sitting still. It will get worse and worse, faster and faster, and I know why now: the water will work away at the old caulking and force its way aft. It's a race against time.

But aren't we moving well!

I think of the Alitalia joke a Pan Am flight attendant once told me: An announcement from the cockpit: "We gotta good news, anda bad news. The bad news is we're lost. The good news is, we're makinga great time."

Later in the morning, the liquid crystal digital display on my short-wave radio starts fragmenting: batteries are low. I change them, but when I turn the radio back on it is silent. A second moment of raw panic this morning. Absurdly, this seems far worse than the leak. The prospect of life without my radio makes me feel lonelier than Robinson Crusoe. The radio is my man Friday, my contact with the rest of the species. Auntie BBC, jazz from the VOA in the evenings, this is the company that has kept me from feeling utterly alone.

I pull the batteries, brand-new Duracells, out of the radio and look at the contact points inside the battery compartment. Nice and shiny, no sign of corrosion. The batteries, fresh from their plastic packaging, look good too. I put them back, slowly, firmly, with the intense telepathic message: *You will work now.* I put the lid back on. Turn the radio on—

Nothing.

I unscrew the back of the radio and pull it off, revealing the inscrutable Japanese interior. I might as well be looking at an atomic bomb. I see no sign of corrosion, which I could expect after years on board. I pick the radio up and turn it upside down: nothing falls out, which is good, but then I realize that if it had I wouldn't know where it came from to put it back. Miserably, I screw the back on.

I feel a terrible cascading fear. I'm undermined, no doubt, by the other, realistically greater problem, but I am undone by the silence from my radio. I feel myself reverting to the baby state I escaped into on the dope boat: I want to blubber and appeal to someone, "*Pleeeaaase!*" More than a thousand miles to go, ten to fifteen days. Cut off from the world. Absolutely, completely, out-of-touch alone.

Almost whimpering, I climb into the cockpit and start pumping. Pumping-pump-pump. The voyage seems too grim now. Suddenly it's no longer fun. I look around at the empty ocean and realize, with a sharpness I've never felt before, how alone I am. Just myself and a leaky boat in the middle of the ocean. Alone, alone, all, all alone.

But isn't this really what you've wanted all along? A real test? To see if you can take it? This is now, at last, a survival situation, mentally and physically. It's perfect. It's going to take everything you've got. Are you going to cave in now, as you did once before, on the *Mary Nell*, when someone else was looking after you, or are you going to rise to this? If you set out across an ocean in a boat like Toad, eager for a whiff of danger and sensation but unprepared to face just such a scenario, you're just a fucking dilettante. This is real. Life or death. Are you up to it, or not?

Why are you here?

In addition to his sailing adventures, Peter Nichols has worked in the film business as a screen-writer, propmaker, and ship-wrangler. This story was excerpted from his book Sea Change: Alone Across the Atlantic in a Wooden Boat, *where you can read about what happens next.*

PART THREE

Heart
of
Darkness

WILLIAM T. VOLLMANN

BLOODSUCKERS

*You never know when you will be called
to be the Good Samaritan.*

WHEN I HITCHHIKED FROM SAN FRANCISCO TO FAIRBANKS,
mosquitoes surrounded me with the hymning hum of a grad-
uation—not right away, of course; not until I got to Canada.
As soon as I was safely in a vehicle they could not affect me
anymore and I rode the familiar thrill of speed and distance,
lolling in the back of the truck, with a beautiful husky kissing
my hands and cheeks, and we slowed to let a moose get out
of the road and at once I heard them again.—A mosquito bit
me.—I was on the Al-Can Highway now. I forgot the night
I'd given up, not even in Oregon, and stayed at a motel, my
face redburned and filthy, my eyes aching; and it had felt sin-
ful to spend the sixteen dollars on the room but it was raining
hard as it had been all day, so no one would pick me up. In
hitchhiking as in so many other departments, the surest way
not to get something is to need it. The more the world dirt-
ied me, the less likely someone would be to take me in.—But
the next morning was sunny and I had showered and shaved,
which was why a van picked me up within half an hour and

took me into Oregon, and as I rode so happily believing that I now progressed, I didn't even consider that the inside of the van was not so different from the inside of the motel; I was protected again. When I remember that summer, which now lies so far behind me, I must own myself still protected, in a fluctuating kind of way, and so a question hovers and bites me unencouraged: Which is worse, to be too often protected, and thereby forget the sufferings of others, or to suffer them one-self? There is, perhaps, a middle course: to be out in the world enough to be toughened, but to have a shelter sufficient to stave off callousness and wretchedness. Of course it might also be said that there is something depressing and even debasing about moderation—how telling that one synonym for *average* is *mean*!

On the long stretch of road between Fort St. John and Fort Nelson, where the mosquitoes were thickest, we came to where the Indian woman was dancing. It was almost dusk, round about maybe nine or ten o'clock. The country was full of rainbows, haze and yellow flowers. Every hour or so we had to stop to clean the windshield because so many mosqui-toes had squished against it, playing connect-the-dots with the outlines of all things. We pulled over and went to work with ammonia and paper towels. They found us as soon as we got out. The driver's head was a big black sphere of mosqui-toes. There were dozens of them in the space between my glasses and my eyes. When we got back into the camper, mos-quitoes spilled in through the open windows. We jittered along at fifty miles an hour over the dirt road until the breeze of our passage had sucked them out. By then the windshield was already turning whitish-brown again from squashed mos-quitoes. The driver did not want to stop again just yet, but I noticed that he was straining his eyes to see through the dead bugs, and I was just about to say that I didn't mind cleaning the windshield by myself this time (I was, after all, getting a free ride), when far ahead on that empty road (we hadn't met another vehicle for two hours) we saw her capering as if she were so happy, and then we began to get closer to her and saw the frantic despair in her leaping and writhings like some half-crushed thing's that could not die. Not long ago I thoughtlessly poured out a few drops of dilute solvent upon waste ground, and an earthworm erupted, stretched toward me accusingly, stiffened and died. But the convulsions of this woman went on and on. Just as her dance of supposed happiness had seemed to me entirely self-complete like masturbation, so this dance of torture struck me as long-gone mad, sealing her off from other human beings, as if she were some alcoholic mumbler who sheds incomprehensible tears. It was not until we were almost past that I understood behind our hermetic windows that she was screaming for help. I cannot tell you how terrifying her cries were in that wild place. The driver hesitated. He was a good soul, but he already had one hitchhiker. Did he have to save the world? Besides, she might be crazy or dangerous. Her yellings were fading and she was becoming trivial in the rearview mirror when he slowed to think about it, and it was only then that we both understood what we had seen, because protected brains work slowly: mosquitoes darkened her face like a cluster of blackberries, and her legs were black and bloody where the red shorts ended. The driver stopped. Mosquitoes began to pelt against the windows.

We had to help her get in. She embraced us with all her remaining strength, weeping like a little child. Her fearfully swollen face burned to my touch. She'd been bitten so much around the eyes that she could barely see. Her long black hair was smeared with blood and dead mosquitoes. Her cheeks had puffed up like tennis balls. She had bitten her lip very deeply, and blood ran down from it to her chin where a single mosquito still feasted. I crushed it.

That afternoon, no doubt, she'd been prettier, with sharp cheekbones that caught the light, a smooth dark oval face, dark lips still glistening and whole, black eyes whose mercurial glitter illuminated the world yet a little longer, shiny black hair waved slantwise across her forehead. That was why the man in Fort Nelson had decided to support her trade. Reservation bait, he thought. She got in his truck, and there were some other men, too; they used her services liberally.

But unlike slow mosquitoes, who pay the bill, if only with their lives, the men had their taste of flesh with impunity. They weren't entirely vile. They didn't beat her. They only left her to the mosquitoes. They let her put her clothes back on before they threw her out—

She'd tried to dig a hole in the gravelly earth, a grave to hide in, but she hadn't gone an inch before her fingers started bleeding and the mosquitoes had crawled inside her ears so that she couldn't think anymore, and she started running down the empty road; she ran until she had to stop, and then the mosquitoes descended like dark snow onto her eyelids. Two cars had passed her. She'd craved to kill herself, but the mosquitoes would not even give her sufficient peace to do that. I'll never forget how I felt when she squeezed me in her desperate arms—I'll never forget her dance.

William T. Vollmann's books include You Bright and Risen Angels, The Rainbow Stories, Whores for Gloria, *and* The Atlas, *from which this story was excerpted. He is the recipient of a Whiting Foundation Award, and lives in California.*

JOHN SUNDIN, M.D.

KIGALI'S WOUNDS

A doctor looks into the darkness.

I'M LIVING AND WORKING AT A RED CROSS FIELD HOSPITAL that was set up a month ago in a converted Catholic convent. It is situated on a hill, looking out over the green hills of Rwanda. Rwanda is known as the Switzerland of Africa, but the comparison stops at the landscape. The country is ravaged by a savage war between the government—Hutu—and the "rebels"—Tutsi. Two tribes, two politics—very complicated. It's war, nevertheless, fought not with planes, bombs, tanks, or missiles but rather with rifles and mortars, and with a fair share of less sophisticated weapons: machetes, clubs, and spears.

Today started at a leisurely pace. There are seven people on the medical team, and we have about two hundred patients staying on the floor and in tents. I am the surgeon, and work with two nurses in our two operating rooms, which were classrooms a month ago. Our cases today included the closure of the scalp over the machete-exposed temporal lobe of a boy. Another: finishing touches on a leg blown off last week by a mine. A woman who, four days ago, was nine months pregnant—until someone clubbed her badly and she delivered a dead baby too quickly. She needed her torn vagina sewn up. A leg that I thought would have to be amputated looked okay, so I will look again in a few days. And this was a good day! I've done maybe twenty amputations of legs, hands, and an eye over the last week.

Sometimes the taste of flesh and pus stay on my palate after the day's work. It's hard to sit down and eat meat, but I do because at night the international team—French, Swiss, Dutch, Danish, Finnish, and me (the American)—sits around a table. We eat what we have, and drink what we can, and smoke like there's no tomorrow. Then to sleep to the sounds of gunfire and awake to start again.

May 15. I'm dragging. To the operating room. Cover a machete cut to the skull—four inches long with exposed brain. Nasty. He will probably die. After lunch I return to my room—sleep is what I need. Three weeks here seems like a year. I check my temperature; I have a fever of 101. That's a good sign—it's not stress alone that's making me feel so bad but some tangible pathogen. Water and aspirin and vitamin C. Fever now 102. Fitful sleep, this side of delirium. Stretchers, thousands of stretchers. Like Chaplin's *Modern Times*—an assembly line of stretchers and wounds, wounds, wounds. There's no doctor here, so I'll have to treat myself. Dangerous. What's wrong with me? the flu? Dengue fever? Encephalitis? Malaria? Nothing is worse than to be sick far from home. My friends nurse me. Aspirin, Fanta, soup. Doctors are the worst patients.

Night falls and my fever rises. Yes, it could be malaria. Kigali is a thousand meters high, but there are still mosquitoes and malaria. We have two drugs here that can treat malaria: Fansidar and Lariam. Neither is to be taken willy-nilly. A complication of Fansidar is called Stevens-Johnson

Syndrome, also known as Watch-every-square-inch-of-your-skin-drop-off syndrome. I saw a photo of it in a medical text. The odds? 1 in 10,000, 1 in 100,000. The odds of being eaten by a lion in New Haven are astronomically low, but if you are the one eaten by an escaped Barnum & Bailey lion then those reassuring odds are only statistics. Lariam—my own stock from Yale—can cause acute psychosis. I'll sleep on it. If my temperature is still up in the morning then I'll do something.

Sleep. Sweet sleep. Sweaty sleep. Mosquito nightmares. The sun again. The thermometer again. Higher, not lower: 103 and pushing 104. Brain-frying time. My head aches to the hair roots. Must treat myself. Fansidar or Lariam? Skin loss or psychosis? What a choice. Convoluted synapses. Feverish thinking. I decide on the Fansidar—all I have to lose is my skin. Better my skin than my mind.

Now the nurse from hell arrives. She's Dutch. Maybe fifty something, and looks like she was sired from stick insects. She's good—don't get me wrong. A veteran of Mogadishu, Kabul, etc. However, I suspect sometimes that she thinks we are in Amsterdam, not Kigali. Limits have to be set.

Anyway, this nurse knocks on my door, enters, and sits on my bed. I know there's trouble brewing. A new patient, twenty something, with a shrapnel wound in his left flank. Blood in his urine. Trouble. The left flank is where the kidney and the big aorta live. I'm dizzy even thinking about getting vertical, but there's no other surgeon. I operate and he may die anyway. I don't operate and he dies for sure. I operate and I am sick for three more days. I don't operate and rest, and can operate in a few days. Too late for him in a few days. Others may come in tomorrow. Must rest. Must get better. Must choose. Crazy place. No lawyers, only limits.

She pushes as she always does: "Well, he will die if we don't operate." I know she's right, but "No, I won't operate today" rolls off my tongue.

Charges: breach of Hippocratic oath. Plea: temporarily crazy place.

Sentence: loss of all skin.

May 16. Recovered from my fever and my Fansidar dose with my skin still intact. The flank wound died as expected. The team was eating together at the time of the news, and we all discussed our limits. The insect nurse is pushing to do more and more and more. Get blood donors! Fight to save every double amputee! It's her nature. The rest of the nurses (French, Swiss, Danish, Finnish) are more willing to accept the limits: very little backup, a sea of wounded, and limited supplies, including blood. Sure we could do a liver resection if we had to, but with no blood, oxygen, or ventilators, the patient is as good as dead anyway. I sense she faults me for not having operated yesterday—but sometimes, *c'est la vie, c'est la mort.*

May 21. Yesterday a man came in with his personality on the stretcher after getting shrapnel to the head. We have a zombie now. A woman buried alive in a mass grave dug herself out after twelve hours. She's pretty freaked out. I would be.

May 25. Bunkered in today. Mortar hit Red Cross compound next door, killing two and wounding five. Hospital staff leaves and wounded pour in. Fifty more today. Putting them everywhere on the ground now. No more tents. Sixty out of one hundred staff have left. Twenty cases to operate on but tomorrow will be another day of shelling. Phillip, our four-pack-a-day Swiss director, reassured us today that we were not a political target, only in a bad geographic place. Politically correct, geographically incorrect.

May 27. The situation is evolving—now very, very tense. Today, for the first time, I feared for my life. Shelling all day, bunkered in. Patients lying on stretchers for three days, waiting for surgery and dying. Patients are dropped off at the gate screaming. Before the military hospital was closed down, we were getting 90 percent Tutsi patients, and the Hutus went to the military hospital. Now everyone comes to us. We are becoming the nexus for these warring, century-old tribal hatreds.

Extremists still exist. The Hutu militia showed up at the hospital today with Kalashnikovs and clubs with spikes. These are the folks who kill Tutsi for sport—and they're in the hospital! They want to know why we treat Tutsi before Hutu. We can't even tell who is Tutsi and who is Hutu. They want to know what happened to one of their men who was brought in yesterday. He's dead. He was a fat man with a small hole up over his liver. There were five others ahead of him with their bellies sliced open. Twenty others with mangled limbs. Now they accuse us of killing this man. They want his body. They take our walkie-talkies. The local staff is in a panic. These are crazed armed killers, the same bunch who killed 150 patients in a Medecins Sans Frontieres hospital in Butare. Two staff leave through the back door saying, "It's finished, it's finished." I am finally really scared. We all are.

The militia take two Red Cross workers, Andre and Ischelle, to find the body, which is already buried in our own mass grave in the compound. They see the body has no surgery marks. They want his shoes. They say he had a million Rwandese francs in them. Not there now. They have murder in their eyes.

The U.N. arrives, only by coincidence. They want some bandages. The militia leaves with the body. They say they will be back. Foreboding. We have no security anymore. Our local staff has left. The military can't be trusted. They're about to be overrun.

I hid in a corner today, fully expecting to be murdered. They wanted the medical team that's "not treating their people."

That's me: I'm the surgeon, the only one. This is really no joke. The locals see it, too. "They don't play games," a local says about the militia. The mortars have been a nuisance—a low probability of being hit—but now we are marked by killers who live down the road.

At Yale, we used to have weekly morbidity and mortality meetings where the surgeons tore one another apart like pit bulls for as little as a wound infection. Tame compared with the jury in this crazy place.

We are no longer safe, and the medical team knows it. Mortars are one thing, but killers are another. Tomorrow at sunrise we will give our decision: We cannot spend another day in the hospital with Kalashs at our heads. We get U.N. protection or we request evacuation as a group. We just can't do any more. Sacrificing our lives isn't in the job description. The chaos is peaking. Order is dissolving.

I'm too tired to be dramatic, but believe me, the situation is very, very, very tense. Please don't tell my mother.

June 11: It's happening: I'm burning out. I really noticed it yesterday while amputating a rotten leg at the mid-thigh— my back and hands sore, my gag reflex twitching. We had fifteen cases between 9 and 1—arms and legs to cut off or dress, a nose and two eyes blown away, a five-year-old leg connected by a thread of flesh. In the beginning we had a schedule. I saw wounds healing and grafts taking. I used to know the patients. Now there are so many wounded that it's assembly-line first aid.

There's another man on the ward with a very bad leg. He refused amputation a few days ago. He missed his chance. He's got the "gas" now—gas gangrene up to his flank. He'll rot from the leg up, like the others. He'll start to smell and the flies will come to feast and the nurses will say do something and

I'll say no. I'll send him to our "hospice" tent and then I'll put him out of his misery.

I've lost my sense of humor. I'm beginning to feel a certain distance. People are beginning to look like insects. Bad sign. The end is not in sight on the military or political front. The end is not in sight for the wounded. But my end is in sight. I'm going to leave at the end of June. Three weeks seem like a very long time. Will I make it? Suddenly the edge has lost its romance.

John Sundin, M.D. practices General Surgery in Key West, Florida, and is still writing.

THE KILLING OF THE CATSIBURERE

In the Amazon jungle many years ago, the price
of being mistaken for a devil was high.

I KNEW MY ORIGINAL ESTIMATE OF THE BEACH'S DEFENSIBILITY
had been wrong. The Indians had somehow crossed the river.
We were in a jam. Jorge—with narrowed eye, the shotgun's
stock seated hard against his jaw—was grimly swinging its
barrel along the front rank of the advancing bravos. He
seemed undecided on a target. Finally, when the gun's front
sight stopped midway through the arc, I knew he had singled
out for his last remaining charge of buckshot an enormous,
predatory-looking Campa brave. The Indian was well out in
front, wearing a basket crown with a white feather rising from
the back of its narrow corona. This time the gun was not
aimed at feathers, but at a man's belly.

"Hold your fire!" I ordered him. I struck down the gun,
which roared out, plowing a furrow across the *playa* up to the
Indian's feet. "It will do no good."

"These devils will burn us at the stake!" he cried out angrily.

With no other choice but to lie in the ooze of those death-trap holes until the unwavering Indians came up and stuck their spears into our backs, I got up in full sight and started toward them as casually as I could. They were only fifty feet away and plainly visible in the moonlight, over a hundred warriors fanned out over the beach with others still slinking out of the somber shadows behind.

They were hard-faced, naked except for purplish-red loincloths and claw-and-tooth necklaces, hideously painted. Fully armed with battle-axes, blowguns, spears, bows and arrows, two of them actually carried nets. They came to an abrupt halt. The closest savages drew back their right arms, but did not throw their saw-edged spears, apparently awaiting a signal from the white-feathered chief.

"Ho! Indios!" I called out, holding my hands palm upward to show they were empty of weapons. I walked slowly forward, came to a stop in front of the tall Indian who was standing well out in front of the others. I recognized him instantly…

"Iye Marangui!" I exclaimed with involuntary surprise. This was the witch doctor we had watched that night in his house near Sutsiki.

The grim face remained absolutely wooden, a complete deadpan, but he opened his maw of a mouth and grunted:

"*Taimroki Matse!*" (White Witch!)

I checked an impulse to extend my hand and shake his own, for this practice is abhorred by Campas who, like certain Moslems, do not wish to contaminate themselves. Instead, I spat at his feet, and pointing at the moon bellowed that its light was good for hunting, that the spirits were subservient to him on such a night, and that we, like all men, must prepare to join Pawa soon.

The customary formalities of greeting over, I turned on my heel and walked back to the pits. Jorge and the two

Indians were uncovering the fire and building it into a huge bonfire of flames. The horde of silent Indians followed me across the beach, gathered in a tight ring around the blaze. Jorge and I, together with José and the 'Opata man, were caught in the center. Iye Marangui stepped in with us and squatting on his heels began a thunderous oration, which from time to time José had to piece out and interpret for me. Apparently the *manso* they had speared at the fire was a "bad" Indian, an evil-eye who had been condemned to die but who had escaped to 'Opata.

When the witchman had broken off his tirade, I asked him a question:

"Where is my guard?"

The witch doctor pressed a great thumb against the side of his throat and grunted significantly. I knew they had killed him.

I continued: "It is a great distance from your house to this beach. How long did it take you?"

"Suns!" he grunted, holding up three fingers, meaning three days.

We then knew that there were secret war trails through what was believed to be a pathless tangle of jungle, trails on which a Campa brave can run fifty miles in a single day. That they had come in three days seemed incredible, but there they were.

I knew that a powerful sorcerer of Iye Marangui's stature had not run a hundred and fifty miles merely to see that a sentence of death was carried out on an Indian he had declared *bruja*. I sensed that our fate was in his hands, but I knew better than to question him directly as to why he had intercepted us, for the Campas are intensely indirect during any form of conversation.

With a wild singsong series of sounds interspersed with grunts, he gave a command to an Indian standing just behind. This Indian instantly leapt forward and held out a very large

and cumbersome bag—a cased coto monkey skin, with the
shaggy brown hair still clinging to it.

Iye Marangui untied a buckskin cord at its neck, and began
drawing out various objects: little packets in bark cloth, small
skin bags, carved green jadeite stones in the form of frogs
(symbol of the Rain God), bundles of feathers and other
items. He started painting his heavy-jowled, flat face. He used
achiote, the bright orange-red paint mixed (in his case) with
snake oil, rubbing it all over his head, shoulders and arms.
From a tiny sack he took a cobalt black paint and smeared it
carefully on his forehead, finishing with a single glaring
Brahmin-like white spot between the eyes. He removed his
white feather *paquitsa* (headdress), and put on instead, over his
own long thick hair a grim anaconda's head, rigidly mounted
so that its mouth was hinged open as if striking. Poorly
tanned, it emitted an incredibly vile stink, unusual for even an
anaconda skin. The snake skin, a mottled black and brown,
which was attached at the back to the headpiece, was about
twenty-four feet long and a yard wide, and this Iye Marangui
carefully coiled around his great body.

A spotted jaguar skin was spread on the sand for him, and
on this the sorcerer sat cross-legged. The mounting flames of
the fire played over him and the ghastly greenish glare from
the moon picked out highlights in the paint. Jorge pointed out
that the snake's eyes were probably diamonds. The stage for
jungle sorcery, red magic, was set...

Iye Marangui began swaying back and forth, his eyes
closed. Sweat broke out in beads on his devilish face, for the
night was sweltering. All at once he cried out in a discordant
chant, which must have continued for several minutes, for
suddenly I realized clouds had blotted out the moon and a
smashing deluge of rain was falling on us. But not an Indian
stirred, though like cats they hate rain. The downpour soon

passed, the moon returned, and only a monotonous drip came from the dank jungle beyond, and the drone of the returning insect hordes.

Suddenly the sorcerer's flint-edged eyes flew open, and the chanting stopped. "I, the Brother of the Serpent, will dream!" he bellowed in a deep voice.

He then set about a self-imposed hypnosis. Certainly in the beach's shadows moved the shade of an old Frenchman named Dr. Franz Mesmer. After a few minutes the *brujo* seemed to have become a disembodied automaton swaying before the fire, into which he stared unblinkingly. The trance was induced quickly, partly through the eardrums, by the intricate sound pattern of a tom-tom beaten by one of the Indians. This was aided by the conventional system of a reflection from some bright object on the retina of the eye, in this case a large quartz crystal held in his fingers. Thus began his savage séance with the jungle gods.

All at once, without warning, the Brother of the Dancing Anacondas began screaming in a tiny voice—the opposite of his usual bellowing tones. José started whispering hurriedly in my ear, sometimes lapsing into Campa: "He is talking to the *catsiburere*, an *itasolenga* (spirit), a malignant man-dwarf, which in adulthood stands only three feet high. It has the hands of a man, also a man's head with white hair. One of its feet is clubbed, and short. Its skin is white. From his shoulders grow read hair and the wings of the white king vulture. It is the worst monster of the jungle. When a man is confronted by the *catsiburere* he becomes paralyzed with fright, and the dwarf falls upon him, and breaks all his bones. It has the strength on a thousand devils, it is *antanukire* (fierce, fiendish), and it eats of the flesh of his victims until the belly touches the ground and the wings and body are dripping with blood."

José was obviously becoming frightened. All about us were

the straining faces of the savages, their hard, narrow eyes staring in fascination at the face of the witchman.

The *brujo's* thin, feeble voice picked up a note of whining, and I nudged José. He turned toward me and began speaking in a very frightened voice: "The *brujo* says—'Man (*champari*) has come from the stars (*enpoguiro*)...and to the silent (*pimagerette*) stars, he will return at death...'"

The *brujo*, that two-hundred-pound hunk of bone and muscle, who had not flinched at the prospect of death from a shotgun, began sobbing and crying out plaintively as if the coils of the anaconda skin were crushing him. Presently his voice rose to a terrific pitch—shrill childish tones of anguish, and he began scratching at his painted red chest with talon fingernails, drawing blood. Tears dripped from his eyes. Then Iye Marangui pitched forward on his face. He was shaking violently from head to foot. He raised his head with a jerk, got unsteadily to his feet. He was still wrapped in the snake skin and he tossed his demon's head this way and that, as if to clear his brain of sleep, hissing all the while. His eyes flew open. His face became ravenous, contorted with a cataleptic insanity, alternately twisting from grotesque expressions of fierceness to those of fawning. One instant he was a snake striking out at us; the next he was a feeding tiger roaring on all fours; then a vampire darting here and there, swooping about the fire, sucking at his own arm.

Here was unbridled art, or sheer madness. He seemed suddenly symbolic of the Campas' *andakangare* (a difficult word—perhaps a mixture of terror and danger), something supernatural. Then in a peak of fury he began running around the circle of Indians, who seemed to be frozen with fright, smelling at each in turn. Abruptly he broke off and leapt toward Jorge and me as we sat near the fire with José and our 'Opata Indian; all the while stomping in a thumping dance around us, smelling at each in turn. Abruptly he broke off and stopped in front of Padre Antony's man, pointing at him with the large crystal still clutched in one hand, hissing, and screaming crazily "*Notqui! Notqui!*"

Now *notqui* merely means "eye," but he was not referring to any ordinary kind of eye, for two warriors sprang forth and dragged the poor *manso* out of our midst, and throwing him hard to the ground with a terrific slam, held him struggling on his back near the fire. There was something malignant, merciless, urgent in their manner. The witchman grabbed up a firebrand, and after the others had brutally forced their victim's mouth open with the butt of a heavy spear, he plunged the burning limb with its flames into the *manso's* mouth, and by screwing it around, forced it straight down into the throat.

The back of Jorge's hard fist appeared from nowhere and knocked me solidly in the chest as I tried to rise, my hand already under my shirt and closed over the .45's grip. "Sit still, you fool! Do you want us all stretched out and killed like that? *¡Las bestias!*"

José said, "This is the killing of the *catsiburere*."

The most terrible cries of anguish came from our poor friend undergoing that awful torture. His legs flew about, twisting this way and that, in what must have been an incredible agony of pain. The smell of burning flesh filled the air. Finally, after a time, a long time, he was still and quiet—thank God the man was dead. The witch rose to his feet a bit weary from his exertions, tossing the firebrand carelessly on the fire. He was satisfied, in fact he shone with virtue—hadn't the devil been driven out of a *catsiburere* who was living in the guise of a man?

"Ah! *¡Está bien!*" cried Jorge. "Now what!"

Leonard Clark had a wild career as an explorer, military intelligence and guerrilla operations expert during World War II, and author. He wrote of his early adventures in the 1937 book A Wanderer Till I Die. *This story was excerpted from* The Rivers Ran East, *published in 1953.*

BILL BUFORD

WHEN IT GOES OFF

*Among the English soccer hooligans,
it's only a matter of time.*

WHAT HAPPENS WHEN IT GOES OFF?

It was around one o'clock, and Robert wanted to show me; he wanted me to see the event close up. Something was going to happen, and Robert didn't want me to miss it. Since eleven that morning, the Manchester United supporters had been gathering at the Manor House—a large, rambling Victorian pub and snooker club in north London—and there were now so many people that the pub had run out of glasses. People were standing on the snooker table because there was no more room on the floor, and others were shouting for drinks from outside because they couldn't get through the door. And then, in an instant, the pub was empty, and everyone was in the street, heading up the Seven Sisters Road, on their way to Tottenham.

Everyone except Sammy, who wouldn't be showing up.

Sammy, Robert was whispering, is said to have killed a man, and there are people out to get him. They will always be out to get him—this year, next year, for ever. Whether he did it or not doesn't matter. They *think* he did it.

The pace was brisk, and Robert held on to my sleeve, tugging me along, urging me on, guide and bodyguard, making sure that I was in front, that I wouldn't miss what was going to happen, and, at the same time, looking out for trouble.

They'll come at you from nowhere, Robert said. Snipers. Knife merchants. They cut you up and then they're gone.

The police appeared—vans, accelerators pressed melodramatically to the floor, their engines whining, coming up from the side-street where they had been waiting for the United supporters—and everyone stepped up the pace slightly in response.

On our right were tower blocks. On our left were tower blocks. It could be Warsaw or a suburb of Moscow, except that everything else was so inimitably characteristic of north London—the film of filth that settled on your skin and the grime from the exhaust fumes and the litter slapped by the wind up against the walls. We passed a doctor's surgery, its doors and windows boarded up, and several buildings black from smoke, with bits of things spread out on the pavement in front: a broken plastic chair, a bed sheet, a pink rubber boot, crinkly empty packets of all kinds—crisps, peanuts, nappies, digestive biscuits, the yellow tissue paper of a cheeseburger. There were bits of plastic—red plastic, clear plastic, white plastic, plastic cups, plastic containers—and food tins and drink tins and endless cigarette butts. Across the street, there was an ice cream van, and I spotted a prostitute hiding behind it, sitting on a low wall, out of view.

Fast now, Robert said, shooing me along, telling me to keep up.

We pressed on, a steady pace, past shops that had been locked away behind metal shutters and wire-mesh cages, small shops, all of them single units—fish'n'chips, kebabs, motor parts, take-away chicken, a café open six a.m. to four p.m., a sandwich shop, a belt shop, a shoe repair shop, new and used furniture bought and sold, GOOD BUYS, a newsagent, another shoe repair shop, an evangelist church, life insurance, women's clothing, cans of household paint (only white emulsion, a lorry-load of white emulsion)—and we then crossed the entrance to the Seven Sisters underground station.

That's where it happened, Robert said. That's where the man was killed.

A supporter's back had been broken, and Robert described him twitching and moaning, legs flapping, unable to stand up.

It was very, very bad, Robert said, and it was probably because I had never heard Robert describe anything he had seen as very, very bad—when I would have described virtually everything he had seen as very, very bad—that I knew this use of "very, very bad" to be a terrible understatement. Two hundred people were involved in a fight on the escalator leading down to the trains, and with Tottenham fans racing up the moving stairs as the Manchester United fans came racing down, someone hit the emergency stop button, and everyone tumbled. Several people were knocked unconscious, and there were many bones broken—arms, legs, the floppy man with his crushed vertebrae—and the traffic along the Seven Sisters Road was backed up from the ambulances that were called in. At the bottom, once everyone had got up, was the dead man.

That's why Sammy is not here today, Robert said. It doesn't matter that it was never proved in court. He can never come to Tottenham again.

The Seven Sisters Road ended in a T-junction just past the tube station, and the long line of United supporters bent round to the left, going up the High Road in the direction of White Hart Lane. And then, on the other side of the street, I saw them: the Tottenham supporters, hundreds, more than a thousand, as many certainly, as had arrived that morning from

Manchester. They, like the police, had been waiting for the United supporters, and—this was why Robert kept pushing me up to the front—the United supporters had known they would be there.

Be ready, Robert said, whispering again, as if the supporters on the other side of the High Road might hear his instructions above the noises of the traffic and the police who were filling up the street with their vehicles and animals.

Any moment now, Robert said. And the walk-run was now verging on a sprint, the two parties, spread across several blocks of the High Road, moving in tandem, trying to get ahead of the police, waiting for the moment to cross.

A dog-handler came racing up alongside the pavement and cut across our path—eight of us now at the front of the crowd, Robert seeming to lead it. The dog-handler was out of breath. He knew what was going on, all the police did, and he would have been dispatched to get to the head of the group to slow it down and prevent it from getting beyond control. He was agitated and jumpy and you could see in his eyes that he knew that at any moment he might find himself in the middle of a riot. He had grabbed his dog by the collar so that, with his other hand, he could use the full length of his chain-leash like a whip.

Get back, he shouted, swinging his chain-leash above his head, cowboy style. Get back, and suddenly my face was stung—a sharp, bright pain across my jaw. The dog-handler had taken to snapping his chain-leash into the faces of the supporters, including my own. I was indignant and shouted at the policeman by his badge number.

We're just minding our own business, I said, we're just minding our own business on our way to a football match. What gives you the fuckin' right to hit me?

He twisted round to look at me, and his face betrayed an

expression of bewilderment and incomprehension, and I could see that he couldn't make sense of what he had just heard: an American shouting out his badge number.

Tell him you're from the press, someone shouted at me from behind my shoulder. Tell him you're going to report him for police brutality.

The policeman dropped his chain-leash to his side and trotted along, led by his dog, and continued staring back at me, his head still twisted round.

Go on, the others were now shouting, tell him you're going to report him.

I have gone too far, I remember thinking. I have let myself become one of them. Here I am, being whipped by a policeman, arguing with him, being urged on by the supporters behind me—by the supporters behind me? By the one thousand supporters behind me: here I am at the front of a crowd, among the people leading it. And then something happened behind us—somebody had crossed the street—and the two long lines, the United supporters on one side, the Tottenham supporters on the other, momentarily converged, a roar going up.

Watch out now, Robert said, watch out for knives. It's going to go off.

But it didn't go off, and it was unclear what had happened—a loss of nerve?—when a supporter appeared, running hard, straight down the middle of the High Road, chased by two policeman, and one caught his heel and the supporter fell and rolled and covered his head, and, just as we passed him, I saw his chin popped backwards by a policeman's boot and then knocked forward as he was kicked by another policeman from behind.

There was another incident further back, but I couldn't see it—the lines of supporters on either side of the street seemed to stretch for a half a mile—and the roar went up again, and everyone turned, ready, but then nothing happened.

Any moment now, Robert was repeating, any moment. He was watchful, waiting for that instant when the thousand United supporters straggling along the High Road would change and know to act in a different way, in unison, as a crowd—as a *violent* crowd. I could see that Robert was actually judging each moment, weighing it, and that the time was not right yet, and that the time was still not right, but that it would be right shortly.

Any moment now, Robert said again.

Something was going to happen, but it was evident that whatever happened would have to involve the police. Had Robert anticipated the police? There were too many—not so many that they were not outnumbered by the supporters—but enough that, having placed themselves down the middle of this road, having positioned their dogs and horses and vans between the two groups of supporters, the police would have to be attacked first. They were in the way—deliberately. It seemed to me that it was one thing to fight those who wanted to fight. It was different thing to fight those who wanted to arrest you. This was not done. You don't attack the police—unless, it follows, you are able to beat them up so effectively that it is then impossible to get arrested. But this, too, was not done: you don't beat up the police. Scattered along this long street, I now realized, were around two thousand people working themselves into a state so heightened that it would allow them to attack the police. They were daring themselves, provoking themselves, asking, as Robert was asking, if this moment was the one that would set them all off.

This road, this ordinary north London thoroughfare, the most direct route into the city, the A10, the very one that led straight back to my home in Cambridge, had taken on a powerful meaning. It separated the supporters of Tottenham from those of Manchester. It separated both from the police. But it also separated them from the experience they were all trying to have. And they knew it. To remain on the pavement was lawful. To step off it was to enter lawlessness. The divide was almost a physical thing. I looked back, taking in the length of this line, this border, and it was as if I could see the lads pressing up against it, testing it, stretching it, wanting to break through it but being unable to do so—*just.* Someone stepped aggressively into the street, but the others whom he was hoping would follow remained on the pavement, and he hesitated, and, having hesitated, lost his nerve, withdrew and disappeared. Someone from the other side did the same—venturing out but finding himself alone—and retreated. This street—such a simple thing—was the line that needed to be crossed for this crowd to become a violent one.

Bill Buford was born in Baton Rouge, Louisiana, and lived for many years in England where he founded and edited the literary magazine, Granta. *He is now the literary and fiction editor of* The New Yorker. *This story was excerpted from his book* Among the Thugs: The Experience, and the Seduction, of Crowd Violence.

BRUCE DUFFY

LOOKING FOR STINGER

Just what every man needs—a surface-to-air missile.

YOU COULD MISTAKE IT FOR A WEEDWACKER, THIS GREEN fiberglass tube weighing just 35 pounds, yet with it a man is a god wielding a meteor—a man who truly owns the sky.

To those who know her, her name is Stinger. Not, you will note, *the* Stinger, but simply *Stinger*, hellfire divinity with her own proper name. Stinger, equal to the swiftest, most heavily armored jet or helicopter, to say nothing of those winged bombs, commercial jets. Stinger the singer: smelling heat, her infrared seeker hits the high note, dreeeeeee—

Lock on. Pull the trigger and behold a 500-story rush, a slithering white star, packing—at near Mach 2—all the kinetic energy of a hurtling Volkswagen, followed by the fireball of one pound of pure C4.

Exhausted and sunburned, I'm driving back to the airport after a day at New Mexico's White Sands Missile Range watching the Marines fire Stingers, when I jolt up. Screaming overhead is an orange-bellied passenger jet, yet all I see now is a target a hundred times larger than the small rockets the

Marines were destroying—destroying with ease—from one and two miles away. But what about TWA Flight 800 exploding at 13,700 feet? Well, if launched from a boat, Stinger—at its very limit—could have achieved its goal.

So what am I doing cramming my head with Stinger lore and launch procedures, bound in a month's time for Pakistan and Afghanistan to find one for sale? Me of all people, Volvo driver, Girl Scout Dad and novelist, off on a fool's errand with all the world's crazies who mecca there in search of toys.

Because, existing as she does at the top of the terror food chain, Stinger remains a major threat to civilian aircraft. At the same time, she's our New Age Medusa, symptom of a binge-and-purge world consumed by wars and awash with arms—arms for sale by people so angry, desperate or casually greedy that, frankly, it's a miracle we've seen as little terror as we have.

"Americans think it's all taken care of now that the cold war is over," one ex-CIA operative tells me. "Well, you slit open the belly of the monster and out they pop, all these horrid, slimy little babies. Drugs. Terror. Weapons. It's organized chaos, and mainstream America can't fathom it. And I can understand, because you have to see it even to believe it."

Peshawar, rotting once-British colonial city in Pakistan, where the forgotten British dead lie in time-tilted rows behind the high walls of the old garrison graveyard on University Road. Sticky with sweat and slapping mosquitoes, I am wasting an hour—anything to keep from thinking about Stinger. Dancing in the gloom, beneath huge, bizarrely wrought trees, are the malarial swarms that probably killed most of them, soldiers, "wives of," nameless infants. Before me there's a whole receiving line as I wade through the swampy growth, followed by an old watchman desperate to be of use, Lifting leafy clumps as I strain to read... *treacherously killed*

July 30, 1883, by a fanatic…In eternal memory of the wives and children of the noncommissioned officers who died during the year of our Lord 1863.

It was Indian then, and Peshawar, ten miles from the Khyber Pass, was the main western garrison in the decades-long battle to subdue the watchman's unconquerable forebears, the Pakhtun. A century later, in the high desert areas where I'm going, the rules haven't changed but the weapons sure have— dramatically since the war in Afghanistan, the old bolt-action Enfields having given way to AKs, mortars and rockets.

Itching and slapping, I wonder what they'd say I was doing wrong, the people who lie here. Because after three tense, confusion-filled days, I can almost hear the Tommies and their ladies scoffing at me. Months and thousands of dollars. Wasted. All wasted on this hapless Yank. Slap.

Certainly, far more knowledgeable people had failed before me. And let's face it: there is an Abominable Snowman aspect to this hunt. From 1986 to 1989, through a notoriously leaky weapons pipeline set up by the CIA and managed by its Pakistani counterparts, the U.S. shipped the *mujahideen* about 1,000 shoulder-fired Stingers. Today, despite a troubled U.S. buyback program, between 100 and 200 are still at large, many for sale on the black markets in the rugged border regions of Pakistan and Afghanistan, home to smugglers, kidnappers, dope kings, arms traffickers and terrorists—guys like Mir Aimal Kansi, convicted in 1997 of killing two CIA employees.

During the war in Afghanistan, American TV networks re-portedly had a standing offer: $60,000 for footage of Stinger bringing down an aircraft. Nada. Zip. And no journalist has since authenticated one in operating order, ready for sale.

So I'd know what I was looking at, my military contacts had carefully led me through the thirteen checks they use to certify Stinger as ready to fire. *LIFE* meanwhile has spared no expense. To compensate for my inexperience, they've assigned veteran photographer Steve McCurry, who covered the war in Afghanistan. They've also sprung for Chris Smith, a British arms control expert who for years now has monitored the toxic spill of death, drugs and fundamentalism unleashed by the continuing turmoil in the region.

Two years ago, Chris says, he got close to Stinger but couldn't lose the Pakistani detailed to keep tabs on him. Blond, ruddy-faced and very British, Chris is my tutor, you might say. Also guiding us is our fixer, a man whom I'll call Anwar to protect his safety—Anwar, whoops-gotta-go, forever clutching his cell phone. Anwar is a veritable Houdini when it comes to disappearing, but he's also brilliantly connected and knows it, unfortunately.

"Before you get too huffy about Anwar," advises Chris, "remember that Anwar is the man here and that without him you are dead. So my advice is to kiss some serious arse."

Fortunately, it is time to break out the kneepads, because at last Anwar has come through—big-time. After weeks of official runaround (that Asian thing, never wanting to say no to your face), we're off to Stinger Central. Off through a back door, even as the Pakistani government, in a bureaucratic no-brainer, has denied us admission to the last place on earth they ever want us to see. This is Darra Adam Khel, a town twenty miles south of Peshawar in the tribal areas, an outlaw region where you can buy virtually any drug or weapon on Earth. Us and not Chicago Chet, the gun freak who had flown clear from the Windy City with his wife, only to be told Darra was now off-limits. Poor guy. He was more downhearted than a kid who'd lost his Mickey ears, stopped like that at the Magic Kingdom. Why, he'd even given Steve several gunsheets— ninja-nut porn filled with assault weapons and prices—to present to the local potentates, along with his business card. Hands across the water.

"Don't kill anybody, huh?" I say, shaking our driver, handsome, maddeningly polite. Farid. Farid prays five times daily, and should, the way he drives.

"As you like, sir," he replies, but only leans more heavily on the horn, scattering goats and men dragging rank, freshly flayed skins. "Fast keeps out the flies, sir."

Blowing through the choked bazaar, we continue our ascent into the lunar mountains of Pakistan's North-West Frontier Province, past the mall-size compounds of the local poppy kings, past camels and nomad encampments, then past Badaber, the U.S. military base from which, in 1960, Francis Gary Powers took off on his ill-fated U-2 spy mission.

This road was a major CIA arms pipeline into Afghanistan, our revenge, bleeding the Russians just as they did us in Vietnam. Introduced relatively late in the war, Stingers were hotly debated at the highest levels of the U.S. government before their deployment in 1986.

No, they didn't single-handedly win the war, but they were far more effective than the CIA-supplied Russian SA-7s and British Blowpipe shoulder-fired missiles the *mujahideen* had been using—credible enough, anyway, that they forced the Russians to fly higher and bomb more inaccurately. For *mujahideen* commanders, Stinger became the ultimate status symbol. And money in the bank.

Which explains why few, if any, have been fired since the Russians left. But the whole equation changed when the fundamentalist Taliban took Kabul and began confiscating weapons. Ever since, surplus arms—Stingers included—have been flowing back into Pakistan, many to the traders here in Darra.

Ahead, we see long green streamers—graveyard flags, beneath which stand nine or ten armed men in black berets, our tribal escort. Jumping into two vans, one in front and one behind, they propel us into town at top speed, horns madly beeping. Kidnapping is another local specialty here.

Inside the compound, Darra's leading elders, or *maliks*, are waiting to greet us—they've even slaughtered a goat in our honor That gunfire we hear isn't celebratory, though. Rather, it's the cash-register sound of buyers testing the goods, spraying the air and back alleys. Dogging us is a political agent, intermediary between the Pakistani government and the *maliks* whose *jirgas*, or tribal courts, deal harsh justice here. And legally, from the destruction of homes to swift executions. Also present is a government press agent who has promised to curtail the ceremonial stuff. Still, not being a stupid man, he's suspicious.

"And please, your story is on what?"

"Oh, arms and the current situation," I say, feigning extreme busyness. "Y'know, the culture, the people…"

Fortunately, just then, five, then ten, then a dozen *maliks* embrace us, two wearing straw hats that resemble enormous popovers. There's even one from London, werewolf-charming, who, to Chris's utter delight, has "the most spot-on British accent." And the food! Hot, juicy goat, and lemon cake washed down by glasses of fresh goat's milk yogurt. Yogurt mixed, rather terrifyingly for me, with the crawling local water by my smiling *malik* host, who watches like Mr. Mom as I dutifully gulp it down. There are no women present. *Ever.*

But hey, guys know what guys like, so after breakfast, up we go to the parapet with two AKs and a sack of rounds, which they begin snapping into banana clips. Wow. Tracer rounds, too, *pop pop poppa-poppa-pop.*

And they're onto us, these guys—oh, they smell secret business to be done, and not in the gun shops, which mainly seem to front the true trade. Meanwhile, on the street, Anwar brings me my first customer.

"To buy? One these *things*?" Nobody utters the S word.

"Well, not exactly to *buy* one, no." As usual, there's a damned crowd around us. Exasperated, I look at Anwar. "You've explained our, uh, *needs*?"

God, I'm out of my league. A sudden, blistering rain is falling, turning the street to mud as the psychedelic smuggler vans, wildly painted like infernal arks, ram west into Afghanistan. In the rain the hypnotically stupid, cross-eyed goats are hugging the buildings. Even they have sense enough to stay out of the rain. Not me. All around me now, I feel a distinct hostility, people eyeing me like a walking price tag, enough to endow a whole village.

Later, the political agent—ostensibly the voice of reason here—is talking about a dispute his people are having with another village. Over electricity. Waving his trigger finger:

"And this will be decided *tonight*! With the heavy weapons!"

"So let me get this straight," I say. "Tonight, you're gonna go home and get your AK—"

"—oh, yes, yes, yes, I have. And rocket grenade, too—"

"—and attack your neighbors? *Because your lights flicker*?"

"But of course." He thinks I'm hilarious. "And why not?"

Perhaps the most disquieting thing about dangerous people is how utterly normal they can seem. Our new Stinger contact, Shahid, is certainly such a man, with his smooth skin and fine white teeth. Let's just say the pseudonymous Shahid is a businessman from the tribal areas.

In more than a half dozen meetings, like a bridegroom, Shahid always wore a white, faultlessly pressed *shalwar kameez*, the cool, collared nightshirt and voluminous trousers that everyone wears in Pakistan. I recall my absurd relief at that first meeting, thinking, *I like this guy.* Yet all I have to do is look out into the barren courtyard of our Peshawar hotel to be forcibly reminded of what's going down. For driving Shahid's white car is a stolid, heavily mustached bodyguard. Even in the worst heat, he always stays with the car, out under the whiteboned eucalyptus, where the gray-crested jackdaws rattle their wings. Looking out, I also note how he keeps the car aimed at the hotel exit, I guess in the event they have to leave suddenly.

Inside, meanwhile, his boss has expertly jazzed us with photographs of Stinger boxes and another picture of a Chinese SA-7 knockoff. He even has a primitive catalogue and two serial numbers that look genuine—and are, it turns out. But so what? Selling numbers is itself a stock piece of flimflam here.

And while Shahid's hustling me, I'm selling him on reports that the U.S. government is paying far more than the $100,000 price he dangled—$175,000, according to one story. But who can they trust? After several rumored stings by ISI (Pakistan's notoriously ruthless intelligence arm), everybody's so jittery that few deals go through, and those that do take forever.

So here's the deal: $2,500 for photographs of one of the three Stingers his contacts allegedly have for sale—photographs or videotape of the fourteen vital points that I've sketched out for Shahid, all to be shot with a current magazine in the background to authenticate the date. Forget having Steve take the pictures—they won't buy it, even when he offers to go in blindfolded.

Of course, it's a miserable deal. With no better options, we're asking to be taken, but there is one inducement that Shahid seems to find genuinely intriguing: If he delivers, we'll try to facilitate a U.S. government buy—at top price. But here, when it seems this argument is getting through, Chris breaks in professorially.

"Er, well, Bruce, I'm sure the CIA is paying the market price. And prices do seem low just now—"

"Chris," I snap, "the Americans are *paying* $175,000."

Enough palavering—I lay it out. Cash, five times the average annual income. Steve busts out laughing. "What a pair of 007s! So you're giving the chief here all the cash? Up front?"

Shahid's English may not be much, but he sure speaks money. Cinching the deal, he rolls my $2,500 in a newspaper, like a hunk of old fish.

Lord, had Shahid's English improved suddenly. And still he thinks we're spooks—spooks posing as journalist bozos in some bizarre scheme. "But why not just buy one?" he asks me at the door. His smile widens. "Not for your government. For your home. Your wife, maybe?"

Afghanistan, the yellow, almost combustible dust. At the border, there is a Stygian feeling about it, as we leave our cars, pay off our drivers, have a dust-caked kid load our gear onto a cart, then sink into rapids of slack-boned refugees and animals, as old men with sticks beat small children to move faster, and bereted soldiers from the famous Khyber Rifles frown and wag their fingers at our cameras. And then I see why.

Packed in white Toyota trucks, in clouds of dust, here come the Taliban, robes and turbans blowing. White battle flags rippling in the wind, they're blazing across the border, off to the front with rifles and pods of green rockets. And with good reason.

Four days before, in Mazar-e Sharif, the Taliban had suffered a horrendous defeat, with three hundred reportedly killed and hundreds more taken prisoner. Yet look where the Taliban reinforcements are coming from—Pakistan. Cannon fodder, too.

Boys barely able to grow fuzz, let alone the required four-inch beards, are roaring in fresh from the Taliban *madrassas* (religious schools) where they've been educated or brainwashed.

Hearing the first reports out of Mazar, our plan had been to do a simple suck-up—stroke the Taliban as conquerors and world statesmen, before turning to our true agenda. After this debacle, though, all bets are off. At this point, we're just going—anything not to go stir-crazy in our crap hotel, waiting on Shahid. It's just Steve and me now—Chris is out: "Dunno a bloody thing about Afghanistan, so I'm off, mate. Lemme know how it goes."

First stop is Jalalabad, a small, relatively unscathed city just across the border. There we're hoping to hook up with a man who had some Stingers once. Sketchy details, said cell-phone Anwar, who also bowed out—another inexplicable family tragedy, courtesy of the most obligingest, dyingest relatives on planet Earth.

Instead, Anwar dispatched not only the portliest Pakistani we'd seen but the only one we'd ever seen drunk. This was Shah, a ringer for Oliver Hardy, who immodestly claimed to have had his wife (one of two) seven times the night before.

"Yes, yes, seven," he insists, holding up seven fat, salacious fingers. "Because I am drunk, and she is already so missing me and afraiding for me, crying. '*You will be kilt!*' Because she know, Shah will be on the front line!"

"Not even a fly," emphasizes the handsome young aide of the Taliban governor of Jalalabad. "If you try, will be very dangerous for you. Believe me." The governor's aide is talking about photographs, which are strictly forbidden, like music, kite flying, even paper bags (which could—they fear—contain a particle of the Koran). Still, it must be said that the Taliban rule of law is no mean achievement. As many told me, hanging and dismemberment are infinitely preferable to the raping, robbery and murder they'd known before.

"Paughhh," mutters Shah as the governor's aide leaves for prayers, "I hate them all, these *beardmen.*"

Yet while the governor and his aide were busily protecting the privacy of insects and the sanctity of paper, not two miles away a major weapons depot had blown up two months before, killing fifty. In Kabul, two days later, we ourselves heard a blast that killed a dozen Taliban. Gathering weapons with the single-mindedness of squirrels, they no sooner build their hoards, it seems, than they blow themselves up.

Shah bounds up, jabbering. It's the governor, just back from prayers. He looks profoundly bored. The dark beard and pale skin, his almost malarial languor—like most Taliban officials I met, he is not quite of this Earth. Obviously, you don't just start off talking Stingers with such a man. So I ask about "conditions," then—when all else fails—America. The governor rouses up.

"Why does America not recognize the Taliban?" he asks. "Look at the suffering, and no help from America. And here when we lose one million people helping you defeat the Russians."

Shah is mopping his face, desperate to go. So I turn to arms.

"Yes," translates Shah, "many we have collected. They are national property and strictly for our protection. We are not Iran." In fact, they hate Iran, which borders them on the west.

"And what about *jihad*?"

"We do not support terrorism, we support Allah."

"Well, your excellency, one thing Americans are very concerned about is these Stingers—"

Stingers. No translation necessary. Blinking with annoyance, the governor summarily denies my request to see the weapons they've collected—if any are even left in Jalalabad.

Shah can't get out of there fast enough, *salaaming* and palming his heart. But, calling after us, here's the young secretary with a burning question. He is inches from my Adam's apple, gaping in wonder. It's my beard, I realize. He's peering under my throat, at the part I carefully trim each morning.

"Why?" he asks thoughtfully, tickling the afflicted area. "Why do you shave this place? No, this hair here Allah wants you to grow. Oh, yes," he beams, "this hair very, very good. Do you know the Koran?"

Naturally, our supposed Stinger contact in Jalalabad falls through. Maybe we'll find him on our return, or maybe we should just pack it in, but on we go, almost wind-driven, like migrating birds.

Banging up the blown-up road to Kabul in a van with a shattered windshield, we're following the Kabul River, here booming in foaming cataracts, there as wide and shimmering blue as a lake. Up the camel-backed mountains, around blind passes, we're beating our bones, jolts so hard I smack my head on the roof, bouncing over tank ruts and sections blown out by massive mines, past destroyed armor and villages reduced to ruins.

Men died here, you remind yourself, men and women and kids plowed under pitiful gray stone shards, many scarcely larger than fingers.

Kabul is the worst, though—ashen, reeking, utterly destroyed for blocks in places. Swarms of beggars. Listless babies and leprous kids with horrible scabs from the biting sand flies that transport some dread filth-borne disease. More horrifying are the ghost women smothered under the *burqahs* which the Taliban force them to wear, widows free to beg but not work, their cricket voices pleading through filmy airholes. Within a day, I'm elbowing kids and even threatening the more insistent with bodily injury. When our driver tries to cheat us out of a few pennies, I order him to stop so I can find the nearest Taliban and have his thieving, malingering ass sent to the front. Or shot, for all I care.

Everybody's a little nutty. Hearing a knock one morning, I find the Egyptian cameraman we'd met coming across the border. Seems the day before, a Taliban commander saw his camera and tried to mow him down with a truck.

"Huge stones he is throwing. Hard. To kill me. Crying *'Kafir! Kafir!'* (unbeliever). And here I am—Muslim. Helpless, while his men stand by with Kalashnikovs." He'd covered the whole war. Many times his life had been threatened. But what had him groping and stammering was the shame of it, to be publicly humiliated in this way by a brother Muslim.

The beardmen even get to Shah, rousted from his bed to pray by the roving religious goons. Near the front, or when we take pictures, Shah is absolutely worthless now, almost addled with paranoia and rumors, marked by lack of beard and our mandatory Taliban translator who whispers against him.

Kabul, city of the dead, where the beggar woman puts her small children in the middle of the road, saying, in effect, alms or death, as cars mindlessly speed by.

Back in Peshawar, there are almost daily meetings to soothe the paranoia of Shahid, so he can allay the paranoia of his contacts who still can't comprehend why we don't just buy one. And eeriest of all, Pakistan and Afghanistan, even the

Taliban—to me now, it all begins to make a kind of lurid, culturally relative sense. Swift justice, because, as they themselves like to say, the people are wild and lawless and fantastic. Weapons, because weapons permeate the culture, as they have for centuries. And really, is it that much crazier than our own homegrown gun culture—us with our Freemen and gangs and camo-clad Walter Mittys?

And what can it possibly mean to them, our subconscious nightmare of a jumbo jet falling through miles of darkness, crashing into the sea? What could that mean to someone who attacks his neighbors over electricity, much less to an Afghan who has known only war and privation?

I'll never forget Shahid's expression when I asked how it felt, selling such things. He stopped and smiled with acute discomfort, not from guilt but from embarrassment at a question so obvious—obvious because money is all the answer necessary, and at last the only question that really matters.

You probably want to know how it all came out. Or maybe you do know, and always did. I wish I'd had that luxury. Anyhow, we got stung. Stung on our professional vanity.

Oh, once at home in America, there were tense calls to Anwar asking how it was going with those *things*. And recently Anwar did connect with the former *mujahideen* contact we had sought in Jalalabad. It turns out he was embroiled in a murky and controversial incident in which as many as thirty Stingers were lost to Iran during a border skirmish in 1987. Nice try, thought the Americans, who suspected that he and his comrades had merely sold them. He claims a CIA team took him to Islamabad for a lie-detector test. "They asked me questions for four hours and eventually gave me a clean chit," he told Anwar. There must be hundreds like him, all with their Stinger stories, their brush with wealth and technological immortality.

As for Shahid, he didn't entirely disappoint. Gentleman to the end, he even faxed me a letter:

> Every character of the story is very clever and intelligent. The business takes place under strick conditions. Time, Date, Day, is not reliable, given by the dealers/Agents or anyone but a sudden telephone call will ask the purchaser to come forward, see and check it. Where about will not be explained. It need one week more. This is due to lack of trust.

Wait, does Shahid betray himself, calling it a "story"? And how *could* it have turned out otherwise? Because even if we'd had a suitcase of cash, how could we have bought one without hiring an army? And how, on their end, would they know they wouldn't get stung—stung like the Afghan warlord known as Rocketi, who after weeks of negotiations with the CIA, lost at least two Stingers to Pakistani paramilitary forces? Rocketi then Ramboed the government by seizing hostages for a year.

Funny. I remember Chris saying he wanted to find this Rocketi chap, and I—clueless then about Rocketi's rep—said that sounded like a *great* idea. And once back in New York, the *LIFE* photo editor told Steve and me that he had something neat to show us—these greasy prayer beads. Pretty, we said. "Bread," he replied. "Didn't I tell you? The last guy we sent to Afghanistan spent six weeks in prison making these…out of *bread*."

So kick me. Hard. But know that she's still out there, Stinger in her waterproof case, with the super argon batteries that will see the Energizer Bunny with both legs in the air.

Stinger, I almost knew ya, baby, and now I do, sorta, with your voodoo tingle. Stinger, whom I always think of now when my flight is boarding. Stinger, as we belly flop off the runway, off in that awful, whoopsidaisy second as we flounder up, 200 souls, and the wheels go bump.

The author of two novels, The World As I Found It *and* Last Comes the Egg, *Bruce Duffy is the recipient of a Guggenheim Fellowship, a Whiting Writer's Award, and a Lila Wallace-Reader's Digest Award. His writings on Bosnia, Haiti, and hoboes have appeared in the pages of* Harper's, LIFE, Discover On-line, *and other national magazines. He lives in Washington, D.C..*

SURVIVING THE CITY OF ANGELS

Some of the deadliest encounters may be closer than you think.

MY MORNING BEGAN IN A TIME ZONE IN ANOTHER PLACE. Five p.m., L.A. time, I found myself a lone passenger on a bus heading north, cutting through left-over desert littered with metallic trash jutting out of the sand like some recently-forgotten, half-buried treasure. The sun shone on those barren scrap-fields, and they sparkled like a stage of fallen stars.

So much luminous waste can make you start seeing things. I could have sworn that dinosaurs (real live versions of those in the La Brea tar pits) were advancing in a state of frozen motion. I blinked. Turned out it was only the sun setting on cranes at rest.

"Where you from?" the bus driver, a guy in his late fifties with a belly which boasted years of taking in the beer, asked. He hadn't spoken before so it took me a moment to come out of myself and respond to him.

"Paris," I finally said, my voice dropping low so he wouldn't get the idea of striking up a conversation with me just because he was bored. Hell, I was tired. What, after a twelve-, thirteen-hour trip?

"What's it like in Paris? Guess it's a real culture shock going there, huh? Guess there's a lot of parley-vous français and wine-drinking going on in that city. I hear they drink a hell of a lot over there. Don't take baths either from what I've been told. Must be one funky place!"

Going to Paris had never produced a shock to my system. Not even the first time. Villages connected by tunnels serviced by reliable trains (when they aren't on strike). Paris, like many of its inhabitants, is thoroughly modern, utterly sophisticated, and hopelessly provincial. What's so shocking about that?

I told the driver that all his guesses were better than any of mine, chuckling so he wouldn't take offense. After all, I was back in America where a chortle or a smile might mean everything. But knowing I couldn't keep up pretenses, I stuck a pair of lightweight headphones in my ears, and plugged into a Walkman playing Gilberto Gil, from which audio-vantage point I viewed my entry into L.A. as though it were no more than a film of my own making. The bus, meanwhile, moved on, stopping frequently (picking up passengers, letting them off), which broke its momentum the instant it seemed to gain some.

I tried to visualize the end of the road; imagine the moment when I would get off, greet the friend at whose home I would be staying. Settle in for the night. But every time the bus covered some small, obscure distance, a length of road seemed to open up to one of two possibilities: either the trip would go on forever, or I'd never get where I was going alive.

Around 6:15 I found myself a lone passenger again. But only for a moment. The bus stopped. Five boys got on wearing colors which signified they belonged, if only to each other. Not one of them paid.

It occurred to me that the driver might comment on their little oversight, *le genre*: "Back in my day when people got on the bus, they paid their fare. Fare was fair. Know what I mean? Nowadays folks don't believe in nothing but a free ride. People just be assuming that without paying a price they can get somewhere. Now ain't that a hell-of-a-way to look at life!"

But the driver's tongue must have sat thick and stiff in his mouth. He didn't say a word as four of the free-riders swaggered to the rear of the bus, as if by silent command. Silence (I was listening carefully) also commanded that I belonged to the leader, a 17- or 18-year-old baby with droopy pants and rotten teeth overlaid in gold, who stood looking down at me like a whip-snapping young overseer.

The boy flashed a smile that glimmered like those metal scrap-fields that had deluded me into seeing things that are not. But this was no time to abandon myself to a space in my head where dinosaurs danced with figments of my imagination.

I stared up at this man-child, to whom life had promised so little. Glowing like luminous waste, violence lay low in his eyes, hiding behind the gold-decked smile. I wanted to smile back but my face got stuck, so I averted my eyes.

"Look at him!" I told myself, "and remember where you are for Christ's sake!" You're not in Paris where flirting doesn't necessarily lead to fucking; where titillation is not a prelude to mutilation; where a man might follow you up the subway stairs (walking a careful distance behind you to get a good look up your dress), invite you for coffee when you've both reached the air, then tell you on the way to a café that he's a cameraman and you're like light to his eyes. This is not Paris where, if a man or two do decide to take you on, you can tell them to make their move as long as they are fully aware that one, two, or all three of you are going to end up dead in a struggle over your body. "This is L.A.," I screamed to give myself a good, hard mental pinch. "You could get shot in the face for looking at that boy the wrong way!

"So look at him the right way," I whispered inaudibly, "or close your eyes and pray, if you remember how."

So many women have met their deaths kneeling. I looked that boy in the eyes. I looked beyond his eyes. Recognized him. I reached out to touch his hand, knowing, explicitly, that gesture might save my life. Besides, with his arm extended, an open palm approaching my lap, the boy's hand was already mine for the taking.

I grasped it firmly. And when I did, the boy's fingers wrapped around my knuckles like a steel coil. Locked in his grip, I heard laughter in the back of the bus, bottles crashing to the floor. I no longer felt the bus moving. The bus driver had turned zombie on me. I was on my own, and had played one empty hand. Now the boy would play his.

"What's your name?"

I heard a slurred voice sing out: *I wanna know your name?* A chorus swooned in the background, gurgling and laughter fizzled in my ears. I wanted my hand back. But I waited. I've waited before. I waited for Christmas when I was little. I waited small eternities for RTD buses (L.A.'s rapid transit bus system) once upon a time when I lived in this tropical, edge-city, sprawl. I've waited hours to be picked up from airports by family who'd forgotten I had come to town. I've waited for phone calls from lovers, for their on-line names to light up my screen.

I waited for my hand. While I did so I told the boy my name. Three times I repeated it because, like most Americans, he couldn't get it in one go.

"Janine."

"Janey."

"No. Janine."

"Jeannie."

"Ja. Say Ja." He said Ja. "Neene. Like mean. That's what my little brother called me when he was a baby."

He said Neene, then put the two syllables together. Smiling, he began to rub his stomach with the satisfaction of a man who's just wolfed down a feast. I wasn't complaining. With both hands on his belly, I had my hand back! I shoved it between my legs, though on hindsight, that wasn't the safest place to keep it.

"My name's Capone," the boy told me.

I swallowed hard to stop myself asking this child if that was the name his mother had given him at birth or some label he'd branded himself with in a violent rite of passage. I made sure the only thing he saw me do was shake my head gently in acknowledgment of what he said, the name falling quietly from my lips.

"Janine, where you stay at? I stay over by the Coliseum."

"I live in Paris."

I will never understand the boy's reaction to this piece of information. He left me, walking tall to the back of the bus, his pants riding the tail-end of his narrow butt. I should have kept my head still, which might have signaled that I considered our encounter a thing of a not so distant past. But when someone whets your curiosity it's hard to close anything, even when fear is fuming in your stomach.

My head turned, and I watched as the boy told his friends, "She stay in Paris." He said it with pride. They sat silent for a moment, as if awe-struck, then watched respectfully as Capone made his way back to me like the Lone Ranger staking out a claim.

There his hand was again, this time reaching for my face. I grabbed it, like I might take hold of a baby's foot, before it could connect with my skin.

"You got some pretty eyes. Anybody ever tell you that?"

He started grinning and teasing me.

"Come on now, they tell you that all the time, don't they?"

I laughed and told him the truth: "Not all the time."

After a moment of silence (he was thinking, rubbing his chin) he asked: "You wanna go with me?"

Now when boys and men tag after you on busy sidewalks speaking nonsense to you and every other female between the ages of 8 and 50, ridiculous things like, *Baby can I come?*, you usually laugh, shake your head (as if in pity) and continue on your way. Or you might ask them in play, "I don't know, can you?" But this boy wasn't playing. His proposition was about as serious as the heart attack I could have had that very moment.

What in the world, I wondered, did this boy see in my face that would have him believe that I would even consider accompanying him and four other drunken boys to some place unknown to me, near the Coliseum? It should have been a joke. He wasn't laughing. Surely this was one of those moments I had to stop and consider who I might be from the world's point of view.

The boy stood there looking down at me, patient. He didn't seem to mind my silent deliberation. He even dropped my hand, as if to say, "Here, take as much of yourself as you need while you make up your mind."

My mind wasn't the problem. You've got to be careful how you say "no" to a man, even one you think you know. How many times had I had to learn that lesson?

I decided that I couldn't. I couldn't tell Capone no.

"I'm thirty-three years old," I told Capone, thinking that might dissuade him. Tell a 40-year old man you're 33 and the fantasy he fancied will evaporate like a late morning dream. But it turns out there's all the difference in the world between a man who needs to suck the youth from a young woman to bolster his own flagging mast and a man-child who's still strong enough to suck and be sucked all on his own juice. Capone all but laughed in my face.

"Thirty-three! Baby, that ain't nothing but a number to me!"

Good thing I have a sense of humor. Our moment of mutual joy bought me some time. A few moments later I served him another line, a true one for what it's worth.

"I can't go with you Capone. I'm going to have an operation the day after tomorrow. That's why I've returned to L.A."

I don't know what I expected Capone's reaction to be. For all I knew he had banged a few bodies deathside in his time. Why should the state of my health mean anything to him?

The grin dropped out of Capone's face. His eyes lost a layer of glaze, making him actually appear sober for a second or so. He extended his arm, reaching neither for my lap nor my face. Touching me lightly on the shoulder he said, as though speaking to a distant cousin (which I may well be) "You take care of yourself, you hear?" A twinge of something southern softened his voice. Probably came from Texas, as a little boy, his family in search of a better life.

"Thanks," I said.

I stared into the boy's face for the last time. Some doors don't shut on their own. You have to help them along, gently. I had to recognize him once more, let him know I did indeed catch sight of *him* behind Capone's golden grin. I sought to speak to the ghost-writer before the boy named Capone changed his mind.

"Thank you."

Capone made his way to the rear, his strut deliberately slow, lazy, and crooked. (Odd how a person can gain strength from pretending to be a cripple). I knew he had to be grinning. Capone had resumed his role. Man has a tendency to survive.

About fifteen minutes later I got off the bus, still *kicking it*, as Capone might have said. Heading down an isolated sidewalk, which ran alongside an abandoned tract, I felt that bus in my back, standing there, the doors probably wide open, like the gates to heaven. Only when I heard the bus pull away did I feel my legs come back to me, as I stumbled around in that lamp-lit dusk breathing that gorgeous, polluted, L.A. air.

And while echoes of drunken laughter and clanging bottles rang in my ears I couldn't help but wonder: Here, in this City of Angels, how many invisible souls remain locked inside the bodies of boys with names like "Capone" merely as a means of staying alive?

Janine Jones grew up a military brat. So there is no place she really calls home, except where she happens to be living. She received a Ph.D. in philosophy from UCLA; lived, on and off, for ten years in France, and traveled throughout Europe. She is now living in Brooklyn, New York, where she makes a virtual living working for a global company located in Emeryville, California.

PART FOUR

Crossing to Safety

ANDREW TODHUNTER

TRANSMISSION

While learning about fear and falling from a renowned rock climber,
the author realizes that his pursuit of danger must have a limit.

AT THIS TIME IN MY LIFE, A WATERSHED OF SORTS, I AM
unwilling to ride a motorcycle on the street. I so abused the
generosity of the Fates that I now fear them as a penniless
gambler fears his creditors. I have outstanding debts in this re-
gard, and with a child on the way, I cannot afford to pay them.

Until recently, I never realized to what degree the middle
class is a moral, rather than an economic, entity, based less on
status than on possessive, life-sustaining love. The moral middle class plays by percentages, because that is the safest bet, and
percentage play—in life as in tennis—is by definition conservative. It is, ironically, the gambler's game. For all appearances,
a true gambler never makes a poor bet. He never goes for the
long shot. If he is a professional, he always bets the sure thing,
and even then he occasionally loses. When the currency in
question is your family's welfare, there appears to be no other
way. There is a deepening to this kind of life, informed by
what the Japanese call *yugen*. An emotion akin to nostalgia,
yugen might be experienced—as philosopher Alan Watts put

it—in an empty banquet hall the day after a wedding. Napkins lie beneath the chairs, the rice crunches underfoot, but the music and the bride and groom and all the guests are gone. The Japanese compare *yugen* to the sight of a ship's sails slowly disappearing around a distant headland, or of geese, in formation, flying into mist. Living a life based essentially upon the protection and preservation of your family is to pit yourself against an enemy—the nature of all things to change and vanish—that you cannot possibly defeat. This is a rich conundrum, offering its own rewards. But it's not nearly as much *fun*, I'm discovering, as riding a Kawasaki GPZ at 120 miles per hour across the Bay Bridge at three o'clock in the morning.

I still consider buying a bike for the track, a high-performance street-illegal machine with no license plates and fat, slick tires as tacky in the heat as licorice. I would drive it to the track on a trailer and pay by the hour to ride. A track is blessedly free of obstructions, and the chance of serious injury or death after a fall is infinitesimal. In full leathers and a new helmet, on a clean, beveled track—free of oil, sand, black ice, potholes, mufflers, telephones poles, reckless pedestrians, and desperate, clinging fathers in Volvo station wagons—I could still allow myself to wind it out. And yet, without the terrible, ambient risk, I wonder, would the enormous speed and the wonderful rhythm of the corners all too soon become monotonous? As I slowed and left the track and rolled the bike onto the trailer, while I lashed it into place for the drive home, to my wife, to my future child, would I feel as I've begun to feel now, in [climber Dan Osman's] company? That I have changed, that another calling—that of family—has waylaid me, that I am equal to its tasks, that I perform my duty, but that I have chewed through my own entrails to do so, that I am no longer, in some essential way, entirely alive?

This is a paltry price to pay, I answer daily, for a wife

beyond all expectation, and for the child she carries—a nameless, genderless child who illuminates the way before us like a brazier. Eventually, perhaps, these vestigial adolescent twinges will subside. I would trade everything I had at twenty again and again for my life now, at thirty. Like the lobsters I used to drag from caves on the floor of the Pacific—wise, ageless creatures, how they fought until they finally surrendered, all at once, and went limp in the hand—I am molting, I hope, into a better form.

Early in my wife's pregnancy, I was top-roping a 5.10 in a climbing gym near our hometown of San Anselmo. I reached the gentle overhang, prepared to move through it—I had climbed the route successfully before—and unexpectedly froze in place. I thought of the baby. The music, cycled perpetually through the gym's loudspeakers, overwhelmed me. I glanced down at my belayer. Her belay appeared sound, but she was chatting with her neighbor, her eyes averted from the route. My motivation to ascend evaporated. The strength drained from my arms. My position—clutching like a salamander to misshapen plastic knobs bolted to a sheet of painted, artificially textured plywood—struck me as absurd. My fear unraveled quickly into panic. I lost all faith in the anchor, the rope, my harness, my belayer, and my ability to climb; I wanted down. I called to my belayer, trying to conceal my alarm, to watch me. I decided to attempt the downclimb, rather than rely on the gear. Clinging to each hold, I descended in horrible, contracted form to the gravel floor.

Sixty feet beneath the surface of the Pacific, alone, I once became trapped in a cave. I started in slowly, rounded a bend, and saw a distant light. Imagining a second entrance, I continued. It was a tight fit; in places, my chest in the sand, my scuba tank scraped against the irregular rock ceiling overhead. When I finally reached it, the opposing aperture was the diameter of a porthole. It struck me then that I might have made a bad decision. With my arms outstretched before me, pushing with bridged fingers, I scuttled backward down the winding corridor. I made steady progress until I stopped short with a thump. I exhaled completely, flattening myself onto the floor of the cave, and pushed again, without result. Just how long have I been down? I wondered. How much air do I have left? My console—equipped with depth and pressure gauges, compass, and computer—was tucked into my vest out of reach; I last checked my gauges before I entered the cave.

I knew the sensation of pulling on an empty tank—we had simulated it in training. The resistance from the regulator stiffens until, at some point in the middle of your last, labored breath, it freezes solid. The valve shuts down and the airspace in the regulator becomes a vacuum; it's like trying to breathe from an empty soda bottle. As a diver, I have often wondered what it would feel like to drown beneath the surface. There, in the cave, I remembered the sensation of the regulator going stiff, stopping, and a wave of claustrophobic terror rose before me. I wanted to bellow, to thrash. An instructor had once observed that panic was a behavior, not an emotion. That it was not fear that killed the trapped or disoriented individual, but the behavior of uncontrolled panic in response. I lay motionless for a moment on the floor of the cave and closed my eyes. I relaxed my limbs completely, and in three breaths the impulse to struggle had passed. I thought the problem through: the flat boot of the tank had caught on an edge that now held me like a barb. I slowly rolled to the left, sliding gently forward and back with my hands, scraping and tapping with the boot of the tank along the rocky obstruction behind me, searching for a slot. No luck. I repeated this process to the right without success. I'm screwed, I thought, and another spasm of fear clutched my chest. I took two huge gulps of air. Think, I commanded. Don't move. Just think. I lay still in the cave until I was breathing evenly, and could no longer feel my heart.

Normally, you could pass such a squeeze by shedding the scuba tank and pulling it along behind you, the regulator secure in your mouth. The passage, in this case, was far too narrow to remove the tank; at first I doubted if I could even work a hand down to feel the obstruction. With a series of contortions I did manage this, and with my right hand I examined the problem. The tank, slightly buoyant and therefore gently elevated at the boot, angled upward just enough to catch a broad flange of rock. By grasping the foot of the tank and drawing it tight against my lower back, then rolling slightly to the right and exhaling while I pushed off with my left hand, I worked the tank under the lip and scraped slowly under the obstruction. I was soon clear of the squeeze, and the remainder of the passage offered no difficulty. As I backed out of the cave, into the light, I checked my gauges. Two hundred pounds; three hundred pounds below the pressure at which divers are encouraged to surface, but enough. I was free, more pleased by my victory over fear than my escape from drowning death at the age of twenty-two.

In the climbing gym, however, I had lost composure. Worse, given the circumstances, the fear was unjustified. At the base of the route I untied from the rope, mumbled something to my belayer, and excused myself. I sat in my car in the parking lot, in the darkness, and wondered, melodramatically, if I would ever climb again.

In the gym you can climb more vertical feet in an hour than you might in a long day at the crags. At the gym there is no hike in from the car, no rope to flake (or uncoil), no hardware to rack, no anchors to place. With a belayer, you simply tie in to the rope and go. Fueled by the music—commonly a blend of traditional and alternative rock—the tempo is quick, the climbing aggressive. Most traditional climbers resort to the gym only when forced, by darkness or poor weather, if at all. But there is a new breed of climber, introduced to the sport in the gym, that climbs exclusively indoors. This individual has never climbed on natural rock, regardless of local availability, and has little or no intention of doing so. There are surfers, I imagine, or will be, who live within a reasonable drive of decent, oceanic surf who have never caught a wave outside a wave pool. No sharks, they might argue. The perfect, consistent wave. Twelve minutes from work. A locker room. *A juice bar.* All too soon, there will be a climbing gym in Yosemite Valley—like a neon wedding chapel erected in the center of the nave of Saint Peter's—and they will pack it in.

Sitting in the car, I unwound the strips of white athletic tape from my fingers. The tape, wrapped around the soft pads between the knuckles, supports the tendons. I rubbed the streaks of residual glue from my ring finger. From the wallet, tucked above the visor, I extracted and replaced my wedding ring. I studied the band of white gold, plain as silver in the light of the streetlamps, and drove slowly home.

For practical reasons, I do not climb wearing the ring; it would interfere with my grip, and could become dangerously wedged in cracks. The soft metal would be damaged, particularly on natural rock. It was a difficult decision, the first time I went climbing after the wedding. I considered taping over it, to protect the metal, but this possessed its own problems. Glue would foul the ring, and the resulting lump would be even more awkward than the ring itself. At first, I wore the ring on a chain around my neck, tucked under my shirt. I soon became afraid of the chain breaking, perhaps in a fall, and of losing the ring forever. Thereafter I strung the ring on my leather watchband and stashed it deep in a pack pocket, or tucked it into the furthest corner of my wallet. Taking it off and putting it back on became a minor ritual. I would study the appearance of my hand in contrast. With ring. Without ring. Removing it, I continue to feel a faint pang of endangerment, as if I am colluding with chaos; seeing it again in its place is as satisfying to the eye as a tarnished copper kettle, its brilliance surfing beneath the labor of a polishing hand. And yet the ring—or what it represents—is heavy; it gives weight.

After a week of inactivity and self-loathing, I continued to climb, but with greater caution. I drove with circumspection. I pondered life insurance. I took up tennis.

As I clung to that overhang and imagined the baby, still small enough then to fit in my closed palm, I felt painfully exposed. In the minute, infinitely fragile fetus, I perceived the frailty of things—myself included—in a way I never had before. Furthermore, I suspected, with the confirmation of this life in utero, my personal exemption from disaster had expired. My luck was up, and the angels had diverted their attentions to the child. They had preserved me through my youth for this transmission; through conception I had passed them on. Get down, said a voice. Get down. There is danger here, and it does not serve.

Andrew Todhunter writes about extreme sports for The Atlantic Monthly. *An amateur climber and adventurer, he usually participates in the sports that he covers. He is the author of* Fall of the Phantom Lord: Climbing and the Face of Fear, *from which this story was excerpted.*

Acknowledgements

We would like to thank our families and friends for their usual forbearance while we are putting a book together. Thanks also to the staff at Travelers' Tales and O'Reilly & Associates, and to Sleeping Lady Retreat and Conference Center in Leavenworth, Washington for a wonderful and supportive creative environment. Finally a special thanks to Rajendra Khadka for his work (and his witty company) during the early phase of the project.

"Pulling Out" by Peter Maass excerpted from *Love Thy Neighbor: A Story of War* by Peter Maass. Copyright © 1996 by Peter Maass. Reprinted by permission of Alfred A. Knopf, Inc. and Macmillan Publishers Ltd.

"Ditching at Sea" by Sebastian Junger excerpted from *The Perfect Storm: A True Story of Men Against the Sea* by Sebastian Junger. Copyright © 1997 by Sebastian Junger. Reprinted by permission of W.W. Norton & Co. and Fourth Estate.

"A Zambian Nightmare" by Anthony Brennan published with permission of the author. Copyright © 1999 by Anthony Brennan.

"The Friendly Bear" by Bill Sherwonit reprinted from the August, 1998 issue of *Backpacker*. Copyright © 1998 by Bill Sherwonit. Reprinted by permission of the author.

"Bulgarian Struggle" by Josie Dew excerpted from *The Wind in My Wheels: Travel Tales from the Saddle* by Josie Dew. Copyright © 1992 by Josie Dew. Reprinted by permission of Warner, a Division of Little, Brown and Company (UK) Limited.

"Python!" by Lyall Watson excerpted from *Lightning Bird: The Story of One Man's Journey into Africa's Past* by Lyall Watson. Copyright © 1982 by Lyall Watson. Used by permission of Dutton, a division of Penguin Putnam Inc.

"Dangerous Liaisons" by John Climaco excerpted from *Epic: Stories of Survival From the World's Highest Peaks* edited by Clint Willis. Reprinted by permission of the author. Copyright © 1997 by John Climaco.

"Incident at Boat Bay" by Jim Nollman published with permission from the author. Copyright © 1999 by Jim Nollman.

"The War" by Sanyika Shakur excerpted from *Monster: The Autobiography of an L.A. Gang Member* by Sanyika Shakur. Copyright © 1993 by Kody Scott. Used by permission of Grove/Atlantic. Inc.

"When It Goes Off" by Bill Buford excerpted from *Among the Thugs: The Experience, and the Seduction, of Crowd Violence* by Bill Buford. Copyright ©1991, 1990 by William Buford. Reprinted by permission of W.W. Norton & Company, Inc. and Secker & Warburg.

"Looking for Stinger" by Bruce Duffy reprinted from the September 1997 issue of *LIFE* magazine. Copyright © 1997. Reprinted by permission of *LIFE* magazine.

"Surviving the City of Angels" by Janine Jones published with permission from the author. Copyright © 1999 by Janine Jones.

"Transmission" by Andrew Todhunter excerpted from *Fall of the Phantom Lord: Climbing and the Face of Fear* by Andrew Todhunter. Copyright © 1998 by Andrew Todhunter. Used by permission of Doubleday, a division of Random House Inc., and the author.

About the Editors

James O'Reilly and Larry Habegger first worked together as late night disc jockeys at Dartmouth College in New Hampshire. They wrote mystery serials for the *San Francisco Examiner* in the early 1980s before turning to travel writing. Since 1983, their travel features and self-syndicated column, "World Travel Watch," have appeared in magazines and newspapers in the United States and other countries. James was born in Oxford, England, raised in San Francisco, and lives with his family in Leavenworth, Washington and Palo Alto, California; Larry was born and raised in Minnesota and lives on Telegraph Hill in San Francisco.

Sean O'Reilly is a former seminarian, stockbroker, and bank slave who lives in Arizona with his wife Brenda and their four small boys. Widely traveled in Europe, he most recently spent time roaming East Africa and the Indian Ocean. He is also at work on a book called *Politics and the Soul: The River of Gold,* which he describes as a "re-examination of classic Greek, Roman, and Christian philosophies as tools for moral excellence in modern society."

TRAVELERS' TALES GUIDES

LOOK FOR THESE TITLES IN THE SERIES

FOOTSTEPS: THE SOUL OF TRAVEL
A NEW IMPRINT FROM TRAVELERS' TALES GUIDES

An imprint of Travelers' Tales Guides, the Footsteps series unveils new works by first-time authors, established writers, and reprints of works whose time has come…again. Each book will fire your imagination, disturb your sleep, and feed your soul.

KITE STRINGS OF THE SOUTHERN CROSS
A Woman's Travel Odyssey
By Laurie Gough
ISBN 1-885211-30-9, 400 pages, $24.00, hardcover
A TRAVELERS' TALES FOOTSTEPS BOOK

✑PECIAL INTEREST

THE PENNY PINCHER'S PASSPORT TO LUXURY TRAVEL
The Art of Cultivating Preferred Customer Status
By Joel L. Widzer
ISBN 1-885211-31-7, 253 pages, $12.95

DANGER!
Ttue Stories of Trouble and Survival
Edited by James O'Reilly, Larry Habegger, & Sean O'Reilly
ISBN 1-885211-32-5, 336 pages, $17.95

Check with your local bookstore for these titles
or call O'Reilly to order:
800-998-9938 (credit cards only—weekdays 6AM–5PM PST)
707-829-0515, or email: order@oreilly.com

$\mathscr{S}$PECIAL INTEREST

FAMILY TRAVEL:
The Farther You Go, the Closer You Get
Edited by Laura Manske
ISBN 1-885211-33-3, 375 pages, $17.95

THE GIFT OF TRAVEL:
The Best of Travelers' Tales
Edited by Larry Habegger, James O'Reilly & Sean O'Reilly
ISBN 1-885211-25-2, 240 pages, $14.95

THERE'S NO TOILET PAPER ON THE ROAD LESS TRAVELED:
The Best of Travel Humor and Misadventure
Edited by Doug Lansky
ISBN 1-885211-27-9, 207 pages, $12.95

A DOG'S WORLD:
True Stories of Man's Best Friend on the Road
Edited by Christine Hunsicker
ISBN 1-885211-23-6, 257 pages, $12.95

$\mathscr{W}$OMEN'S TRAVEL

SAFETY AND SECURITY FOR WOMEN WHO TRAVEL
By Sheila Swan & Peter Laufer
ISBN 1-885211-29-5, 159 pages, $12.95

$\mathcal{W}$OMEN'S TRAVEL

WOMEN IN THE WILD:
True Stories of Adventure and Connection
Edited by Lucy McCauley
ISBN 1-885211-21-X, 307 pages, $17.95

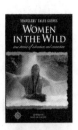

A MOTHER'S WORLD:
Journeys of the Heart
Edited by Marybeth Bond & Pamela Michael
ISBN 1-885211-26-0, 233 pages, $14.95

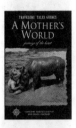

A WOMAN'S WORLD:
True Stories of Life on the Road
Edited by Marybeth Bond
Introduction by Dervla Murphy
ISBN 1-885211-06-6
475 pages, $17.95

——— ★ ★ ★ ———
Winner of the Lowell
Thomas Award for Best
Travel Book—Society of
American Travel Writers

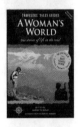

GUTSY WOMEN:
Travel Tips and Wisdom for the Road
By Marybeth Bond
ISBN 1-885211-15-5, 123 pages, $7.95

GUTSY MAMAS:
Travel Tips and Wisdom for
Mothers on the Road
By Marybeth Bond
ISBN 1-885211-20-1, 139 pages, $7.95

$\mathscr{B}$ODY & SOUL

THE ROAD WITHIN:
True Stories of Transformation and the Soul
Edited by Sean O'Reilly, James O'Reilly & Tim O'Reilly
ISBN 1-885211-19-8, 459 pages, $17.95

——★ ★ ★——
Small Press Book Award Winner and Benjamin Franklin Award Finalist

LOVE & ROMANCE:
True Stories of Passion on the Road
Edited by Judith Babcock Wylie
ISBN 1-885211-18-X, 319 pages, $17.95

FOOD:
A Taste of the Road
Edited by Richard Sterling
Introduction by Margo True
ISBN 1-885211-09-0
467 pages, $17.95

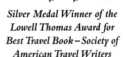

——★ ★ ★——
Silver Medal Winner of the Lowell Thomas Award for Best Travel Book – Society of American Travel Writers

THE FEARLESS DINER:
Travel Tips and Wisdom for Eating around the World
By Richard Sterling
ISBN 1-885211-22-8, 139 pages, $7.95

COUNTRY GUIDES

AMERICA
Edited by Fred Setterberg
ISBN 1-885211-28-7, 550 pages, $19.95

JAPAN
Edited by Donald W. George
& Amy Greimann Carlson
ISBN 1-885211-04-X, 437 pages, $17.95

ITALY
Edited by Anne Calcagno
Introduction by Jan Morris
ISBN 1-885211-16-3, 463 pages, $17.95

INDIA
Edited by James O'Reilly & Larry Habegger
ISBN 1-885211-01-5, 538 pages, $17.95

FRANCE
Edited by James O'Reilly, Larry Habegger
& Sean O'Reilly
ISBN 1-885211-02-3, 517 pages, $17.95

COUNTRY GUIDES

MEXICO
Edited by James O'Reilly & Larry Habegger
ISBN 1-885211-00-7, 463 pages, $17.95

THAILAND
Edited by James O'Reilly
& Larry Habegger
ISBN 1-885211-05-8
483 pages, $17.95

——★ ★ ★——

Winner of the Lowell
Thomas Award for Best
Travel Book—Society of
American Travel Writers

SPAIN
Edited by Lucy McCauley
ISBN 1-885211-07-4, 495 pages, $17.95

NEPAL
Edited by Rajendra S. Khadka
ISBN 1-885211-14-7, 423 pages, $17.95

BRAZIL
Edited by Annette Haddad & Scott Doggett
Introduction by Alex Shoumatoff
ISBN 1-885211-11-2
452 pages, $17.95

——★ ★ ★——

Benjamin Franklin
Award Winner

REGIONAL GUIDES

HAWAII
True Stories of the Island Spirit
Edited by Rick & Marcie Carroll
ISBN 1-885211-35-X, 375 pages, $17.95

GRAND CANYON
True Stories of Life Below the Rim
Edited by Sean O'Reilly & James O'Reilly
ISBN 1-885211-34-1, 375 pages, $17.95

CITY GUIDES

HONG KONG
Edited by James O'Reilly, Larry Habegger & Sean O'Reilly
ISBN 1-885211-03-1, 439 pages, $17.95

PARIS
Edited by James O'Reilly, Larry Habegger & Sean O'Reilly
ISBN 1-885211-10-4, 417 pages, $17.95

SAN FRANCISCO
Edited by James O'Reilly, Larry Habegger & Sean O'Reilly
ISBN 1-885211-08-2, 491 pages, $17.95

SUBMIT YOUR OWN TRAVEL TALE

Do you have a tale of your own that you would like to submit to Travelers' Tales? We highly recommend that you first read one or more of our books to get a feel for the kind of story we're looking for. For submission guidelines and a list of titles in the works, send a SASE to:

Travelers' Tales Submission Guidelines
330 Townsend Street, Suite 208, San Francisco, CA 94107

or send email to *guidelines@travelerstales.com*
or visit our Web site at **www.travelerstales.com**

You can send your story to the address above or via email to *submit@travelerstales.com*. On the outside of the envelope, *please indicate what country/topic your story is about*. If your story is selected for one of our titles, we will contact you about rights and payment.

We hope to hear from you. In the meantime, enjoy the stories!